The Digital Revolution in Health

Health and Innovation Set

coordinated by
Corinne Grenier

Volume 2

The Digital Revolution in Health

Edited by

Jérôme Béranger
Roland Rizoulières

ISTE

WILEY

First published 2021 in Great Britain and the United States by ISTE Ltd and John Wiley & Sons, Inc.

ISTE Ltd
27-37 St George's Road
London SW19 4EU
UK

www.iste.co.uk

John Wiley & Sons, Inc.
111 River Street
Hoboken, NJ 07030
USA

www.wiley.com

Library of Congress Control Number: 2021932939

British Library Cataloguing-in-Publication Data
A CIP record for this book is available from the British Library
ISBN 978-1-78630-695-1

MIX
Paper from responsible sources
FSC® C013604

Contents

Foreword

Advocacy for a European Reference Framework for Digital Ethics

When inventing the binary code 170 years ago, human beings certainly did not imagine that they would themselves become a sequence of 0s and 1s. Today, algorithms are omnipresent, intrusive, and have no qualms about entering people's intimacy. This digital transformation then introduces a change in contextual reference points and perspectives focused on information and its potential for financial valuation.

Consequently, these technological innovations irremediably lead to ethical and moral questions relating to appropriateness, security, non-discrimination, free will, confidentiality, bias, and autonomy in relation to human beings. Under these conditions, we are convinced that in order to understand and accompany this digital revolution, we must reason in transversality – in *continuum* – and not in a silo, because everything is articulated and interwoven within a sociotechnological system. It is at this point that an ethical approach takes on its full meaning!

Since the Enlightenment and the emergence of the Encyclopedia, human civilizations have tended to separate and isolate, if not to compare, the exact sciences (mathematics, physics, chemistry, etc.) and the humanities and social sciences (HSS; philosophy, sociology, anthropology, etc.). Today, when HSS specialists think and talk about a digital world that escapes them, former scientific experts are developing technical innovations without really being aware of their impact and consequences on society. In our opinion, the main weakness relative to the digital word lies there!

Consequently, without a decisive and modern contribution from the scientific community, this amounts to leaving the question of the meaning, legitimacy, and responsibility of digital systems only to a few predominant market players who do not have the vocation or quality to think about the good of humanity. The great thinkers of another time like Plato, Pascal, Aristotle, or Descartes, who were at the same time great scientists and philosophers, no longer exist! Now, the scientific philosopher has become an endangered species, or is even already extinct. In this period that gives up thinking globally and simultaneously about innovation, technology, and meaning, it seems essential to (re)educate, train, and orient scientists towards HSS in order to open them to fundamental reflections for the well-being of our contemporary society, and philosophers towards the exact sciences to improve their knowledge of a digital humanity.

If you think about it, to have a well-structured ethical reasoning, you have to be Cartesian and rigorous from a methodological and architectural point of view. Under these conditions, half a millennium after the last great multi-disciplinary intellectuals such as François Rabelais ("science without conscience is but the ruin of the soul") and Leonardo da Vinci ("to do in order to think and to think in order to do") we can see that their maxims are more topical than ever. It therefore seems clear that we must strive to return to a transversal and holistic perception in order to answer the following question: How should we approach the world today and in the future?

Pluridisciplinarity and coordination must once again be the key to success in the face of hyper-specialization due in large part to globalization and international competition, in order to accompany and strengthen this digital humanity that is looming on the horizon. It is, therefore, necessary to succeed in marrying the digital and the ethical, by establishing a bridge between the two until they are no longer distinct. The "and" becomes the "is". This approach, centered on Ethics by Design (from the design stage), will enable us to provide a positive and fearless framework for the technological innovation at the heart of its genesis. In this context, it seems essential to set up a European reference framework for digital ethics in order to establish a common base of responsibilities, awareness, and simple actions relating to the socio-ecological impact of digital technology. This shared repository would then be composed of principles, rules, and ethical recommendations whose objective would be to bring confidence to citizens in the face of the expansion of digital technology.

Finally, a few centuries after the European cultural movement leading to the emergence of the Enlightenment, which proposed to overcome obscurantism and promote knowledge, Europe could once again be the initiator of a new, more transversal vision and standardization approach to digital transformation, the watchword of which could be – on this 500th anniversary – “digital technology without ethics is nothing but the ruin of humanity”. This digital revolution would then enter a century that could be called the century of “Intelligences”. Moreover, when you think about it, “being a beacon” does indeed mean “being intelligent”!

Dominique PON
Director of the Clinique Pasteur, Toulouse
In charge of the government’s digital worksite for the *Ma santé 2022* plan

Stéphane OUSTRIC
General Practitioner and University Professor
President of the Departmental Council of the Haute-Garonne Medical Association
National Delegate for Health and Digital Data for the CNOM

Jérôme BÉRANGER
Founder of ADELIAA (Algorithm Data Ethics Label)
Researcher (PhD) associated with Inserm 1027
BIOETHICS Team – University of Toulouse 3

March 2021

Acknowledgements

To our friend Corinne Grenier, without whom this confluence would not have been possible; to her listening and her great professionalism.

Also, a big thank you to our co-authors for their expertise and finesse of analysis on their respective themes.

Finally, thank you to our loved ones for their patience in this time spent away from them writing and exchanging on this exciting topic.

Introduction

Digital technologies are supporting the changes in our healthcare system (mainly the aging of the population and the sharp increase in chronic diseases) and sometimes bring about major changes in the organization and functioning of our healthcare system, particularly in the processing of health data (artificial intelligence). Not only do they make it possible to modernize current organizations, but also to imagine radically new practices (diagnosis, prevention, therapeutic education).

The main events in digital health technologies involve computerization, digitization, and technical networking involving management, organization, and delivery of care and services. Technological advances have made it possible to process, store, and disseminate information in all its forms – oral, written, or visual – increasingly freeing us from any fear of distance, volume, and time. Initiated in most industrial countries since the early 1990s, the implementation of information and communication technologies (ICTs) is increasingly supporting the various transformations taking place in the field of health.

In less than two decades, the Internet and mobile telephony have revolutionized our modes of communication. The healthcare sector is now facing a major change, fueled by the explosion of knowledge in biomedical sciences, biomechanics, nanotechnology, "cyborgization"[1], clinical applications, and the standardization of certain technologies like genome

---

Introduction written by Jérôme BÉRANGER and Roland RIZOULIÈRES.

1 This term refers to the implementation of neuroprosthetics in the patient's body to combat neurodegeneration or tetraplegia.

sequencing. The health data produced, collected, and stored throughout the patient's care pathway are now massive. Big Data are increasingly feeding the medical "data-sphere". Coupled with the progress made in ICT[2], this evolution around these large volumes of data is set to become a revolution.

We are now entering the era of medicine "4.0" based on Big Data, algorithms, blockchain, self-learning expert systems, and artificial intelligence (AI) to move towards a more individualized, personalized, and predictive medicine. Big Data from connected devices and tools of all kinds and interpreted by expert systems can only be managed by machines that, thanks to AI, can communicate with each other and create new ways to serve humans. This new medicine follows the medicine Hippocratic[3] (a singular physician-patient symposium) of Antiquity, medicine 2.0 (medical forums via the Internet)[4], and medicine 3.0 (health applications on smartphones and connected devices) of the 2000s. Since then, healthcare professionals and patients are always on the lookout for information on the pathologies observed, treatments, and care to be provided or on preventive actions. To do so, they still mainly use websites to inform and educate themselves. We are seeing the emergence of communities of patients as well as more and more healthcare professionals via community platforms (mono or multi-specialty) and active groups on open social networks such as Twitter, Facebook, and LinkedIn. For healthcare institutions, the Web is becoming an indispensable tool in the relationship with patients. This involves tools and services on their websites and an increased presence on social media such as YouTube, Twitter or Facebook. These communities of healthcare professionals promote sharing between colleagues and peers, particularly of clinical cases or expertise, multidisciplinary collaboration, etc. Thus, this digital technology is an opportunity to develop less traumatic and expensive medicine and much more preventive, participative, and personalized medicine.

---

2 Cloud computing, search engines, data mining techniques, Very Large Database, datacenters, Open Data, indexing robots, multi-agent systems for automatic data indexing, CRM (Customer Relationship Management), profiling and innovative approaches to data acquisition, semantic web tools, connected devices, bioinformatics, biometric devices, computational nanotechnologies represent essential elements on which Big Data relies.

3 Note that in the Hippocratic Oath, the text invites doctors to practice their profession with the best knowledge of the technologies of their time.

4 The doctor-patient couple is subject to the interaction of society as a whole (other patients, other health professionals as well as insurers and political power). From that moment on, the singular colloquium became plural. But it is always human beings who interact with each other using digital means as a medium.

This new digital world is constantly studying the real world with the aim of creating predictability and predictability. This connected medicine provides a better understanding of both infectious and chronic diseases at the population level, innovative approaches to patient diagnosis and treatment, improved research into diseases and their therapeutics, and optimized monitoring of diseases and risk factors. Under these conditions, the range of possibilities is considerable, and we can only glimpse today the major changes generated by the advent of digital technology in healthcare. This convergence between technological innovation and scientific research, between digital technology, mathematics, and medical progress, will have direct repercussions on medical practice and the doctor-patient relationship, which until now has been based mainly on the medical act. Thus, this information technology has a profound effect on social relationships, human beliefs and the very nature of knowledge. It is transforming the practice of medicine. From now on, medical communication no longer consists only of delivering a precise diagnosis, but also in evaluating all the interactions implemented by patients and the systems that accompany them (family, social environment, caregivers). Under these conditions, the meaning of medical information is considered to be an object of sharing and exchange at the crossroads of relationships and patient management processes.

The objective is neither to put these ICTs on trial in the doctor-patient relationship, nor to make the slightest value judgment on the subject, but rather to identify the issues and limitations, so that they do not become more harmful to the healthcare user than they will be beneficial to him or her. Thus, the performance and possibilities of technologies related to medical information raise new problems for health professionals of a judicial, medical, and reparational nature related to new requirements for the legitimacy of the right to information, causing a certain disorganization and upheaval in the doctor-patient relationship. In addition, there is a real awareness and ethical questioning of confidentiality, the right and freedom of access, security, accountability, free will, autonomy, and medical secrecy that surround the use of medical information via ICTs. Finally, there is the advantage of greater ease of interpersonal communication and medical performance for some, greater uncertainty about security, confidentiality, accessibility, medical data protection, and social justice for others; this digital medicine leaves no one indifferent!

Therefore, this book leads us to question this digital revolution within the healthcare system. What are the challenges, the stakes, and the integration of this digitization of medicine in the healthcare system (Part 1)? What are the repercussions and consequences of this digital medicine on the mentalities and social values of the digital actors in the relationships between professionals and patients (Part 2)? Finally, one of the major questions raised by this book is how the technological modernization of the use of digital data can be accompanied by an ethical-legal awareness of the actors of the health system (Part 3).

I.1. The health system and digital technology: challenges, issues, and transformations (Part 1)

The public authorities and the private sector (particularly the insurance and mutual insurance sectors) have a normative and financial position. As such, they have the legitimacy to support creativity and digital innovations in health. They can frame and encourage this movement. However, for too long, good ideas and innovations have remained confined to the services, institutions, or local networks that gave birth to them, generating compartmentalization and incompatibilities that are harmful to a controlled "urbanization" of information and management systems. Our healthcare system needs these innovations in order to overcome the difficulties of coordination between professionals, to cope with a growing proportion of elderly people at home or in institutions and patients with chronic diseases as well as to enable citizens and patients to be more involved in their care.

Paradoxically, healthcare professionals have a great many digital tools and services at their disposal in their daily practice, whether for patient care or administrative management. As these tools are offered by various institutional and private players on geographical scales that are sometimes inconsistent with the health and life paths of patients, the result is a lack of transmission of patient data to coordinate the process. And the coordinator does not always exist, or perhaps very little, except for complex cases, with the added bonus of remuneration that is poorly adapted (lack of patient packages or pathologies). Above all, however, the practice comes up against fragmented and often poorly interoperable application frameworks. Thus, each use often corresponds to a tool, which greatly complicates daily professional practice. This phenomenon means that the most basic expectations and needs of healthcare professionals (medical and paramedical) are not met or are met in too fragmented a manner: information exchanges between individuals around a patient, coordination of professionals, exhaustiveness of information available on care pathways, simplification of administrative procedures.

These phenomena are described on several fields of analysis and experiences in the first part. The institutional approach and the experience of the authors shed light on the dysfunctions and the creative organizational tinkering that the actors operate.

I.2. The digital and transformations in the relations between professionals and patients (Part 2)

Traditionally, the healthcare system places the consumer/patient as an object of care provided by professionals, the "knowers". The consumer/patient is often reduced to a passive role in the construction of their care pathway and has extremely little control over the use of their health data. In addition, users currently have only a very limited panel of digital health services compared to the uses they can develop in other sectors. The digital shift in health, as defined by the WHO, must therefore have the essential objective of repositioning users as the primary beneficiary of digital health services by giving them the means to be a real player in their own health.

Moreover, while health concerns all citizens, the ethical framework within which digital health must be used remains unclear. The interests and limits of the use of digital technology in health deserve to be explored in greater depth.

Finally, the ethical dimension in the use of digital technology in health is explored in the specific context of the development and promotion of public health in West Africa, particularly with epidemics such as Ebola.

I.3. Supporting digital health (Part 3)

Innovation, whatever its form (technical, organizational, etc.), implies an organization of uses upstream and downstream of the implementation of innovation. However, the modes of production and dissemination of innovation in digital health are being overturned by new practices between players, shedding light on support and governance methods that encourage their success, create difficulties in disseminating them, or block them.

On the one hand, digital healthcare support must deal with new approaches to innovation in the public sector, particularly innovation approaches open to new actors and collaborations, which consist of mobilizing the resources, expertise, and knowledge of a variety of actors to discover, develop, and implement new ideas. The quality of the innovation is then potentially enriched by the participation of this variety of actors, which gives rise to organizational innovations in terms of governance and management of relations between the players, taking into account their different identities and cultures. The construction of a common language and shared practices is an in-depth work, in perpetual movement and recomposition.

Moreover, the need to support digital healthcare has led to a redefinition of ethical governance and responsibility. The case of AI is shaking up codes and practices. Ethics must be addressed on the side of practitioners as well as users/patients.

Finally, the launch of digital technology in Europe highlights the fact that governance and the speed of development are not the same as in the Americas. The reason for this is certainly cultural, but also legal: a legislative framework that European countries have chosen to give themselves, which can be improved, but which has the merit of existing. For telehealth, the French concept is unique compared to that of other European neighbors, whereas for the processing and use of data, it is the European states that together have opted for a unique framework compared to the one launched in the United States. Moreover, this gives rise to major geopolitical conflicts over the use of health data and its appropriation by third parties outside the national/European territory.

Thus, these three parts illustrate the upheavals that are taking place as a result of the digital revolution in healthcare. In order to develop a transversal and ethical reflection, our book is based successively on the digital revolution, the "data-sphere" and its digital applications, the legal framework and ideas to move towards what can be called a "digital trust of society". By highlighting a background framework based on ethical and technical reflection, this book aims to provide the first elements of an evolutionary path that will contribute to significant changes in mentalities and ways of working, as well as strategic and organizational transformation, a transformation that must have a "human face" for this digital revolution in health, the goal being to find a certain coherence and meaning in this landscape of perpetual technological evolution. Technology cannot be a goal in itself, let alone in health. It must above all be oriented towards the patient, who is as much as possible at the center, and provide the best possible healthcare for the patient. Finally, the aim of this book is to raise awareness among all the players in the healthcare system and to promote a culture oriented towards involvement, appropriation, and responsibility in digital healthcare.

PART 1

The Health System and Digital Technology: Challenges, Issues, and Transformations

Introduction to Part 1

As financers and builders of standards, public authorities and the private sector (particularly insurance and mutual insurance companies) must support the creativity and development of digital innovations in health, and provide a framework and encouragement for this movement. For too long, good ideas and innovations have remained confined to the services, institutions, or local networks that gave rise to them, generating compartmentalization and operational incompatibilities. Our healthcare system needs these technological innovations to overcome the difficulties of coordination between professionals, to deal with the growing proportion of elderly people in homes and institutions and patients with chronic diseases. Digital technology must also help citizens and patients to be more involved in their healthcare.

At different territorial scales and in particular to manage the city-hospital link, healthcare professionals have many digital tools and services at their disposal in their daily medical practices, whether for patient care or administrative management. However, these tools are offered by various institutional and private players on geographical scales that are sometimes inconsistent with patients' health and life paths. Above all, however, practice comes up against fragmented and often poorly interoperable application frameworks. Depending on the history of each organization, a tool often corresponds to each use, which greatly complicates daily professional practice. This phenomenon leads to the most basic expectations and needs of healthcare professionals (medical and paramedical) not being met or being met in too fragmented a manner: exchanges and sharing of information

---

Introduction written by Roland RIZOULIÈRES.

between caregivers around a patient, coordination of professionals, completeness of information available on care pathways, simplification of administrative procedures, etc.

We analyze the challenges, issues, and transformations of the healthcare system through digital technology from three perspectives. The first component deals with the digital integration of health territories from an organizational analysis perspective. The second part develops the digital experience within the city-hospital journey of cancer patients, with an organizational and ethical analysis. Finally, the last section looks at the experience of a tool for coordinating players, a connected health record, from a sociological and organizational perspective.

1

Digital Integration and Healthcare Pathways in the Territories

1.1. Introduction

At the beginning of March 2018, French ministry work on the "digital" project of the *Stratégie de transformation du système de santé* (STSS), on the theme "Accelerating the digital shift", aimed to produce by the end of June 2018 an operational roadmap covering the 2018–2022 period and aimed at strengthening the digital shift in the health system. In the long term, however, digital technology is responding to two strong but unfinished challenges: better integration of healthcare and better coordination of care.

The management of patients is becoming more complex, in particular due to the increasing prevalence of chronic pathologies, the accumulation of co-morbidities, psychosocial problems, and the aging of the population (Perone *et al.* 2014; Huard 2018). The difficulty in applying the recommendations of practice guidelines for such complex patients has been shown; in fact, by combining health, social, and environmental issues, they have specific properties (Wilson *et al.* 2001; Waldvogel *et al.* 2012). Complex patients are complicated not only because of their multiple pathologies but also when their different problems intertwine and interact, creating a new situation that is more difficult to manage. It becomes a unique case for which interventions must be rethought (Boyd *et al.* 2012) and adapted not only to the specificities of the pathologies and above all to the priorities and resources of patients and their environment.

Chapter written by Roland RIZOULIÈRES.

Patient management in this context of epidemiological transition has been the subject of various conceptualizations, including the Chronic Care Model (CCM; Figure 1.1) proposed by Wagner *et al.* (1998) and Bodenheimer *et al.* (2002a, 2002b). In order to respond to the diversity of problems and the multiple skills required, these models recommend individualized care, requiring on the one hand an adapted healthcare system (Bodenheimer *et al.* 2009) and, on the other hand, a coordinated interdisciplinary approach (Schibli 2012; Gittel 2014).

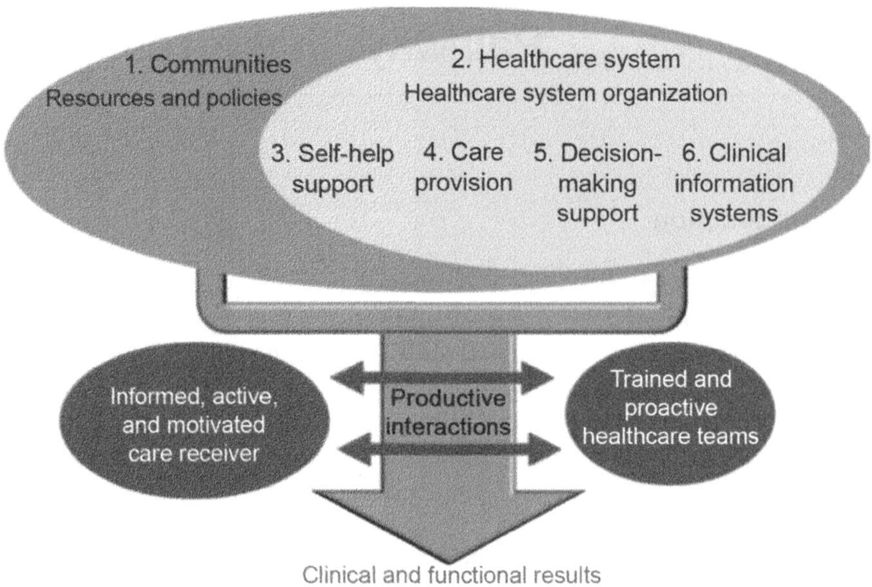

Figure 1.1. *Long-term chronic care model (Source: Perone et al. 2014). For a color version of this figure, see www.iste.co.uk/beranger/health.zip*

The consequence of this integrated and coordinated approach is the *need for digital tools on the territory to* ensure exchanges between professionals and patients/caregivers. It is precisely on this point that our reflection focuses. However, while the digital revolution brings great changes, digital tools are primarily based on organizational changes and often reveal organizational difficulties rather than representing the "Holy Grail" for all our problems.

Integration of care can be defined as a set of techniques and organizational models implemented to enable the transmission of information, the adoption of common operating modes, and collaboration between the health, medical, and social sectors. It can intervene at the level of financing, the administrative organization of the territory, and the functioning of healthcare structures.

The immediate goal of integration is to reduce the fragmentation of medical and social services in order to facilitate patient access to services that meet their needs. Its longer-term goal is to enable better care outcomes and better use of health resources.

The Chronic Care Model (Wagner 1998) conceptualizes the totality of conditions that influence the quality of care for a chronically ill person: funding, policies, laws, training, communication systems, information, resources, etc. This model postulates that changes in these different areas will have an impact on the practice of caregivers and on the care of sick people.

It also suggests that changing practices at the caregiver level requires action at the overall health system level. It may thus prove relevant to act on the legislation surrounding the methods and conditions for financing services, on the communication systems available to enable caregivers to communicate with patients, on the organization of training systems, on the recognition of the usefulness of support structures offered to patients, etc. The report also suggests that, in order to change practices at the caregiver level, action must be taken at the global level of the health system. Furthermore, this model shows the importance of proactive and interdisciplinary teamwork.

It is part of a clearly collaborative perspective in which the person being cared for participates actively in their care.

Integration alone does not improve care outcomes. It must be combined with “case management” procedures, that is, the explicit identification with an individual, or a group, of coordination activities whose flexibility and workload are beyond the capacity of primary healthcare professionals in their daily practice.

We will look at how digital healthcare is helping to improve the health and life course of patients and their caregivers, while raising the organizational issues inherent in our historically siloed healthcare model.

1.2. What lessons can be learned from integrated American and Swiss models?

In general, the study of internationally integrated health systems is situated from the perspective of organizational critical analysis in the management of chronic diseases. Issues of efficiency and cost-effectiveness (cost containment) are the two main drivers. The digital issue generally remains in the background. However, as Christian Bourret (2003) points out, "in the United States, 30% of medical errors are said to be due to problems related to information processing, in particular patient identifiers. This shows the importance of health information and the extent to which its control, optimal use, and quality of data are at the heart of the evolution of health systems and the improvement of the quality of care."

Jane Grimson *et al.* (2000) identify "the inability to share information across healthcare systems and organizations as one of the major barriers to care coordination and cost containment." Some of the reasons for the limited or non-implementation of information technology in the health sector are the complexity of medical data, data entry problems, security and privacy issues, the lack of a unique national patient identifier in many countries, and a general lack of awareness of the benefits of information technology. Many models are experiencing these difficulties. Obviously, we cannot analyze them all in this chapter. We will focus on two of them: the HMO (Health Maintenance Organization) in the United States and the Swiss model of the Delta network (Huard and Schaller 2010a, 2010b, 2011a, 2011b). The HMO was chosen for its historical character and the Swiss model for its effectiveness in chronic disease management (Huard 2019).

1.2.1. *The cradle: the United States*

The United States has been experimenting with integrated systems at least since the 1950s and has seen a significant evolution in the organization of its most familiar model, the HMO, since the 1990s. However, the HMO is not the only model in the United States. Since the country has not historically had compulsory health insurance, it is the private sector that has strongly structured the health system. Obamacare has only partially changed this dominant state of affairs.

The other interesting model in the United States concerns the territorial structuring of medical homes in town medicine, the PCMH (Patient-Centered Medical Home). The reflection initiated on the management of chronic diseases based on the Chronic Care Model has been extended in the United States by focusing on the organization of primary care, which will allow us to better understand the notion of *digital healthcare territory* in the United States, a notion that is imperfectly covered by HMOs.

1.2.1.1. *Evolution of health maintenance organizations: from managed care to disease management*

We start with the oldest of these integrated models, embodied by HMOs. "HMOs have been in existence since the early 20th century in the United States and are partnerships between private insurers and healthcare providers. Initially, they offer a care pathway, financed by the associated insurance, and structured as a gatekeeping system: a general practitioner refers the patient, if necessary, to the hospital or to specialists in the network" (Parel 2016, p. 3). They developed from the 1973 HMO Act adopted by the Nixon administration (Gruber *et al.* 1988). The HMO Act led to the unprecedented development of Managed Care.

HMOs can be described as an integrated system of health maintenance, production of healthcare, and health insurance (Duhamel 2002):

– *a health maintenance system:* in this network paid by capitation, the insurer and the healthcare provider take full responsibility for the expenses of their members covered by the contract and, therefore, have every interest in keeping their clients as healthy as possible. Prevention and health education are important elements of the programs put in place and are considered long-term investments;

– *an integrated care production system:* for its subscribing population, the insurer is responsible for organizing access to care through a set of selected professionals (health professionals, providers employed or contracted by the insurer). Access to care is prioritized and coordinated. The group of physicians working for an HMO is multidisciplinary and organized into one or more medical centers, depending on the geographical area served. The notion of *healthcare territory* is still rather fluid. The medical staff includes primary care physicians and specialist physicians. For less common specialties, the insurer establishes contracts with specialists either within or outside the network. The size of the structure varies considerably, ranging from 100 to 1,000 doctors. As a result, the insured party's access to care is very strongly limited to network providers. Except in emergencies, if the insured party consults a doctor outside the HMO, he or she is subject to a substantial, if not exclusive, financial contribution to the payment of services (Duhamel 2002). It is clear that the notion of *healthcare territory* remains vague for the HMO, insofar as it is linked to the area served by the insurer and by patient movements, which are known to be significant throughout the United States, compared to the French;

– *for the insured party, a global and integrated coverage:* the affiliation to the network is voluntary and for a fixed period of time. It is insured against the payment of a fixed annual lumpsum payment, which is made by prepaying the insurance premium deducted monthly from the salary. In return, all the care covered by the contract is paid for by the network (third-party payer).

The backbone of the information system (IS) is the patient's shared medical record. For example, Kaiser Permanente, the largest American HMO, has set up a cooperation with Epic Systems Corporation for the implementation of a shared medical record for its patients, as a central element of a policy to improve the quality and efficiency of care (Bourret 2006).

At the end of the 1990s and the beginning of the 2000s, it appeared that the so-called managed care systems were running out of steam. They came up against reactions of rejection from professionals and policyholders, and their effectiveness, even in terms of controlling expenses, was questioned. Without totally abandoning these tools, private insurers will turn to disease management based on a philosophy radically different from that of managed care. It is no longer a question of controlling the delivery of care, but of trying to obtain optimal care for the potentially most expensive patients, based on the conviction that this improved care can result in significant savings in terms of hospitalization (Bras 2007, p. 118).

Disease management is used for pathologies where there are proven gaps between practices and recommendations, and where patient behavior is a determining factor in health outcomes (Bras 2007). The main diseases managed are diabetes, heart failure, coronary artery disease, asthma, and COPD (chronic obstructive pulmonary disease).

> There are organizations where disease management is implemented under the authority of the physician by his or her employees. This type of intervention can be found in integrated organizations such as Kayser or the Veterans Health Administration. Several conditions must be met to implement it. (Bras 2007)

First of all, the physician must be part of a team and have collaborators to whom he or she can delegate contact with patients; the transfer of tasks is, therefore, essential. Second, the physician and his team must have an efficient information system to organize contacts with patients according to their situation and risk level. Finally, physicians and their teams must have an interest in developing such a practice, where they do not simply wait for the patient, but where they can be called upon to intervene with the patient independently of his or her requests (Bras 2007). To achieve this, a system for evaluating and rewarding clinical performance is, therefore, necessary so that teams can devote energy to disease management. There is a need for an integrated information system built on an organization where people are at the forefront and where profit-sharing is more valued than is strict control. The organization of staff motivation is as important as the strict standardization of the information system and the coding of this information.

Moreover, disease management involves the manipulation of many nominative data on patients, and there may even be some data that must be processed without the patient's consent (creation of the initial file). The integrated interface calls for a secure and well-structured authorization structure for the handling of this highly sensitive data.

1.2.1.2. *Patient-centered medical home*

Applied to the primary care sector, the Chronic Care Model gave rise in the United States to the Patient-Centered Medical Home (PCMH), which is an approach adapted to the specificities of community medicine, which was experimented in doctors' offices in the early 2000s. As in the Chronic Care Model, the emphasis here is on harmonizing practices around evidence-based medicine, the use of information and communication technologies (computerized records, shared information systems, etc.), and patient involvement (Kilo and Wasson 2010; Bras 2011a, 2011b; Sebai and Yatim 2017).

The CDMHP clearly identifies the patient's family physician as the primary point of contact for all the teams involved in the patient's care. The organizational challenge is thus twofold. On the one hand, it is a matter of promoting the coordination of patient care and, on the other hand, facilitating interprofessional cooperation, not only at the office level but also at the level of the entire healthcare system, and throughout the patient's care pathway (Sebai and Yatim 2017).

This PCMH model partially corrects the difficulties of disease management in patient follow-up. The limitations of the disease management model, in which patient follow-up is carried out outside the practice, reinforce the interest in an approach in which the practice itself is reformed to integrate the patient follow-up function.

After reviewing several definitions, Bras states that:

> The goal of the PCMH is to promote a primary care practice based on teamwork under the authority of the physician and the intensive use of new communication and information technologies, including the use of "registries" to manage the patient's care plan. This type of organization should make it possible to better monitor the care provided in order to ensure that it corresponds to the best standards, to increase the possibilities of interaction and communication with patients, particularly to encourage their participation in the care process, and to better coordinate the intervention of the various stakeholders in the care process. (Bras 2011b, p. 29)

Pierre-Louis Bras notes that the introduction of modern information and communication tools was not a simple operation limited to the adoption of a turnkey tool. Physicians had to accept a transformation of their role with regard to patients and develop leadership qualities with regard to their collaborators, breaking with traditional management methods (Bras 2011b, p. 31). Once again, we see that the digital tool can only be made possible by human and organizational qualities that confine the tool to its status. Not everything revolves around the digital. It enables change towards an integrated model, but it also reveals the underlying organizational dysfunctions.

1.2.2. *The Swiss model of the Delta network*

Created in 1992, the *Réseau de soins Delta* (RSD, Delta Network) has grown steadily to reach today more than 700 primary care physicians in French-speaking Switzerland and ensures the health of more than 250,000 patients spread over five cantons.

It is important to note that the RSD retains the office model as physicians continue to practice in their offices, and the activities are those of primary care medicine. The RSD relies on many physicians with widely dispersed practice locations.

It works as follows (Huard and Schaller 2011b):

– the RSD remains driven by the small team of promoters from the beginning;

– each insurer working with the RSD offers its insured parties the opportunity to join the network and choose a treating physician from the RSD list. It is this attending physician (the gatekeeper) who decides to refer them to other service providers if necessary;

– the RSD negotiates a global capitation with each insurer, the amount of which is less than the average cost of reimbursements made by the insurer for all of its insured parties;

– the general practitioners of the canton can join the RSD by signing a charter and by committing themselves to participate in the quality circles that the RSD organizes in different areas of the canton, five times a week;

– the operation and results of these quality circles are one of the specific characteristics of the RSD. Each quality circle brings together, for one hour, at lunchtime, the same doctors, ten or fifteen in number, with a doctor who has been trained for this function;

– these quality circles contribute to the significant reduction in the cost of care for RSD patients compared to cantonal averages;

– the cost reduction has led to a positive result so far, that is, a surplus available to the RSD;

– this surplus is used in two ways. Firstly, it is used to finance joint activities: steering and management of the whole system (a high-performance computerized information system called "Delta data", which provides doctors with a wide range of information). Secondly, the balance of the surplus is used to remunerate doctors for their participation in quality circle sessions;

– the RSD is an innovative, high-profile device with an impressive list of services for policyholders.

The dynamic process can be seen on two levels:

– *cost reduction process*: cost reduction compared to the cantonal average is the central feature of the RSD, as it makes the network attractive to all the actors involved in its activity. The reduction of costs is indeed at the origin of:

- reducing premiums and the interest of the insured party,

- the reduction of the amount of refunds and interest from insurers,

- the increase in the number of insured members and the interest of physicians;

– *dynamic processes of reinforcement*: the central process just described is reinforced by several complementary processes.

Firstly:

> the surplus generated by cost reduction is first used to finance common services (steering, management, information system, case management program project, disease management, etc.) that contribute to the quality of patient care. However, some of these services directly concern the insured party. For example, for a large number of prevention and wellness activities, access is free or at a reduced rate, because RSD covers all or part of the cost paid to providers. Naturally, these benefits are an important reason for enrolling policyholders and contribute to increasing the number of policyholders, even though the number of policyholders determines the size of the RSD's revenues. (Huard and Schaller 2011b)

Secondly, a dynamic process develops between the number of insured parties and the number of physicians. On the one hand, the operation of the RSD results, as we have just seen, in an increase in the number of insured parties who join the scheme. This increase allows the RSD to recruit new physicians (Huard and Schaller 2011b).

The increase in the number of doctors is a new factor in the increase in the number of insured people, because it broadens their choice by offering them a more extensive list in which they are more likely to find a doctor they know or whose practice is located close to their home (Figure 1.2; Huard and Schaller 2011b; Huard 2019).

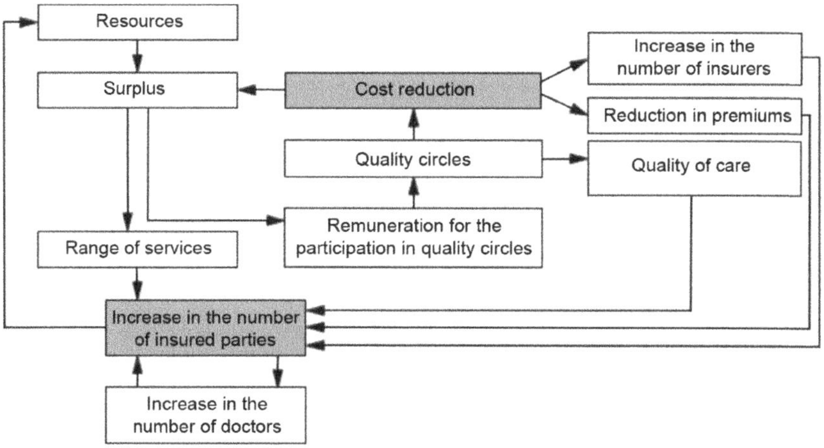

Figure 1.2. *Dynamic processes of Delta network development (Source: Huard and Schaller 2011b)*

As shown in Figure 1.2, all these dynamic processes are articulated with each other. They are recursive and cumulative and explain how the RSD has developed so far.

In this dynamic process, there is a loop concerning efficiency (investment and size) and another concerning attractiveness to professionals and patients. But insurers may also be interested because they negotiate, with the network, capitations that are lower than average costs, because if their insured members are satisfied, they will remain in the insurance that allows them to access the services offered by the network.

The issue of digital integration was not dealt with directly by Huard and Schaller. It was supplemented by interviews. It appears implicitly in their published articles. This indicates that the organizational stakes are more important than the digital tool, which only plays the role of facilitator. The information system (a very high-performance computer system called "Delta data") remains relatively little analyzed in the literature.

For Huard, coordination implies (1) that the information necessary for the convergence of activities is available (information on the activities that can be mobilized, on patients, on the stages and modifications of the patient's journey) and (2) that the participants take this information into account in their decisions (Huard 2019, p. 47).

With the extension of the Delta network to five cantons, it is obvious that the organization of digital technology plays a decisive role in the structuring of the network.

The analysis of the French case, for its part, places the cursor much more clearly on digital integration.

1.3. Digital technology as a challenge for territorial integration in the context of healthcare in France

To evoke the concept of the healthcare territory, let us return to the concepts of space, place, and their relationships that have long been debated in geography and geographic economics (notably by the ASRDLF, *Association de science régionale de langue française*). Theories in geography, for example, consider space as a geographical location that has no social connection for a human being, whereas places are spaces created by human experiences (Relph 1976; Tuan 1977). However, these concepts are not disjointed (Pérez *et al.* 2016): individuals give or derive "meaning" from knowledge of their environment and organize the world around them. Place is also the spaces where individuals focus intentions, experiences, and actions in a space (Seamon and Sowers 2008).

In health research, space is considered a dimension of reference for studying unhealthy behaviors, disease risk factors, and health problems (Chaix *et al.* 2013). Alternatively, place represents a container of either a population's health demand or healthcare activities (Poland *et al.* 2005). Information and communication technologies (ICTs) and digital technology have stimulated the development of new medical devices and the introduction of innovative organizational models that can improve healthcare delivery and healthcare pathways. Conceptually, they require enriching ways of thinking about the relationship between space and place of care. In addition, digital innovations are opening up new research opportunities to better define the health needs of an aging and healthy population, to track their evolution over time, and to provide appropriate services at the local level.

However, studies conducted to date show that the spread of digital healthcare is not homogeneous and can have both positive and negative effects. For patients, digital applications help overcome the limitations imposed by the geographical distribution of services and improve accessibility to care. They enable the transition to integrated, person-centered care. In practice, however, since the appropriation of digital healthcare is gradual and context-dependent, the diffusion of technologies may exacerbate existing disparities or create new ones.

1.3.1. *Healthcare territories: starting from the patient-user rather than from the offer of health and medico-social actors?*

Healthcare territorialization is a process of transformation of health systems aimed at setting up a planning policy based on the diversity of production methods in the developed areas and the decompartmentalization of resources and activities. In France, the 2009 Hospital, Patients, Health, Territories law was a pivotal step that continues with the current reforms (Loi de santé 2016, Plan Ma santé 2022). In other countries, although the stages and methods of implementing reforms vary, the logic inherent in the transformations of healthcare systems may seem similar: the rise of the "local" as a space for management and action, normative discourse on proximity to offset health inequalities, the multiplication of intermediaries in the organization and activity of healthcare, and the spread of management models inherited from New Public Management. Because of the diversity of the systems, their arrangements, and the types of action carried out according to countries, sectors, and structures (hospitals, doctors, specialists, etc.), the aim here is to gain a better understanding of the reorganization of spatial, temporal, and organizational scales induced by this process of territorialization. The acceleration of reforms in France constitutes our case study and allows us to better understand how public policies evolve and modify their actions over time to respond to demographic and health challenges.

Our reflection on France is based on two key ideas. The first idea is linked to the fact that the current logic of calls for tenders by the supervisory authorities (ARS, etc.) breaks up and compartmentalizes; between convergence and interoperability, the road ahead will be long and difficult.

The second key idea is territorial; if we take the logic of the care pathway, we need to look at how to situate the territories experienced. For Vigneron, we have five healthcare territories, but few current IS systems are based on this territorial anchoring. Only one course receives a positive response to this territorial problem: the complex pathway (*territoire de santé numérique*, TSN [digital healthcare territory], *plateforme territoriale d'appui*, PTA, [territorial support platform], *méthode d'action pour l'intégration des services d'aide et de soin dans le champ de l'autonomie*, MAIA [method of action for the integration of assistance and care services in the field of autonomy], *parcours de santé des personnes âgées en risque de perte d'autonomie*, PAERPA [healthcare pathway for elderly people at risk of loss of autonomy] etc.).

The tools and systems designed to organize coordination between actors at the territorial level stemming from the latest legislation show that the healthcare system remains compartmentalized between city care on the one hand and hospital care on the other.

Thus, while "the structuring of the healthcare pathway must be patient-centered, adapted to territorial needs, and take into account social and environmental specificities (healthcare offer)" (Veran 2017, p. 48), it must be noted that this pathway remains fragmented from an organizational and digital point of view through the implementation of current tools and systems.

These tools and devices are mainly:

– in the field of urban care, TSNs, primary care teams, and territorial health professional communities, as well as territorial support platforms;

– in the case of hospital care, the GHT (*Groupement Hospitalier de Territoires* [Regional Hospital Grouping]).

For information systems, there is a compartmentalization of digital tools; information systems are linked to the territorial perimeter of the devices, despite the national *e-parcours* (e-pathway) tools. We are in a logic of calls for tender on a territorial level, which places public action in a logic of successive calls for tender, without much coherence:

– the tools developed within the framework of the TSNs served as a prefiguration of the territorial information system for the route and coordination (National Agency for Performance Support, ANAP);

– territorial support platforms (PTAs) and *communautés professionnelles territoriales de santé territorial* (CPTS [health professional communities]): what digital tools and funding? The e-Term Plan remains very evasive on these points;

– the GHTs: the HOP'EN plan remains confined to the public bodies of the GHTs, independently of the path of actual patients.

Thus, tools and services can be seen to be intertwined; the territorial level of information systems crosses the launch of national services (DMP-type tools, shared medial folder), regional and local services developed through experimentation, and a regional governance (GRADES) that is beginning to take shape.

Launching national services remains fragmented to date: services and tools for sharing and exchanging health data such as the DMP, secure health messaging (MSSanté), and the implementation of the unique patient identity integrating the national health identifier (*identifiant national de santé*, INS).

Patient referral tools (ROR Viatrajectoire) are well accepted regionally.

The tools for coordinating pathways, a legacy of the TSNs (e.g. PAACO Globule), remain confined to experimental digital healthcare territories.

Why then develop national services in addition to local tools? The interoperability goes beyond the framework of the GHTs. The convergence of public healthcare institutions is not limited to the limits of the GHT. "Indeed, the ecosystem of a healthcare pathway must reflect its ability to communicate with other players in the territory, such as local medicine, healthcare networks, and the medico-social sector," explains the Deputy Director of Innovation at Enovacom. The constellation of players with very heterogeneous information systems makes interoperability even more complex. Thus, the practice of interoperability standards is practically non-existent in the medico-social sector. Tools such as the shared medical record or secure healthcare messaging must enable exchanges between all these players. All that remains is to launch them.

Theoretically, according to the *Ma Santé 2022* report, we will eventually have a global target schema for the architecture of the health information system, with interoperability and interconnection to smart devices.

Today, we can note one exception – the regional e-health platform SISRA, which integrates all ISs at the regional level. But the digital integration in progress cannot hide organizational problems (FHF report "*Renforcer le lien ville-hôpital*" from March 2018).

1.3.2. *An exemplary structuring of the territory? The TSN program and the E-Parcours*

Included in 2013 in the Ayrault government's digital roadmap, the TSN (*Territoire de soins numérique*, Digital Care Territory) program was allocated a national budget of 80 million euros as part of the Future Investment Program (*programme d'investissements d'avenir*, PIA) for the 2014–2017 period. This program has had the distinction of being co-managed by the Ministry of Health and the Ministry of the Economy of France. However, make no mistake about it, it was a matter of starting from the field, the local level, and their innovations in order to bring best practices to the fore.

The TSN program aimed to strengthen the coordination of healthcare professionals and innovative patient care organizations by financing the development of digital service packages in pilot territories.

Five projects were selected in 2014: XL ENS (*Landes espace numérique de santé*) for the Nouvelle Aquitaine region, eTICSS (*Territoire innovant coordonné santé social*) for the Bourgogne-Franche-Comté region, TerriS@nté ("*Le numérique au service de la santé en métropole du Grand-Paris*") for the Île-de-France region, PASCALINE (*Parcours de santé coordonné et accès à l'innovation numérique*) for the Auvergne-Rhône-Alpes region, and OIIS (*Océan Indien innovation santé*) for the Indian Ocean.

Each of the five projects was developed around specific priorities: the fight against chronic diseases for OIIS, the city-hospital relationship for eTICSS, the articulation of information systems with TerriS@nté, healthcare at home for XL ENS-Santé-Landes and tools for exchanges between healthcare professionals with PASCALINE, but always with the main objective of better management of the patient pathway through interdisciplinarity and digital innovation. The examples of the PASCALINE and TerriS@nté projects show the potential of digital technology to improve the link between patients and medico-social professionals.

1.3.2.1. *Case study: TSN PASCALINE*

We analyze in more detail the project entitled PASCALINE, which focused on a territory of 235,000 inhabitants between the eastern districts of Lyon (Rhône) and Bourgoin-Jallieu (Isère).

The PASCALINE program is structured around the implementation of two territorial support platforms (PTAs) in April 2016 in northern Isère and in September 2016 in eastern Lyon, and a digital device for exchanging and sharing health information, which aimed to converge the tools used to coordinate the paths within the PTAs, the MAIAs (methods of action for the integration of aid and care services in the field of autonomy) and health networks.

For any public or private healthcare establishment in the territory, the interaction between the establishment's hospital information system and the territory's tools is essential so that the establishment's professionals can communicate with all of the territory's healthcare players.

In order to respond to this problem, digital tools make it possible to communicate with:

– city professionals (doctors, nurses, masseur-physiotherapists, pharmacists, other city and medico-social actors, actors of the coordination of the routes), thanks to the solution MonSisra;

– the coordination cells for the MesPatients solution;

– the patient, via the provision of the myHOP patient portal;

– the other establishments in the territory.

The system is, therefore, available in several different interfaces, depending on the user's profile, and is based on the Zepra application (for *Zéro échange papier* in Rhône-Alpes), opened in 2010 in the region for the secure exchange of information from the electronic patient record (EPR) and software used by the various healthcare players.

Despite its common usage and perceived attractiveness, the qualifier "integration" or "integrated" in the context of information systems remains notoriously slippery because "individuals often have a different understanding of the meaning of the word" (Gulledge 2006, p. 5), or it can "mean everything to everyone" (Wainwright and Waring 2004, p. 229).

We thus have several different levels here in the construction of the integrated model, with different uses and different entry and authorization levels for practitioners according to their function (medical, medico-social, etc.) and even for users.

These are:

– connecting hospitals: Zepra, which predates the TSN, was already used to connect hospital practitioners from the computerized patient record;

– connecting urban healthcare: the MonSisra tool is aimed at urban healthcare professionals and enables them to manage the coordination and sharing of information for all healthcare pathways, including complex situations. It is both a secure health messaging system (MSSanté) and a portal for accessing patient histories and all e-health services deployed in the region (ViaTrajectoire, the operational resource directory (*répertoire opérationnel des ressources*, ROR), the tool for managing multidisciplinary cancer concertation meetings (*réunions de concertation pluridisciplinaire en cancérologie*, RCP), or the electro-technical vaccination record);

– homogenizing coordination tools: the MesPatients tool is a version of the Rhone's exchange and sharing system for coordination structures. It allows interaction between the different people involved in patient care, the sharing of the patient's file, and the development, monitoring, and evaluation of the patient's personalized health plan (*plan personnalisé de santé*, PPS) and individualized service plan (*plan de service individualisé*, PSI);

– offering digital services to patients: the third brick of digital services developed as part of the TSN program is aimed at patients and offers them a single access point to their health information through the regional MyHop portal;

– proposing a follow-up tool: ViaTrajectoire is a tool for following up on referrals in follow-up care and rehabilitation, home hospitalization, long-term care, residential facilities for the elderly or for people with disabilities.

The operator chosen for the structuring of this territory's IS is public (GCS SIRA).

1.3.3. *What lessons can be learned?*

First of all, in order to benefit from TSN's tender logic to finance digital projects, it is necessary to start from the field rather than from a top-down logic, and from related services developed in partnership mode.

The originality of the TSN program in Auvergne-Rhône-Alpes was to entrust the steering of the development of additional digital services to partners such as the Regional Union of Health Professionals (*Union régionale des professionnels de santé*, URPS), private doctors and the i-Care Innovation Cluster.

The i-Care Cluster has taken charge of the organization, management, and development of the innovation incubator in order to allow for the experimentation of innovative health solutions to improve user experience and facilitate exchanges between professionals. The primary objective is to contribute to the development of new solutions in the field of health and medico-social care in the PASCALINE experimentation area, in order to optimize the journey of users and healthcare professionals. The secondary objective is to promote the implementation in the field of innovative solutions by maximizing the chances of success for routine use thanks to the Living Lab method applied to health.

1.3.4. *PTAs and CPTS: the Alpha and Omega of healthcare territory structuring?*

Now, with the passage to the e-pathway, the notion of a TSN is taken up on a more basic scale to be set up by the PTA and CPTS; the Ministry of Health wants an unthinkable acceleration of the movement, subject in particular to the condition that the private practitioners set up the projects themselves (CPTS).

Organizing and simplifying coordination are the watchwords of multifaceted reforms, but there is a tendency to complicate rather than simplify (Bloch and Hénault 2014).

"The question of coordinating healthcare and assistance for the elderly has long been the subject of public attention, and has given rise to the creation of numerous measures since the 1960s and especially the 1980s"

(Bloch and Henault 2014). Bloch insists on the fragmented and particularly stacked nature of the structures.

There are many support mechanisms for coordinating the pathways, which are not very clear: local information and coordination centers (*centres locaux d'information et de coordination*, CLIC), method of action for the integration of aid and care services in the field of autonomy (MAIA), networks, PAERPA, etc.

Measure No. 6 of the national health strategy, the territorial component carried by Norbert Nabet, indicates that all the coordination mechanisms for complex cases within the PTAs must be merged (Pribile and Nabet 2018).

Territorial support platforms (PTAs) become the place where all the existing coordination mechanisms (MAIA, PAERPA, CLIC, PRADO, healthcare network, etc.) are merged, on which they rely to organize the path of complex patients. Access to these systems, by patients or professionals, is through a single point of contact, which then activates the intervention best suited to the patient's situation. The PTAs thus constituted complement the simple coordination mechanisms set up at the local level that will be developed.

The PTA gradually integrates all the devices that will have emerged in the territory within the framework of territorial animation, and may also eventually include the function of regulation, advice and guidance of patients. It will also be necessary to define a financing model that will enable these platforms to have the necessary human resources as their active file develops.

The expected benefits for the patient are:

– users (patients or caregivers) are no longer left alone to coordinate their journey;

– within a territory, the offer of coordination is legible and graduated;

– the number of patients integrated into the coordination devices is significantly increased, allowing more patients to stay at home or in close proximity;

– healthcare professionals no longer have to carry out the task of finding the most appropriate coordination mechanism themselves;

– better coordination of the pathways reduces the use of emergency services and accommodation structures (health or medico-social), which are thus listed on their missions.

In terms of support, the PTAs will be able to benefit from the €2 billion investment plan announced on May 24, 2016, one of the priorities of which is the development of digital technology between the city and healthcare institutions and support for the territorial organization of care in order to promote relevant healthcare pathways and healthcare at home.

1.3.5. *Launch of SNAC in regions*

The national strategy provides for support over five years for the development of digital services to support coordination (*services numériques d'appui à la coordination*, SNAC), and a multi-year funding of €150 million, of which €20 million is planned in 2017 in the FIR, is proposed to support:

– firstly, the ARSs to define and implement the regional strategy for digital services and the coordination that they will have built with all the players involved in the patient and user journey;

– secondly, the ARSs for the progressive launch of these digital services to the healthcare, medico-social, and social actors involved in the coordination of the pathways, throughout the territory, particularly (but not exclusively) to support the coordination support missions as defined by the Decree No. 2016-919 of July 4, 2016, relating to support functions for professionals for the coordination of complex healthcare pathways.

Ultimately, and fundamentally, the measures put in place, beyond the specificities of each, represent opportunities to launch new national and regional calls for tenders, in order to finance the launch of digital healthcare. It can be said that the framework was set with the TSN, the launching of an IS on the territory for all the players and service launches. But the government did not want to generalize this experiment as it stands. The *e-parcours* program follows the TSN program. However, its purpose is not to generalize the TSN program but to accompany and generalize the coupled device of PTA and CPTS.

1.4. Digital integration and aging in France: from health pathway to life pathway

The INSEE's demographic projections (Blanpain and Buisson 2016) tell us that in 2030, nearly 30% of the French population will be 60 years old and over and 12% will be over 75 years old. At the same time, INSEE forecasts show a trend towards a strong increase in the number of dependent elderly people. For metropolitan France, this increase would amount to 40% between 2010 and 2030 and 100% between 2010 and 2060. The number of dependent elderly people would rise from 1,150,000 in 2010 to 1,550,000 in 2030, and then to 2,300,000 in 2060 (Cour des comptes 2016).

This demographic evolution suggests that the EHPADs will be more and more medicalized and will welcome people with more and more serious pathologies, notably neurodegenerative disorders. It will not be possible to build EHPADs up to the level of this demographic pressure, as healthcare at home is becoming a major issue.

Strategic documents at the national (Ministry of Health), decentralized regional (ARS), or departmental level set as a priority the optimization of healthcare at home for the elderly. These orientations are shared by the CNSA, the ASV law, the PRS of the ARS and echo above all the demographic problem of the rise of the elderly and the aspirations of this new aging generation. This demand to "age at home" is a strong factor to be taken into consideration in the future evolution of the accommodation offer for elderly people with loss of autonomy.

Of course, healthcare at home covers many types of housing situations, from initial housing to various more collective but non-medicalized modalities, including independent residences.

Developing healthcare at home involves coordinating the healthcare and life pathways. If we refer to the literature on coordination, and in particular the work of Marie-Aline Bloch and Léonie Hénaut (2014), the field of coordination of the seniors' healthcare pathway is one of the most complex, which is a multi-layered structure. Today, there is an extremely fragmented and uncoordinated supply of homecare services.

The players appear to be particularly fragmented and a multitude of systems have been developed in France (CLIC, gerontological networks,

MAIA, PAERPA). Despite the improvement and goodwill of all those involved in homecare, there are still many disruptions in healthcare and treatment that all too often lead to hospitalization, with the consequences we know about when people return home (destabilization, loss of autonomy). It is, therefore, necessary to guarantee continuity of service in any situation and at any time of the day or night.

The integration of the health and life course essentially poses the problem of digital patient monitoring on several levels: (1) the difficulty of the interoperability of existing information systems in healthcare and medico-social structures, (2) a complex course that is generally well taken care of (TSN, PAERPA, etc.) but not by the person in need of care before dependency and the prevention part, which leaves much to be desired, (3) the appropriation of digital tools by patients/caregivers, and finally (4) the challenge of tomorrow is healthcare at home (home automation, e-health, coordination of professional actors and caregivers), detection of frailties and management of the outside world.

If the organizational difficulties of the public players persist, as nature abhors a vacuum, the private players will be there to compensate (Ramsay Santé, Groupe SOS, Croix Rouge, or locally specific private groups). The risk remains that this will always lead to a situation of inequality of access between those who can afford to pay for access to these services and those who cannot.

1.5. Conclusion

The health ecosystem is facing complex and multiple challenges: an increase in chronic diseases, an aging population, and the all too recent introduction of issues that were neglected in the past (prevention, health promotion, aging disability, etc.). Digital technology makes it possible to follow the patient along a path of health and life. However, organizational problems are revealed by the irruption of digital technology, which cannot solve human problems. There is still a long way to go before healthcare regions fully invest in the digital integration that is essential for the management of healthcare and life pathways, especially for those most in need. The French case, paradoxically, focuses on the digital issue, whereas the model is the least integrated compared to the American cases (HMO and PCMH) or the Swiss Delta network. This perhaps shows a willingness on the part of public authorities to place a lot of hope in digital technology, failing to move towards a model that is *de facto* more integrated and difficult to reform by stacking up. It is to be feared, as we have emphasized on many occasions, that digital technology will only bring to light the organizational dysfunctions of our French healthcare structures in the face of the challenge of aging and chronic diseases. This does not, however, prevent the success of certain territorial models such as those of the TSNs.

1.6. References

Amat-Roze, J.-M. (2011). La territorialisation de la santé : quand le territoire fait débat. *Hérodote*, 143(4), 13–32.

Ankri, J. (2013). De la coordination à l'intégration : petite histoire d'une recherche permanente de défragmentation du système d'aide et de soins aux personnes âgées. *Actualité et dossier en santé publique*, 85.

Argoud, D. (2016). Les gérontotechnologies sont-elles une innovation sociale ? *Retraite et société*, 75(3), 31–45.

ARS Centre (2014). Cadre d'urbanisation des Systèmes d'information partagés de santé en région Centre [Online]. Available at: https://www.sante-centre.fr/portail/gallery_files/site/1637/2463/2464.pdf.

Baudier, F. (2019). Crise à l'hôpital et dans les EHPAD, même combat : abattons les murs ! *Santé Publique*, 31(2), 293–295.

Bergoignan Esper, C., Bringer, J., Budet, J.-M., Vigneron, E. (2019). *Les groupements hospitaliers de territoire : un moyen d'organisation de l'offre de santé*. Berger Levrault, Boulogne-Billancourt.

Bertillot, H. and Bloch, M. (2016). Quand la "fragilité" des personnes âgées devient un motif d'action publique. *Revue française des affaires sociales*, 107–128.

Blanpain, N. and Buisson, G. (2016). Projections de population à l'horizon 2070. Deux fois plus de personnes de 75 ans ou plus qu'en 2013. *Insee Première*, 1619(November).

Bloch, M.-A. and Hénaut, L. (2014). *Coordination et parcours : la dynamique du secteur sanitaire, social et médico-social*. Dunod, Paris.

Bodenheimer, T., Wagner, E.H., Grumbach, K. (2002a). Improving primary care for patients with chronic illness, part 1. *JAMA*, 288(14), 1775–1779.

Bodenheimer, T., Wagner, E.H., Grumbach, K. (2002b). Improving primary care for patients with chronic illness, part 2. *JAMA*, 288(15), 1909–1914.

Borgès Da Silva, G. and Borgès Da Silva, R. (2005). La gestion intégrée des soins : l'expérience de Kaiser permanente et de Veterans health administration, aux USA. *Revue médicale de l'Assurance Maladie*, 36(4).

Bourquard, K. and Coat, A. (2009). Une démarche d'élaboration de cadres d'interopérabilité ou de sécurité pour les systèmes d'information en santé. *Pratiques et organisation des soins*, 40(4), 283–296.

Bourret, C. (2003). La santé en réseaux. *Études*, 399(9), 175–189.

Bourret, C. (2004). Réseaux de santé et nouveaux métiers de l'information. *Documentaliste-Sciences de l'Information*, 41(3), 174–181.

Bourret, C. (2010). Évaluation et communication des nouvelles organisations d'interface : le cas des réseaux de santé. *Communication et organisation*, 38(2010), 77–88.

Bourret, C. (2016). Nouveaux métiers d'intermédiation dans les organisations d'interface en santé. *I2D – Information, données & documents*, 53(3), 32–33.

Bras, P. (2007). Le disease management. In *De l'observance à la gouvernance de sa santé*, Laude, A. (ed.). PUF, Paris.

Bras, P. (2011a). Peut-on réformer l'organisation des soins de premier recours ? *Les Tribunes de la santé*, 30(1), 113–126.

Bras, P. (2011b). Réorganiser les soins de premier recours : les maisons médicales centrées sur le patient aux États-Unis. *Pratiques et organisation des soins*, 42(1), 27–34.

Buttard, A., Dos Santos, C., Tizio, S. (2012). Networking healthcare. From a competitive call to a medical cooperation as a guarantee of a found confidence. *Recherches en sciences de gestion*, 93(6), 21–43.

Calvet, L. and DREES (2016). État de santé et dépendance des personnes âgées en institution ou à domicile. *Études et résultats*, 988.

Chaix, B., Meline, J., Duncan, S., Jardinier, L., Perchoux, C., Vallé, J., Merrien, C., Karusisi, N., Lewin, A., Brondeel, R., Kestens, Y. (2013). Neighborhood environments, mobility, and health: Towards a new generation of studies in environmental health research. *Revue d'épidémiologie et de santé publique*, 61S, s139–s145.

Chambaretaud, S. and Lequet-Slama, D. (2002). Managed care et concurrence aux États-Unis, évaluation d'un mode de régulation. *Revue française des affaires sociales*, 11–37.

CNOM (2015). De la e-santé à la santé connectée. White paper [Online]. Available at: https://www.conseil-national.medecin.fr/sites/default/files/cn_pdf/janvier2015/master/sources/projet/MEDECINS_sante_connectee.pdf.

Coldefy, M. and Lucas-Gabrielli, V. (2012). Le territoire, un outil d'organisation des soins et des politiques de santé : évolutions de 2003 à 2011. *Question d'économie de la santé*, 175.

Collos, J. and Delomier, C. (2012). Usage et non-usage des objets communicants dans le cadre du maintien à domicile : la relation des personnes âgées avec les TIC. *Gérontologie et société*, 35/141(2), 41–55.

Cour des comptes (2016). Le maintien à domicile des personnes âgées en perte d'autonomie [Online]. Available at: https://www.ccomptes.fr/fr/documents/32712.

Couturier, Y., Gagnon, D., Salles, M., Belzile, L. (2011). L'évaluation multidimensionnelle de la perte d'autonomie des personnes âgées. In *Usagers ou citoyens : de l'usage des catégories en action sociale et médico-sociale*, Jaeger, M. (ed.). Dunod, Paris.

Curtis, S. and Learmonth, A. (2013). Place shaping to create health and wellbeing using health assessment: Health geography applied to develop evidence-based practice. *Health and Place*, 24, 20–22.

Czernichow, P. (2015). Un système de santé plus intégré pour mieux prendre en charge les maladies chroniques. *Santé Publique*, s1(HS), 7–8.

DGOS (2016). Instruction no. DGOS/R5/2016/392 du 2 décembre 2016 relative aux équipes de soins primaires (ESP) et aux communautés professionnelles territoriales de santé (CPTS). Document, DGOS.

Duhamel, G. (2002). Le système de santé et d'assurance maladie américain. Action avec les médecins concernant la qualité des soins et la régulation des dépenses en ambulatoire. IGAS report, 2002-073, April.

Eliot, E., Lucas-Gabrielli, V., Mangeney, C. (2017). Territorialisation sanitaire et décentralisation : état des lieux et enjeux à partir du cas français. *Revue francophone sur la santé et les territoires*, June.

Grimson, J., Grimson, W., Hasselbring, W. (200). The SI challenge in health care. *Communications of the ACM*, 43(6), 49–55.

Gulledge, T.R. (2006). What is integration? *Industrial Management & Data Systems*, 106(1), 5–20.

HAS (2013). Efficience de la télémédecine : état des lieux de la littérature internationale et cadre d'évaluation [Online]. Available at: http://www.has-sante.fr/portail/upload/docs/application/pdf/2013-07/efficience_tlm_vf_2013-07-18_14-48-38_743.pdf.

Huard, P. and Schaller, P. (2010a). Améliorer la prise en charge des pathologies chroniques – 1. Problématique. *Pratiques et organisation des soins*, 41(3), 237–245.

Huard, P. and Schaller, P. (2010b). Améliorer la prise en charge des pathologies chroniques – 2. Stratégie. *Pratiques et organisation des soins*, 41(3), 247–255.

Huard, P. and Schaller, P. (2011a). Innovation organisationnelle et prise en charge des maladies chroniques. 1. La coopération entre partenaires distants. *Pratiques et organisation des soins*, 42(2), 111–118.

Huard, P. and Schaller, P. (2011b). Innovation organisationnelle et prise en charge des maladies chroniques. 2. Deux études de cas. *Pratiques et organisation des soins*, 42(2), 119–126.

Hugues, L. (2014). L'accompagnement global par le gestionnaire de cas pour un changement dans la situation de la personne âgée. *Vie sociale*, 6(2), 145–165.

IGAS (2018). Déploiement des communautés professionnelles territoriales de santé. IGAS report, 2018-041R.

Jacquet, M. (2019). Le virage numérique à l'hôpital : un processus de transformation globale. *Gestion & finances publiques*, 1(1), 37–43.

Kilo, C.M. and Wasson, J.H. (2010). Practice redesign and the patient-centered medical home: History, promises, and challenges. *Health Affairs*, 29, 773–778.

Kodner, D.L. (2012). Soins de santé intégrés – quoi, pourquoi, comment, quoi éviter ? *Symposium national sur les soins de santé intégrés*, October [Online]. Available at: http://www.conseilcanadiendelasante.ca/tree/symposium2012/P1_IntegratedHealthCare_Kodner_FR.pdf.

Levesque, J.-F., Feldman, D., Dufresne, C., Bergeron, P., Pinard, B., Gagné, V. (2009). Barrières et éléments facilitant l'implantation de modèles intégrés de prévention et de gestion des maladies chroniques. *Pratiques et organisation des soins*, 40, 251–265.

Lie, M. and Brittain, K. (2016). Technologie et confiance : le point de vue des personnes âgées sur un système de télésurveillance à domicile. *Retraite et société*, 75(3), 47–72.

Longépé, C. (2004). *Le projet d'urbanisation du S.I.*, 2nd edition. Dunod, Paris.

Loubat, J.-R., Hardy, J.-P., Bloch, M.-A. (2016). *Mettre en œuvre une plateforme de services en action sociale et médico-sociale*. Dunod, Paris.

Parel, V. (2016). Le développement des réseaux de soins dans l'Amérique de Richard Nixon. Les enseignements du Managed Care américain depuis le HMO Act de 1973. *Histoire, économie & société*, 35th year (3), 125–142.

Pérez, S., Laperrière, V., Borderon, M., Padilla, C., Maignant, G., Oliveau, S. (2016). Evolution of research in health geographics through the International Journal of Health Geographics (2002–2015). *International Journal of Health Geographics*, 15(3).

Perone, N., Filliettaz, S., Budan, F., Schaller, P., Balavoine, J., Waldvogel, F. (2015). Concrétiser la prise en charge interdisciplinaire ambulatoire de la complexité. *Santé Publique*, s1(HS), 77–86.

Poland, B.P., Lehoux, D., Holmes, A.G. (2005). How place matters: Unpacking technology and power in health and social care. *Health and Social Care in the Community*, 3(2), 170–180.

Pribile, P. and Nabet, N. (2018). Repenser l'organisation territoriale des soins. Stratégie de transformation du système de santé. Report, Ministère des Solidarités et de la Santé, France.

Relph, E. (1976). *Place and Placelessness*. Pion, London.

Schaller, P. (2014). Éléments pour une gestion stratégique d'une maison de santé. *Santé Publique*, 26(4), 509–517.

Seamon, D. and Sowers, J. (2008). *Key Texts in Human Geography*. Sage, London.

Sebai, J. (2018). Les plateformes territoriales d'appui : une réforme partielle de plus pour répondre au défi de la prise en charge ambulatoire des patients complexes ? *Les Tribunes de la santé*, 58(1), 103–113.

Sebai, J. and Yatim, F. (2017). Les maisons de santé pluriprofessionnelles en France : une dynamique réelle mais un modèle organisationnel à construire. *Revue française d'administration publique*, 164(4), 887–902.

Sirven, N. (2013). Fragilité et prévention de la perte d'autonomie. Une approche en économie de la sante. *Irdes, Questions d'économie de la santé*, 184.

Sirven, N. (2014). Mesurer la fragilité des personnes âgées en population générale : une comparaison entre les enquêtes ESPS et SHARE. *Irdes, Questions d'économie de la santé*, 199.

Sirven, N. and Rapp, T. (2016). Vieillissement, fragilité et dépenses de santé. *Irdes, Questions d'économie de la santé*, 216.

Somme, D., Trouvé, H., Passadori, Y., Corvez, A., Jeandel, C., Bloch, M., de Stampa, M. (2013). Prise de position de la société française de gériatrie et gérontologie sur le concept d'intégration. *Gérontologie et société*, 36/145(2), 201–226.

Takagi, J. (2006). L'évolution du management des médecins américains. *Revue française de gestion*, 168–169(9), 55–81.

Tuan, Y.F. (1977). *Space and Place: The Perspective of Experience*. University of Minnesota Press, Minneapolis.

Vigneron, E. (2005). Une conscience géographique de la santé. *Sciences humaines*, special edition 48(March–April–May).

Vigneron, E. (2019). Le territoire des GHT : bilan, réflexions et propositions. In *Les groupements hospitaliers de territoire : un moyen d'organisation de l'offre de santé*, Bergoignan Esper, C., Bringer, J., Budet, J.-M., Vigneron, E. (eds). Berger Levrault, Paris.

Wagner, E.H. (1998). Chronic disease management: What will it take to improve care for chronic illness? *Effective Clinical Practice*, 1(1), 2–4.

Wagner, E.H. (2004a). Effective teamwork and quality or care. *Medical Care*, 42, 1037–1039.

Wagner, E.H. (2004b). Keynote address *NICS Heart Failure Forum 2004*, National Institute of Clinical Studies [Online]. Available at: http://www.nhmrc.gov.au/nics/data/mediacache/879850011538245621 47/NICS%20Heart%20Failure%20Forum%20Report.pdf.

Wagner, E.H., Austin, B., Davis, C., Hindmarsh, M., Schaefer, J., Bonomi, A. (2001). Improving chronic illness care: Translating evidence into action. *Health Affairs*, 20(6), 64–78.

Wainwright, D. and Waring, T. (2004). Three domains for implementing integrated information systems: Redressing the balance between technology, strategic, and organizational analysis. *International Journal of Information Management*, 24, 229–246.

2

Digital Technology in a Cancer Patient's Primary-Secondary Care Journey

2.1. Introduction

The interface between private practice and hospital medicine is an important issue in the organization of care, enabling all patients to receive care, and also to return home in good health. The different caregivers must coordinate and collaborate closely for optimal care.

Some of the main sources of change in the health system are computerization, digitization, and technical networking affecting the management, organization, and delivery of care and services. Technological advances have made it possible to process, store, and disseminate information in all its forms, whether oral, written, or visual, increasingly free of all constraints of distance, volume, and time (Carré and Lacroix 2001). New technologies are modifying the way information is exchanged, how documents are searched, and even interpersonal relationships. Digital applications are becoming more and more integrated into the patient's primary-secondary care journey.

This chapter looks at different points in the management of patients, using cancer as an example. Indeed, the very history of the disease and the health organization developed to improve the care of the patient suffering from cancer make it possible to show concrete examples of models or

---

Chapter written by Marie-Ève ROUGÉ-BUGAT.

inadequacies in the primary-secondary care literature. The examples of digital interventions taken in this chapter allow for a preliminary critical reflection. This chapter does not intend be exhaustive in terms of covering all digital interventions in the care of a cancer patient.

2.2. Organization of cancer care

2.2.1. *Cancer plans*

In France, three successive plans have been implemented to address the major public health challenges of cancer. The first Cancer Plan (*Plan cancer I*) from 2003–2007 laid the foundations for the organization of the healthcare offer and developed prevention and research support. The second Cancer Plan (*Plan cancer II*) from 2009–2013 drove the improvement of the quality of life of people with cancer, the reduction of health inequalities, and has emphasized the role of the general practitioner in the care of cancer patients. The third Cancer Plan (*Plan cancer III*) from 2014–2019 aimed to optimize regional and territorial organizations for more efficient care. It seeks to improve primary-secondary care coordination and the exchange of information between professionals. It advocates the need to generalize the computerization of cancer care processes in primary care and secondary care and to improve the sharing and secure exchange of information between professionals.

2.2.2. *Primary care actors*

The primary care team (general practitioner, pharmacist, and nurse), must form a close-knit trio, within which fluid communication is ideal for better management of the cancer patient. This coordination around the patient will allow for optimal therapeutic compliance and quality of life for the patient. To achieve this, tools, particularly digital tools, have been created and are available on several information channels.

2.2.2.1. *General practitioners*

The management of cancer patients involves general practitioners both during the acute phase of treatment and in the post-treatment follow-up. Putting the general practitioner at the heart of care was the proposal of the

Cancer Plan II (2009–2013). This plan considered the situation of the general practitioner to be important but problematic, as he or she is often excluded from the care of patients with cancer. The general practitioner or "primary care ambulatory specialist" (HPST law[1] (Ministère de la Santé 2009), Article L. 4130-1 of the French Public Health Code) is one of the strong links in our healthcare system. Through their specific role in the care and orientation of patients in the healthcare system, general practitioners, clinicians specializing in primary care, become central in the organization of the provision of ambulatory care. The general practitioner is the user's first contact with the healthcare system. He or she is responsible for the overall care of the patient, the continuity of care over time, according to the patient's needs, and ensures the efficient use of the health system's resources. This is done in particular through the coordination of care and the management of the use of other specialties and other caregivers. The general practitioner cares for individuals in the familial, environmental, and cultural context, using in particular the knowledge and confidence accumulated through repeated contact.

The general practitioner will successively go through prevention, screening, diagnosis, treatment, sometimes remission, relapse, then evolution and end of life. However, even recent history of medicine teaches us that general practitioners have not always found their place (Summerton 2000). With the permanent progress of systemic treatments, their administration in day hospitals (outpatient care) and the increasing use of new drugs such as targeted therapies or immunotherapy, sometimes delivered in primary care pharmacies and both associated with new side effects, the pressure on primary care medicine is increasing. These technical advances have consequences on the activities of hospital and primary care healthcare professionals, who must adapt to the "ambulatory shift" in cancer management and its involvement in daily life.

The interface between hospital medicine (hospital, clinic, or cancer center) and primary care medicine is an important issue in the organization of care allowing all patients to receive care and also to return home in good condition. It involves close collaboration between the various caregivers.

---

1 "*Hôpital, patients, santé, territoire*" (Hospital, Patients, Health, Territory) reforming the hospital and relating to patients, health and territories, also known as the Bachelot law, enacted on July 21, 2009.

2.2.2.2. *Home care nurses*

Registered home care nurses provide care intended to maintain or restore the health of sick people. They monitor the state of health of patients and act either on their own or according to the doctor's prescriptions: interviews with patients and their family, therapeutic education, preparation and distribution of medicines, technical care (dressings, samples, blood pressure, injections, etc.). Nurses intervene in the patient's home and are therefore ideally exposed to the material and familial environment.

As part of the therapeutic follow-up, the nurses organize the taking of treatments and can thus follow the patient on a daily basis. It is thanks to them that patients can organize their medication intake according to meals and that they can be alerted to possible interactions. Nurses will also be able to identify polymedication and inform general practitioners and pharmacists. They will also witness the appearance of adverse effects and the possibility of healthcare at home. They are the daily link between all those involved in healthcare at home, and must, therefore, be easily proposed and involved in the management.

2.2.2.3. *Dispensing pharmacists*

Some cancer therapies are available in pharmacies, especially those administered orally. However, these drugs are not without side effects and risks of drug interactions that the pharmacist must prevent and control with each dispensing.

The dispensing pharmacist is one of the best-placed actors to study the patient's prescription in order to rule out drug interactions and to limit polymedication, especially for elderly cancer patients (Rougé-Bugat *et al.* 2017). Several research projects are currently underway in this field in order to set up a "drug reconciliation" with the help of hospital and pharmacy pharmacists. The dispensing pharmacist is the only caregiver who knows how much non-prescription treatments are being used.

2.3. Regional health organization for patient management

2.3.1. *Healthcare supply*

The supply of healthcare is organized within the region with highly specialized services of high technological level (neurosurgery, cardiac surgery, treatment of serious burns, organ transplants). Within the care structure, the file is computerized and collects administrative, medical, and paramedical information for each patient.

The second level includes specialized services, within "healthcare territories" and more recently around territorial health professional communities (*communautés professionnelles territoriales de santé*, CTPS). The CPTS are made up of health professionals grouped together in the form of one or more primary care teams, actors providing primary and secondary care, and medico-social and social actors. The aim is to improve the supply of care and the coordination of healthcare pathways beyond the scope of each healthcare professional's patient, with the involvement of actors other than the independent ones. This level organizes healthcare pathways requiring a hospital technical platform (maternity, surgery, oncology, cardiology) and specialized medico-social services, in particular for the treatment of certain disabilities. There is no specific organization for information sharing at this level that is well identified. Some groups of professionals, even from different disciplines, may decide on a common work software, but there is no obligation to do so.

Local services, particularly primary care, are organized as close as possible to home, within the "healthcare pool" and the primary care teams (*équipes de soins primaires*, ESP) created in 2016 by the Touraine law. They are the first level of care for general practitioners. Their objective is to ensure better coordination of their action and thus contribute to the structuring of healthcare pathways. Computerization has spread to medical practices with the medical record and the necessary organization around administrative issues (health insurance card, archiving of reports, biology, work stoppages, accidents at work, declaration of the attending physician, etc.). The grouping of professionals in group practices and increasingly in nursing homes requires them to use a common work software. This is a considerable asset for the transmission of information at this level.

For cancer patients, the hyperspecialized care is offered in secondary or tertiary care centers. Thus, even if these hyperspecialized structures offer healthcare for all cancer patients, the distances to be covered in a territory to provide care can be very important. The organization of treatment is sometimes delegated to the care centers of the "healthcare territories" at the heart of the CPTS, which requires an imperative need for coordination. The patient's return home after the specific treatment of his or her illness requires organization in the "healthcare pool", at the heart of the ESPs. The link between this regional hyperspecialized care offer, the CPTSs and the ESPs must be clear.

2.3.2. *Transmission of information*

Useful information must reach the various stakeholders involved in patient care in a timely manner. In order to enable the articulation and exchange of information between these three levels of supply of care, physicians historically "write" to each other.

Primary care physicians write a so-called addressing letter. The content of this letter aims to give information on the history, the current clinical presentation, the result of the various examinations if necessary, and the diagnostic suspicion, and is entrusted to the patient. On the other hand, the so-called addressing letter is not, at present, replaced by its digital equivalent. The development of support platforms or case managers can help physicians use the right care pathway for patients in complex situations. They do not replace the necessary transmission of information.

Hospital doctors write a letter describing the diagnosis, the results of the examinations carried out, the treatment chosen and sometimes the monitoring or follow-up to be carried out. The development of digital technology does not modify the content necessary for care, but transforms the vector of these letters. The development of secure messaging makes it possible to do away with paper when patients return home. Primary care physicians receive the necessary information for the next step in care. It remains to ensure that this information arrives in time: this is why the obligation to send the mail on the day the patient is discharged from the hospital sector (mail sent on "D0") has been introduced. However, these measures are currently applied very unevenly throughout France. They depend on the internal organization of the department concerned and the availability of doctors to finalize the letters of request. Moreover, the content of the letters is not always informative about the practical steps to be taken (Rougé-Bugat *et al.* 2016a). A national in-depth study on this subject would make it possible to improve the transmission of information from secondary care to primary care.

The Cancer Communicating Record (*dossier communicant de cancéroligie*, DCC) is a specific medical record for cancer patients. It has been developed by the regional cancer networks and is accessible *via* their websites, particularly for multidisciplinary consultation meetings (*reunions de concertation pluridisciplinaires*, RCP). It is during these MCRs, which have been mandatory since the Cancer Plan I, that patient files are discussed in order to propose the best therapeutic strategy. The DCC, therefore, makes it possible to carry out RCPs between different care structures. The DCC can be considered as a means of bringing hospital structures together. It can be accessed by login and password, and in some regions, by the CPS[2] card. The DCC is now accessible to healthcare at home professionals in certain regions. Access is sometimes possible not only for general practitioners, but also for office-based pharmacists and private nurses. The information contained in the DCC is mainly represented by RCP sheets, operative, and anatomopathological reports, but increasingly, the file is completed by the personalized care program (*programme personnalisé de soins*, PPS) and the patient's personalized post-cancer plan (*plan personnalisé de l'après-cancer*, PPAC). The "primary care team" players (general practitioner, nurse, pharmacist) can therefore log on to obtain the information they want. This is the limit of this digital tool. Indeed, we need to look at things more globally, because these caregivers do not only take care of cancer patients; the consultations successively go through very different reasons for consultation. If each specialty has its own file to consult, the consultation day will quickly become a "puzzle" for the caregivers.

2.4. Theoretical pathway of a cancer patient

The different stages of the process are characterized by different dedicated times; the patient consults his or her general practitioner, the diagnosis is made, the patient's file is discussed in RCPs, and then the patient benefits from the announcement system. A PPS is given to the patient, then specific treatments are initiated (Figure 2.1).

The RCP is done in the form of a face-to-face meeting or videoconference allowing an interactive exchange by simultaneous transmission that gives the possibility of simultaneous connection of several

---

2 The CPS or *carte de professional de santé* is an electronic professional identity card dedicated to the healthcare and medico-social sectors.

sites in interactive link. These RCPs are still the current practice of meetings between different cancer specialists. The primary care actors cannot, as it stands, participate in them. Experiments, notably on myelodysplasias, show that it is feasible and useful to integrate the general practitioner of the patient concerned at the cost of a very cumbersome organization for the hospital and the doctor. The constraints are, for the general practitioner, to be free at the time when he or she is in the middle of consultations with the constraints related to the care (several reasons for consultations, emergencies, etc.) and the connection is working. For the hospital doctor, it is necessary to draw up a list of patients scheduled for RCP, identify the GPs, contact them, propose the meeting schedule, and finally connect with them to discuss the files. This organization would require a specific budget to be feasible in current practice.

Since the Cancer Plan II, the announcement is formalized by the "announcement system". This device includes the announcement of the diagnosis and the announcement of the therapeutic decision as formulated by the RCP. This institutional system is made up of four successive stages. The first announcement stage is medical, including the announcement of the diagnosis and treatment. The second stage is the time of care accompaniment or "nursing consultation". It allows patients or their relatives to have access, according to their choice, to available caregivers who listen, reformulate, and give information. The third allows the patient to be supported and guided in his or her steps, particularly social ones, as well as a meeting with specialized professionals (psychologist, physiotherapist, etc.). The fourth stage is the link with the general practitioner's medical services. The patient and his family have had exchanges with the hospital teams, but the patient will continue to be monitored by his or her general practitioner. Communication between the team and the general practitioner is, therefore, essential. The reality and quality of these exchanges are, for the patient, a guarantee of security and continuity of care.

Once treatment is decided, a personalized care plan (PCP) is given to the patient. It includes the different phases of treatment (including surgery, radiotherapy or chemotherapy), the treatment sites, and the names of the doctors responsible. It also includes the contact details of the people to be reached in case of difficulties and the associations that the person or his or her family can contact. For patients, it plays a dual role–as a tool for dialog with caregivers and as an operational diary of the therapeutic pathway.

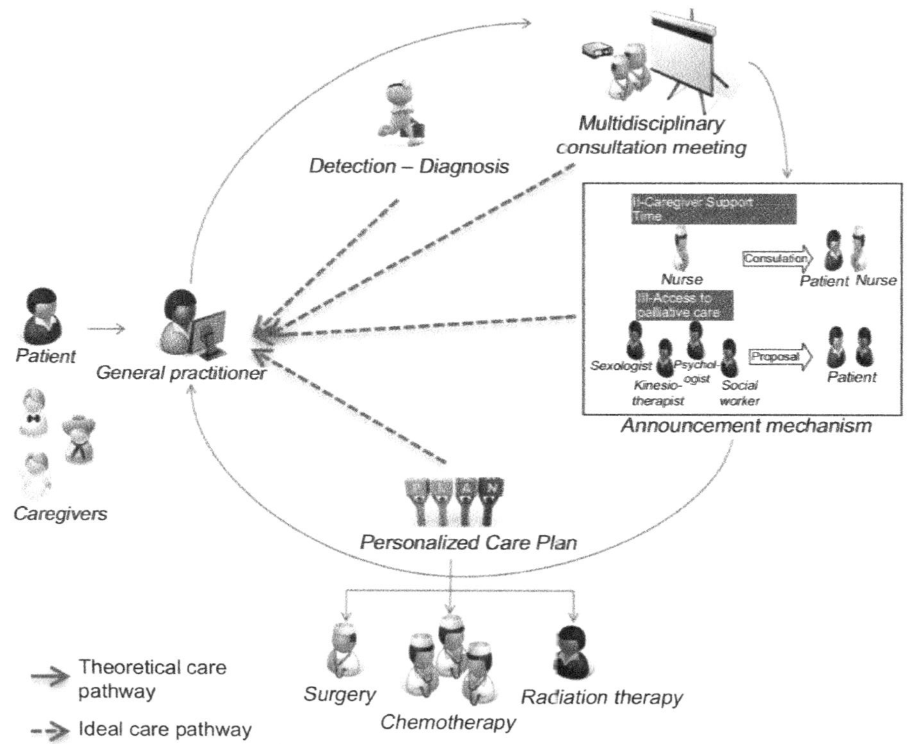

Figure 2.1. *Summarized pathway of the cancer patient. For a color version of this figure, see www.iste.co.uk/beranger/health.zip*

We will address the issue of digital in the primary–secondary care literature according to the care pathway of the cancer patient, that is, successively for the announcement of the cancer, for the management of the adverse effects of the treatments, and for the follow-up of the disease.

2.5. Cancer announcement

The relationship between caregiver and care receiver is changing and evolving towards a more collaborative decision between physician and patient. This relationship presupposes an understanding of the situation on the part of patients and, therefore, appropriate qualitative and quantitative information. The announcement of a serious illness is always a test for the patient. The way in which this announcement is made has an impact on the patient's experience and his or her relationship with the medical profession (Reich *et al.* 2001; Higuchi 2007). The Cancer Plan II took this problem into account by imposing the "announcement mechanism" (*dispositif d'annonce*, DA). This is one of the major measures of this plan. The aim of the DA is to enable the patient to benefit from the best conditions of information, listening and support. There is a linkage phase with the local medical services; however, in practice, the general practitioner is often sidelined by this system. About 19% of doctors declare that they are delegated by the doctor who made the diagnosis to make the announcement, to the disregard of the DA, since the ambulatory practice makes it impossible to provide the time for self-care and access to palliative care after the medical announcement. About 18% specify that the announcement is made by the patient himself (Rougé-Bugat 2016b), making the fourth step of the announcement mechanism obsolete. The private nurse and the patient's dispensing pharmacist are only called upon if the need is identified by the hospital care team. No information is systematically transmitted to them.

General practitioners describe a sequence in the announcement. They prepare the announcement by making a "pre-announcement", then refer the patient to the hospital team, and then review patients "post-announcement", after the official institutional announcement by the DA has been made (Rougé-Bugat *et al.* 2016b). The private nurse and the pharmacist are led to reformulate the disease or treatment components with the patient. They do this without having received any particular information document, but according to their experience and the treatments to be administered. The information is often given to them by the general practitioner, whom they must ask for it. An interprofessional digital tool would make it possible to give the minimum information to the various primary care actors. The creation of such a tool depends on the specialist sector, but must be carried out in consultation with professionals in the outpatient sector.

The advertisement cannot be scanned or digitized. It is unthinkable that such a special and decisive moment as the announcement could be replaced by an artificial or robotic intelligence. In future projections, the precision of diagnostic algorithms or medical decision support or prescription algorithms will be a major contribution that will have to be tamed in order to bring these instruments into practice. The announcement will be based on these tools.

2.6. Management of treatment-related adverse events

Adverse reactions can occur at any time and the general practitioner must be able to identify them and manage patients who request it. How can a systematic collection of adverse events from the patient be organized? A multitude of digital applications is emerging, whether for monitoring patients at home after surgery or for therapeutic follow-up. They are developed by pharmaceutical laboratories or healthcare structures. They all propose that the patient provide information on a regular basis. Experiments show that patients actively participate in the collection of information. But who collects this information? What will happen if patients do not re-enter follow-up data? Who will be alerted to the appearance of an undesirable effect: the oncologist, the nurse coordinator, the healthcare pathway coordinator, the advanced practice nurse, the independent nurse, the pharmacist, the general practitioner? What will happen outside the working hours of the identified referrals?

These questions are not yet clear-cut and do not seem to have obvious answers. This is the great limit of digital monitoring applications. However, programs such as STAR (Symptom Tracking and Reporting), which allows patients to report adverse treatment effects, have been shown to extend life and improve quality of life (Cowan *et al.* 2016).

Another way of doing this is to set up a trio around the patient consisting of a private nurse, a pharmacist, and a general practitioner, all three chosen by the patient for his or her follow-up. This human organization allows for dispensing the treatment and its administration at home when it is adapted. Daily monitoring by the home care nurse and weekly monitoring by the general practitioner ensures compliance and the appearance of undesirable effects. Preliminary results show a feeling of safety among patients and caregivers, a role for primary care providers in the active phase of care, and a great fluidity in exchanges. This raises the question of the willingness to develop digital tools that forget the existing and efficient professional organizations closest to patients.

Summary sheets have been created in several French regions to provide information on the expected adverse effects according to the chemotherapy protocol and to provide a suggested course of action for doctors, nurses, or pharmacists. The sheets were used in 56% of adverse reaction cases and enabled 93% of general practitioners to manage side effects. The use of the sheet has an impact on the number of hospitalizations and divides by ten the risk of being hospitalized for an adverse event (Rougé-Bugat *et al.* 2015). How can these sheets be disseminated? The most effective means of communication should be considered. Is it more judicious to use letters, e-mails, faxes, specific websites, or to transmit the sheet to the patient as is the personalized care plan (PCP)? The activity of caregivers in close proximity leads them to see patients with a wide variety of pathologies throughout the same day. The consultation of dedicated sites, each linked to a pathology, such as the DCC for cancer patients, during the consultation seems illusory. Caregivers would have to be asked to connect to different sites depending on the pathology in question in order to look for information that would be useful to them at the time of the consultation. This is an unrealistic obstacle course. In the absence of a high-performance DMP, it seems inevitable that the information will be transmitted from "secondary to primary care". The development of an application called AKO@dom seems to be an accompanying solution intended for patients with metastatic cancer who are treated at home by oral therapy. It would be initiated by the oncologist, and would make it possible to coordinate and secure the implementation of treatment at home. This application has not yet seen the light of day and is still under development and experimentation. Its operation will be based on the training of home healthcare professionals for the most complex and isolated cases.

The new coordinated care pathways offer city medicine an important role in the care of cancer patients. Interprofessionality is the key word in this situation. The ideal follow-up seems to be a shared follow-up with a complete integration of the primary care from the active phase of the treatment in order to apprehend the patient as a whole.

2.7. Patient follow-up

2.7.1. *After cancer*

When patients are cured or in remission of their disease, the general practitioner continues to accompany patients in this "after cancer" phase. INCa[3] published a study involving 4,349 people two years after their diagnosis. It reveals that the quality of life of patients is degraded, that they have not always returned to work, and that they feel discriminated against due to cancer. The classic follow-up includes check-ups and consultations with the oncologist, initially every three to six months. In these disease-focused appointments, the doctor focuses on the risk of relapse. Innovative devices seek to identify the physical events and psychosocial disorders that impact the quality of life of patients after cancer. This generally involves filling out an evaluation grid, by the general practitioner, recording somatic events and sending it to the oncology team. Depending on the devices, a part collating possible psychosocial events is carried out by the hospital team. Synthesis is carried out by the oncologist who then sends a report to the general practitioner so that he can plan the actions to be taken with the patient.

The exchange of information goes from "primary to secondary care" and from "secondary to primary care". The success of one of these devices, called AMA AC (*assistance des maladies ambulatoires après cancer*, for assistance to outpatients after cancer), is due to the cohort of patients identified in a pathology that is not very prevalent: lymphoma (Compaci *et al.* 2015). This allows the general practitioner to complete the part of the AMA AC that is his or her responsibility on a voluntary basis and the dedicated funding of hospital staff to collect psycho-social events and ensure the synthesis of the file. It is, therefore, difficult to envisage extending this type of intervention to all cancer patients.

3 The *Institut national du cancer* (INCa) is a French public interest group responsible for coordinating scientific research and the fight against cancer.

2.7.2. *Alternating monitoring*

Patient monitoring is warranted because early detection of a relapse is often associated with a better prognosis. Surveillance is usually radiological and more or less biological and clinical. In France, the second Cancer Plan (2009–2013), in Measure 18, Action 18.2, proposed to "develop recommendations on monitoring shared between hospital physicians and attending physicians, with a first priority concerning breast cancer [...]". Several alternating monitoring interventions were thus implemented, particularly in England (Grunfeld *et al.* 1999; Grunfeld 2006). These interventions have shown that patients have welcomed this type of cooperation (Grunfeld *et al.* 1999), while maintaining an effectiveness comparable to the classic model, both in terms of detecting recurrences and in terms of survival and quality of life (Grunfeld 2006). In France, several experiments of alternate or shared follow-up have been initiated. For regions that have already set up this type of monitoring, the available results mainly concern the good acceptance of patients and physicians.

In theory, alternating surveillance would allow the oncologist to reduce the number of patients managed in follow-up visits. The specialist could delegate the follow-up while identifying a preferred contact person. This sharing of surveillance would enhance the institution's relations with the local physicians. Alternating monitoring would allow the general practitioner to remain involved in the management of their patients, to be the patient's easily accessible contact, and to work in a network with specialized professionals. Patients, for their part, would have easier access to a dedicated consultation. Contact with their general practitioner would provide patients with continuity of care, avoiding the need to visit an oncology center, while maintaining quality follow-up and facilitating discharge from patient status.

Not all cancer pathologies lend themselves to shared surveillance. Women with breast cancer have been followed in different alternating surveillance programs with varying degrees of success. The physician oncologist (gynecologic surgeon, medical oncologist, or radiotherapist) proposes the alternating surveillance program to his or her patient. The general practitioner or medical gynecologist designated by the patient is informed by the oncologist. A follow-up consultation summary document should be completed by the physicians at the scheduled follow-up consultation. It is this document that is the main determinant of the success or failure of the alternating follow-up programs. One difficulty of the scheme for alternating physicians (general practitioners or gynecologists) is to identify the follow-up consultation. The patient may consult for many reasons and on a recurrent basis during the six months between the initial consultation and the monitoring consultation. This makes it difficult for the doctor to know when to carry out this consultation. The interface for filling in the follow-up document was envisaged to be on paper or in digital form. The paper was sometimes lost and then had to be entered by a third party. The dematerialized form, because of the necessary security of the data, required an identifier and a password, not very suitable for a traditional consultation in a private practice. The DCC was sometimes the dematerialized interface, with a good success rate when the connection was made directly via the doctor's CSP (without a login and password). The DMP (shared medical file) may make it possible to erase technical malfunctions. The identification of the consultation and its traceability were factors of failure. On the other hand, some experiments have been successful and are still in progress in certain departments or in certain healthcare centers.

This shows a difficulty for private doctors to comply with a tool that is not part of their daily practice, even if it allows information to be transmitted from "primary to secondary care".

Applications are being developed to detect early recurrences. In particular, there is MoovCare for lung cancer, for which the patient must answer a simple questionnaire every week (Denis 2006). The medical team is alerted and can restart treatment. It is a direct interface between the patient and the specialist care team, without the involvement of the general practitioner.

2.8. Ethics to support the primary to secondary care journey

According to Comte-Sponville, there are four major orders structuring society: the technical-scientific order, the legal-political order, morals, and ethics. There is a hierarchy in the orders (Comte-Sponville 1994). The technical-scientific order is incapable of limiting itself. It is limited from the outside by a second order that is superior to it, the legal-political order, but just as incapable of limiting itself as the preceding one, and which is in turn limited by a superior order, the order of morals, which is open from above to a fourth order, the order of ethics.

2.8.1. *Deontology*

Article 60 of the Code of Medical Deontology (Article R.4127-60 of the French Public Health Code) specifies that the general practitioner "must propose the consultation of a colleague as soon as the circumstances require it or accept that which is requested by the patient or his or her family and friends". General practitioners must have access to a specialist to reinforce the level of technical-scientific knowledge necessary for the patient's care. The specialist is not obliged to call upon his or her colleague specialist in general medicine to reinforce the level of environmental, economic, and familial knowledge necessary for the care of the patient, in particular when returning home, announcing the diagnosis or announcing the evolution of the condition. Is a reversibility of this obligation not desirable? Isn't it conceivable that the specialist doctor should, in turn, have access to the general practitioner for his or her field of expertise?

At the end of the consultation, the medical specialist "informs the attending physician in writing of his or her findings, conclusions, and possible prescriptions by notifying the patient." Moreover, Article 64 of the Code of Medical Deontology[4] requires that "when several physicians collaborate in the examination or treatment of a patient, they must keep each other informed." The information is not always passed on to the primary care actors, and it is sometimes the family that informs the doctor of the diagnosis (Rougé-Bugat *et al.* 2016b). In turn, when the general practitioner is asked to keep the specialist informed of his or her consultation, he or she does not always do so. Beyond deontological violations, how can the sharing and transmission of information be improved? The implementation of the DMP should make it possible to improve the transfer of information.

As digital is not always a facilitating innovation, human organization is sometimes simply necessary. The actors in the field are present and fulfill their functions if they are properly informed. The training of healthcare pathway coordinators, through a professional Master 2 in care pathway coordination carried out by two faculties in France (Toulouse and Marseille), will surely be one of the elements to improve the quality of communication between specialized structures and urban medicine. They will be able to create a consultation dedicated to the organization in the patients' living areas. In this way, the coordinators would provide a link not only with the

4 Article R.4127-64 of the French Public Health Code.

primary care actors, but also with the care sectors potentially concerned for ad hoc care. The patient's care pathway would be marked out and the primary care providers would be informed and consulted in real time for the organization of care around their patient.

Deontology represents the social requirement in the techno-scientific order, just as equity represents morality in law (Comte-Sponville 1994). In medicine, it is the codification of the moral rules of the profession. The council of the order, either departmental (administrative) or regional (disciplinary), must ensure that the deontology (written in the code) is respected. The national council has the function of writing the new codes. It is the 1995 code that is still in force, even if it has been slightly reworked to erase the inconsistencies that arose when new laws and decrees were published. The sharing of information and relations between colleagues of different specialties will surely be a deontological issue of the future.

2.8.2. *Ethical questioning*

Ethics questions behaviors and thus accompanies the procedure to be followed. in a situation of medical morality. Ethics poses the question: "How can we best act?" Ethical spaces bring together people (professionals or not) thinking about possible answers in a given situation.

Ethical reflection must feed the university training departments on the scope of action and coordination of general medicine. Oncology specialists should certainly extend their reflection to the organization of care beyond their reference structure. The territory, the "healthcare pools", can inspire their reflection on a more coordinated sharing of follow-up closer to the patients' living environment. The individual exercise extends to the necessary multi-professional work. Cancer patients are a population highly adapted to this model of care. Multi-professional homes can be a model of teamwork.

The internship in medical oncology is not yet part of the compulsory internship in general medicine. Projections predict that in 2025 one out of two patients with cancer or who have had cancer will participate in general medicine consultations. A training course in oncology could train future general practitioners in multi-professional collaborative work, in the management of complications of cancerous disease, in the adverse effects of treatments, and make them aware of the tools available (files, regional cancer network) and existing devices (DA, DCC). In the same way, the general medicine internship is not yet part of the mandatory internships of the other medical specialties, including oncology. However, knowledge of patient management outside the hospital would allow for more realism in the orientation or feasibility of the care prescribed to the patient. A better mutual knowledge of each other could lead to better trust between general practitioners and medical oncologists.

2.8.3. *Impacts and consequences of digital technology on the healthcare pathway*

The reality of a patient's healthcare journey is now complex, in particular with technical issues relating to the management of information systems focused on the primary-secondary care network. The digitization of medicine is becoming the target of many ethical issues, such as doctors' deontology and their role in relation to better informed patients, medical secrecy, confidentiality, protection and security of the patient's digital record, respect for privacy (fraud, theft, loss), the risk of forgetting that there is a human being behind the numbers and pixels, and the sharing of responsibility (between the doctor and a help or support system), equal access for all (an essential factor of social equity) with a risk of aggravating inequalities in access to the most efficient techniques, the risk of imposing care carried out by robots on disabled or elderly people against their will (free and informed consent), slowness in the adoption by practitioners of available technologies, discrimination and bias in certain algorithms from decision support systems, the free will of the health professional, etc.

In this context, we can ask ourselves whether this medicine might not lose its essence because human relationships are disrupted by these new technologies. How does digitization contribute to relational, behavioral, and organizational changes between the healthcare professional and the patient? Hasn't technological development trivialized the "sacralization" of medical information by making it increasingly accessible to all? Will this modernization of information and communication tools, illustrated by the example of telemedicine, not relegate clinical and therapeutic practice to the background?

This digital medicine must obey on the one hand ethical principles such as beneficence, autonomy, non-maleficence, and justice, and on the other hand ethical rules relating to transparency, explicability, confidentiality, integrity, common good, respect for the person, responsibility and quality that guarantee credibility, trust, universality, inclusion, coherence, and relevance of the digital. It must also be usable and beneficial, that is to say, it must be integrated into an accessible program for solving problems of a multiple nature: organizational, strategic, human, health, territorial, and economic. It is, therefore, essential that each digital project be the subject of a multidisciplinary consultation involving all the players directly and indirectly concerned in the healthcare process, as recommended in the French Ministry of Health's *Ma santé* 2022 plan. In our view, the "digital" modernization of patient healthcare must, therefore, be accompanied by an "ethical" modernization that will lead to digital medicine with a human face. This necessarily involves an ethic oriented towards the quest for the meaning of the technical tool, and whose major objective is to take into consideration the human interplay in order to control any deviations and possible risks.

2.9. Conclusion

The new coordinated healthcare pathways offer so-called "town" or local medicine an important role in the care of cancer patients. The ideal follow-up seems to be a shared follow-up with full integration of the general practitioner in the active phase of the treatment of the disease in order to understand the patient as a whole. This follow-up will be better thanks to inter-professional collaboration not only between healthcare centers and primary care providers (primary-secondary care), but also between the primary care professionals themselves. The vision of each person and the care of the patient at different stages of the journey allow for more comprehensive care and closer monitoring of the difficulties presented by the patient.

Physicians most certainly underestimate the importance of technology, both in their daily practice and in their communication with colleagues, other healthcare professionals and patients. New information and communication technologies are changing the way in which information is exchanged, how literature is searched, and even interpersonal relationships. Their prospective development is very important and all fields of activity are impacted by the introduction of these technologies. One of the major challenges of communication within the medical profession lies in primary-secondary care communication. The emergence of digital applications in the new coordinated healthcare pathways between primary and secondary care is becoming crucial. These applications must provide solutions to clear issues, following a detailed analysis of the demand from the various players and the constraints they face. The development of practical and digital tools, standardized by national authorities, will probably improve their accessibility and give confidence to primary care professionals in the management of cancer patients.

Technological innovations raise ethical questions. They risk generating serious consequences if we are not able to provide answers to the questions they raise. In particular, it will be necessary to ensure that the confidentiality and integrity of the data that will circulate is respected. These technological innovations and tools, whether digital or not, will generate Big Data. Companies involved in the processing and market of Big Data will have to face strict regulations and rules.

2.10. References

Carré, D. and Lacroix, J.-G. (2001). *La santé et les autoroutes de l'information*. L'Harmattan, Paris.

Compaci, G., Rueter, M., Lamy, S., Oberic, L., Recher, C., Lapeyre-Mestre, M., Laurent, G., Despas, F. (2015). Ambulatory Medical Assistance-After Cancer (AMA-AC): A model for an early trajectory survivorship survey of lymphoma patients treated with anthracycline-based chemotherapy. *BMC Cancer*, 15, 781.

Comte-Sponville, A. (1994). *Valeur et vérité, études cyniques*. PUF, Paris, 224.

Cowan, R.A., Suidan, R.S., Andikyan, V., Rezk, Y.A., Einstein, M.H., Chang, K., Carter, J., Zivanovic, O., Jewell, E.J., Abu-Rustum, N.R., Basch, E., Chi, D.S. (2016). Electronic patient-reported outcomes from home in patients recovering from major gynecologic cancer surgery: A prospective study measuring symptoms and health-related quality of life. *Gynecologic Oncology*, 143(2), 362–326.

Denis, F. (2018). Web-mediated follow-up and prognosis in lung cancer patients. *Medical Sciences*, 34(6–7), 590–594.

Grunfeld, E. (2006). Looking beyond survival: How are we looking at survivorship? *Journal of Clinical Oncology*, 24(32), 5166–5169.

Grunfeld, E., Fitzpatrick, R., Mant, D., Yudkin, P., Adewuyi-Dalton, R., Stewart, J., Cole, D., Vessey, M. (1999). Comparison of breast cancer patient satisfaction with follow-up in primary care versus specialist care: Results from a randomized controlled trial. *British Journal of General Practice*, 49(446), 705–710.

Higuchi, N. (2007). Telling of the cancer diagnosis and the law. *Nihon Hoshasen Gijutsu Gakkai Zasshi*, 63(10), 1208–1210.

Ministère de la Santé (2009). Loi HPST [Online]. Available at: https://solidarites-sante.gouv.fr/IMG/pdf/vademecum_loi_HPST.pdf.

Reich, M., Deschamps, C., Ulaszewski, A.L., Horner-Vallet, D. (2001). Disclosure of a diagnosis of cancer: Paradoxes and misunderstandings. *Rev. Med. Interne*, 22(6), 560–566.

Rougé-Bugat, M.E., Lassoued, D., Bacrie, J., Boussier, N., Delord, J.P., Oustric, S., Bauvin, E., Lapeyre-Mestre, M., Bertucci, F., Grosclaude, P. (2015). Guideline sheets on the side effects of anticancer drugs are useful for general practitioners. *Support Care Cancer*, 23(12), 3473–3480.

Rougé-Bugat, M.E., Dufosse, V., Paul, C., Oustric, S., Meyer, N. (2016a). Communicating information to the general practitioner: The example of vemurafenib for metastatic melanoma. *Journal of the European Academy of Dermatology and Venereology.*, 30(12), e192–e194.

Rougé-Bugat, M.E., Omnes, C., Delpierre, C., Escourrou, E., Boussier, N., Oustric, S., Delord, J.-P., Bauvin, E., Grosclaude, P. (2016b). Primary care physicians and oncologists are partners in cancer announcement. *Support Care Cancer*, 24(6), 2473–2479.

Rougé-Bugat, M.E., Bourgouin, M., Gérard, S., Lozano, S., Brechemier, D., Cestac, P., Cool C., Balardy, L. (2017). Drug prescription including interactions with anticancer treatments in the elderly: A global approach. *Journal of Nutrition, Health and Aging*.

Summerton, N. (2000). Diagnosis and general practice. *British Journal of General Practice*, 50(461), 995–1000.

3

A Smart Health Record for Better Coordination: A Sociological Analysis of the Organizational Dynamics of the Calipso Project

3.1. Solving health problems through better coordination

3.1.1. *A context conducive to home automation technologies in healthcare*

The healthcare landscape in France, and in the majority of other countries, is marked by major changes in the way patients are cared for and in the way healthcare pathways are formalized. Changes in the demographic characteristics of the population and the increase in chronic diseases are combined with patterns of action that are changing, in particular under the impetus of public policy.

Cost rationalization is a vector for major organizational changes, such as the "ambulatory shift" that began in the early 2000s (Pérodeau and Côté 2002). This measure aims to "free up beds" in institutions and promotes the home hospitalization system (*hospitalisation à domicile*, HAD) where hospital teams take care of patients directly at home (Sentilhes-Monkam 2005). More generally, we are witnessing the questioning of a medicine described as hospital-centric (Vezinat 2019). The phenomenon of keeping people at home is encouraged by other dimensions, such as the aging of the population, which

---

Chapter written by Valentin BERTHOU.

is accompanied by the willingness of people to stay in their homes as long as possible[1]. Congruently, the rise of digital devices in healthcare, starting with the shared medical record (*dossier médical partagé*, DMP) (Mathieu-Fritz and Esterle 2012) or telecare tools, is contributing to the redefinition of healthcare methods and professional practices (Mathieu-Fritz and Gaglio 2018).

In this context, the multiplicity of actors and the technicalization of healthcare acts increase the complexity of care. New priorities are emerging and since the 1980s, we have been witnessing a real call for (better) coordination of the actors, acts, and structures (Aubry 2007), gradually moving towards an integrated care system[2] that attempts to take into account the different dimensions of care (Shaw *et al.* 2011). Coordination is systematically presented by its proponents as a guarantee of improved patient care and should result in substantial financial savings by maximizing the efficiency of the patient's journey while simplifying it. The aim is to implement "formalized coordination" (Robelet *et al.* 2005), that is, standardization of care procedures. Furthermore, the implementation of health networks (Polomeni and Larcher 2001) has led to a broadening of the definition of health to justify the obligation to resort to multi-professional care (Blanchard 2004). The issues at stake therefore concern the ability of professionals to coordinate their actions to maximize the effectiveness of these systems.

As part of the HAD system, an administrative team attached to the hospital provides technical support for coordination between the actors. Hospital coordinating physicians build the management strategy (the "personalized health plan") to guide the caregivers and adapt the actions according to the patient's complaints and environment. However, the majority of interventions in the home take place outside the HAD, which mainly treats complex clinical cases and outpatient surgery patients. The majority of inventions are carried out by independent professionals – also grouped under the term "city medicine[3]" (e.g. attending physicians, nurses, physiotherapists, etc.), which

1 Cour des comptes (2016). Le maintien à domicile des personnes âgées en perte d'autonomie. Une organisation à améliorer, des aides à mieux cibler [Online]. Thematic public report, July 12, 2016. Available at: www.ccomptes.fr.

2 World Health Organization (2016). Integrated car models: an overview [Online]. Working document, Health Services Delivery Programme, Division of Health Systems and Public Health. Available at: http://www.euro.who.int/__data/assets/pdf_file/0005/322475/Integrated-care-models-overview.pdf.

3 The term "city medicine" groups together practitioners who work outside the hospital setting (although not all do this).

overlaps with the majority of "frontline" professionals (frontline healthcare workers). In this area, the coordinating bodies and actors are much less formalized and less centralized than for HAD care. The transmission of information is more artisanal, more inter-personal, and traditional liaison tools are used (telephone, paper notebook, mail, etc.). This operation is problematized by the actors of the Calipso project (for *cahier de liaison informatisé pour un parcours de soins optimisé*, or computerized liaison notebook for an optimized care pathway) as a weakness that will constitute the main development axis of a multidisciplinary digital liaison notebook.

Another improvement, identified by health professionals, is the lack of continuity between city medicine and hospital. Thus, the French Hospital Federation insists on the need to simplify the exchange of information between these two professional spheres by, for example, making it mandatory to transmit a patient's medical results from the general practitioner to the hospital and vice versa[4]. More particularly, emergency hospitalizations and/or home returns appear to be the two most chaotic stages in the information flow. There has been a revival of interest in city-hospital collaboration with the desire to better formalize healthcare networks under the effect of an aging population (Fournier 2002). However, many players in the field, particularly the professionals of the Calipso project[5], consider that the situation is still not satisfactory and that digital technologies in healthcare are relevant levers for improvement that need to be developed.

3.1.2. *A digital liaison notebook to facilitate the transmission of information*

The Calipso device is intended for professionals as well as the patient's family and friends, like caregivers. Although the tool does not specifically target the elderly, they remain the majority target since the tablet is designed for people receiving healthcare at home. The Calipso tool is part of a strategy to support healthcare at home, sometimes referred to as "aging well"[6], and is an application installed on a touch-sensitive tablet. Several functionalities co-

---

4 Rapport Jardry pour le compte de la Fédération hospitalière de France (FHF): https://www.fhf.en/Press-Communication/Espace-presse/Communiques-de-presse/Ville-hopital-des-pistes-pour-renforcer-les-liens.

5 The Calipso project was financed by the "digital economy" program of the Grand Est Region.

6 When there is no academic reference, the words or expressions in quotation marks are those of the actors in the field.

exist, but the main one is the provision of a digital link notebook where each person in a patient's entourage can write a comment (Figure 3.1).

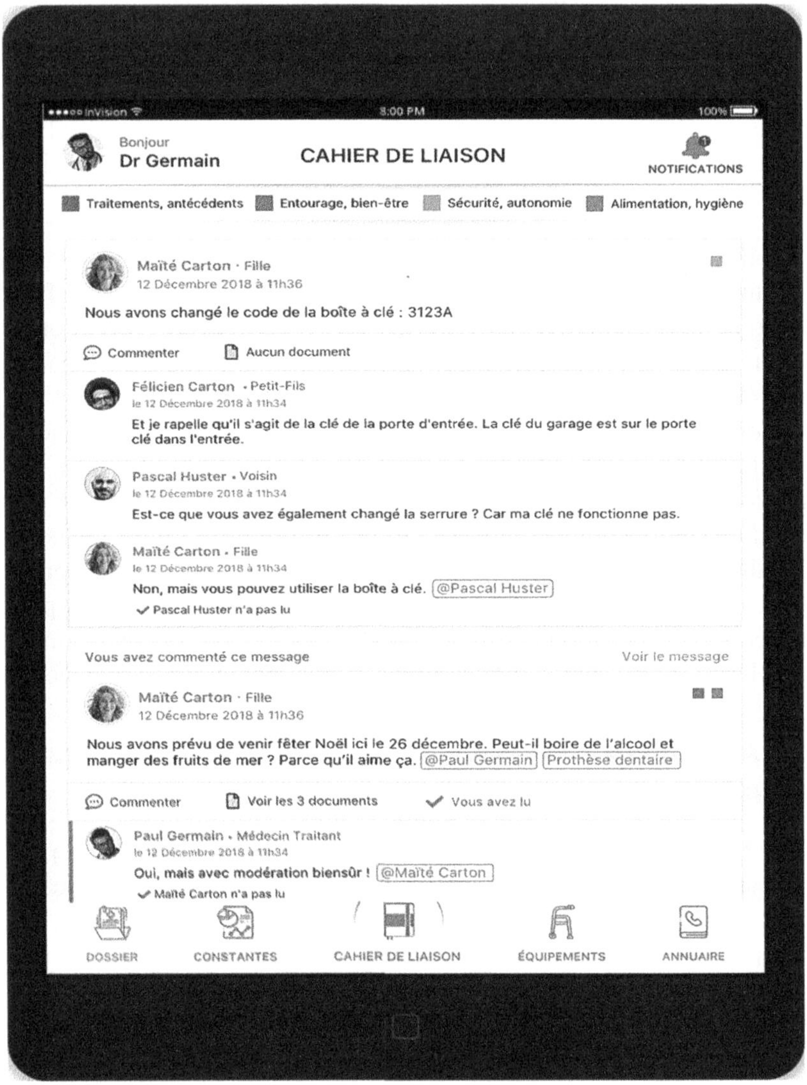

Figure 3.1. *Main page of a hypothetical logbook in French, opened with the session of an attending physician ("Dr. Germain"). The five icons on the bottom panel give access to the five functionalities of the tablet: the patient record (dossier), the table of constants (constants), the liaison notebook (cahier de liaison, current page), the equipment section (équipements), and the directory (annuaire). For a color version of this figure, see www.iste.co.uk/beranger/health.zip*

The objective of the Calipso project is the collaborative design of a digital liaison notebook to increase city-hospital coordination and to constitute a "common information space" (Schmidt and Bannon 1992) to improve the quality of healthcare. Although this project is located in the Department of Aube, attempts to build shared electronic files have been made in other countries, involving collaborative systems close to the Calipso technological architecture (Archer *et al.* 2011).

This chapter focuses on the study of the dynamics of the project (2019), which is unique because of the particular organization of its actors. The different partners are linked by a common institutional history and driven by a desire to anchor their actions in a palpable reality. Under these conditions, a tension oscillates between the development of a utilitarian technology and a concern for conceptualization to provide objective and reflective frameworks for professional healthcare activities. We will therefore study, through the dynamics of the project, how the ambitions of the actors to modify the practices of professionals in healthcare at home networks are crystallized in a socio-technical device. In particular, the aim is to identify the work of transformation undertaken by the actors involved to change the definition of conventional healthcare towards a more "multidisciplinary" healthcare.

This chapter highlights an iterative process in which the actors construct new problems and project their intention in the technical realization of a device (and its impasses). We will see that the project's progress is not linear, as the adjustments were so important due to internal controversies within the team and the re-qualification of the issues following the feedback from the users. In this context, particular attention will be paid to the way in which usage scripts are constructed (Akrich 1990) in the first instance, and then how the designers renegotiate them, deal with them and override them despite the formalization of a technology. In order to do this, the chapter proceeds to a twofold level of analysis: on the one hand, the institutional springs that preside over the intentions of the actors are studied, and on the other hand, the situated activities of the design activity.

Our status as a sociologist "embedded" in the project makes us a witness and an actor in the implementation of this technology. Charged with conducting a sociological investigation into the launch of the device, we propose several analyses of the behind-the-scenes production of a sociotechnical artifact being developed and the difficulties encountered in a project that claims to be multidisciplinary. Thus, after reviewing the institutional trajectory of the project (section 3.2) and the positioning of its actors (section 3.3), we will return in more detail to the development of the Calipso technology (section 3.4), with particular emphasis on one of the controversies (section 3.4.3) and by questioning the conditions of interdisciplinarity required to carry out an experimental phase (section 3.4.4).

3.2. Historicity of the Calipso project

3.2.1. *A bundle of information for thinking about the digital liaison notebook*

In projects before Calipso, researchers had shown the importance of the paper liaison notebook in the care of patients at home. It constitutes a central information medium for professionals providing healthcare at home (Abu Amsha and Lewkowicz 2014). It is mainly filled out and consulted by the auxiliaries[7] and nurses. Handwritten comments refer to the acts of care provided and observations on the patient's health status like recording physiological constants, for example a blood pressure measurement. The notebooks also make it possible to trace the activities of professionals who sometimes carry out an actual "reporting" work of daily activities, transforming the notebook into a communication medium. However, the exchange of information is limited to transmission between members of the same profession, as notebooks are rarely shared.

The observational work in previous academic projects had led to the coexistence of several types of notebooks – even in the same patient – ranging from standardized versions of auxiliaries to more home-made versions in the form of notebooks. The aggregation of information on their characteristics had led to the proposal of an update: a unified and "multidisciplinary" model. This new notebook was presented as a "medical, social, and family" liaison notebook, demonstrating the deeper desire to place the patient's health within a system of actors broader than the scope of medical professionals alone. The idea put forth was based on an "overall" health taking into account the relational structure of the patient and the

7 These auxiliaries are called "personal care assistant", "personal carer", or "professional caregiver".

importance of social and family support for his or her health. The notebook was intrinsically designed as a collaborative tool, since it already responded to a logic of centralization and fluidity of information, two factors that were supposed to allow for better coordination. A digital mock-up was developed, acting as a "proof of concept" and prefiguring the Calipso application.

3.2.2. *Territorial anchoring of the project in an already established network of actors*

In order to understand the technological and intellectual ramifications of the logic behind the creation of the Calipso tool, it is important to briefly review the genesis of the project and clarify the territorial context of its creation.

Faced with a situation of medical desertification, the department of Aube (north-eastern France) began several years ago to develop telemedicine tools to compensate for the lack of health professionals and their geographical dispersion. The MyGHT[8] project is one of the answers. It is a digital portal whose objective is to connect professionals and patients in the territory via a directory that allows them to carry out teleconsultation procedures. The Aube Medical and Shared Care Project (2017–2022) estimates that "as of June 2017, MyGHT has 10,000 registered patients and 500 subscribing healthcare professionals, including 76 pharmacies out of the 95 in the healthcare basin, and is continuing to develop."[9]

Login to the MyGHT portal is done through an individual account. MyGHT and Calipso applications are based on the same company and technical bridges have been designed to interconnect the two systems. For example, the MyGHT account for healthcare professionals is a counter that will eventually serve as a remote access point for the Calipso liaison notebook.

These territorialized projects are the result of collaborations between the industrial, academic, and hospital worlds. They have been built in filiation and at each stage a technology has been added or transformed. The

8 GHT: *groupement hospitalier de territoire* (regional hospital group). See: https://www.myght.net/.

9 https://www.ch-troyes.fr/le-projet-medical-et-de-soins-partage-du-ght-de-laube-et-du-sezannais-approves, p. 14.

composition of the actors of a new project is partly conditioned by the previous results of this socio-technical configuration, as well as the organization and technological orientations. The Calipso liaison notebook does not represent a technological breakthrough, as the environmental uses are in line with the continuity of the paper version by adding some functionalities.

It can, therefore, be said that this socio-technical configuration is largely subject to effects of technological dependence on the pathway (Liebowitz and Margolis 1995; Castaldi and Dosi 2006).

3.3. Collaboration as an object of study and theoretical framework

The Calipso project is unique in that it is in a double scope of collaboration. As we will see, collaboration is claimed by the project team as a methodological principle structuring the project. It is driven and formalized by academic researchers through theoretical approaches that conceptualize and legitimize it. The dynamic includes non-academic actors who also recognize themselves in a shared and contributory functioning. But the collaboration does not stop there, since it is also at the heart of the project and its objective.

3.3.1. *A multidisciplinary team to carry out a project "in Living Lab mode"*

Calipso is a collaborative project led by four partners: a team of researchers-leaders, mainly from CSCW (Computer Supported Cooperative Work, see below), a local hospital community, a computer engineering services company that develops the technical part of the system, and an association of independent healthcare professionals. The organizational dynamic is based on a longstanding cooperation between the stakeholders marked by precedents[10].

---

10 For example, the PICADo project (2012-2016, http://www.madopa.fr/projets-en-cours/projet-picado/), which studied the modes of collaboration of liberal health professionals and showed the importance of the link notebooks in their care practices, or the HADex project (2016–2018, http://www.madopa.fr/projets-en-cours/hadex/), which focused on the study of the functioning of the home hospitalization system and which prefigures the development of the Calipso application.

The theoretical and methodological approach developed in the project by CSCW researchers is inspired by the operation of Living Labs[11] in the health and autonomy sector (Nesti 2017). This approach advocates the development of a product according to user-centered and incremental methodologies (Eriksson *et al.* 2006; Bergvall-Kåreborn *et al.* 2009; Almirall *et al.* 2012). Concretely, it is a matter of giving users a voice – here, it is mainly health professionals and caregivers – and translating expectations and needs to build the project guidelines. A comparison of several Living Labs reveals strong disparities in the mobilization of users (Berthou and Gaglio 2020); however, the projects carried out there are often the result of collaborative work with a sustained focus on promoting "bottom-up" logics. Moreover, the Living Lab approach advocates a trial-and-error approach to product design and the use of experimentation in real situations. These orientations are presented as the guarantee of a development in adequacy with the field constraints and offering a strong flexibility to resize the product according to the technical hazards and the returns of use. Let us now see how the precepts of the Living Lab approach are concretely materialized in the Calipso project.

The development of the project is structured around mixed co-piloting and is nourished by the experience of its members, particularly health professionals who are daily confronted with healthcare issues. The project was also guided by the results of previous work (mentioned in section 3.3.2) from the time its initial objectives were drawn up. Institutional anchoring is ensured by the multi-positionality of its actors, whose trajectories often reveal an important experience that has led to the constitution of extensive socio-professional networks. For example, one of them holds the position of chief emergency physician and is also president of the Council of the Order of Physicians. The Living Lab approach acts as a methodological framework that curbs strong differences of opinion and maintains an organizational balance.

Another level of reflexivity is built through a sociological survey conducted longitudinally at the different phases of the project. It is on this

---

11 In the abundance of definitions on Living Labs, we can cite that of the collective work in Quebec on these entities and whose repercussion in France has been important: "A Living Lab is a research method in open innovation that aims at developing new products and services. The approach promotes a process of co-creation with end users under real conditions and is based on an ecosystem of public-private partnerships" (Dubé *et al.* 2014, p. 11).

basis that this chapter is written. The survey aims at analyzing in real time the process of co-design and launch of the system. Two schematic stages follow one another in the survey: first, the identification of the actors in the field and professional routines in order to establish a mapping of practices and actors in order to establish an initial point of comparison; second, an analysis of uses during and after the launch of the technological device. The challenge is then to highlight the key points of the phenomenon of appropriation or non-appropriation of the Calipso tool, as well as the detour of use or the possible modification of practitioners' professional routines.

The survey is based on multi-site ethnographic work (Marcus 1998). And insofar as this evaluation mission is commissioned, it can be qualified as an intervention sociology (Herreros 2001). Here, the sociologist is expected to take a distanced look at the practices of the actors in order to create reflexivity in the project and also to be directly involved in the launch actions and to participate in the co-design. In this way, their contribution is transverse to the project and is not limited to a detailed analysis of downstream uses of the project.

3.3.2. *What theoretical framework for dealing with complex situations? Knotworking, the core of reflection on the activity*

The Calipso project is a multidisciplinary project with stakeholders from a wide range of backgrounds. The theoretical framework of the researchers is strongly anchored in the CSCW. This branch of computer science has the particularity of playing on both the technical design of prototypes and the study of the uses of technologies. The two aspects are constantly recombining and changing, particularly within university laboratories where technologies are developed. In terms of its materiality, CSCW's object of study is very much focused on "communication machines" and cooperation processes (Cardon 1997; Elmarzouqi *et al.* 2008). The theoretical bases of this branch of computer science are particularly heterogeneous (management sciences, design, cognitive psychology, industrial design, etc.), and consequently offering a malleable analytical framework that seems to correspond well to the aspirations of the Calipso project. More precisely, one of the key concepts mobilized is that of knotworking, which stems notably from the work of Y. Engeström (2008). Following the work of L. Suchman

(1997) on "coordination centers", Engeström proposed to broaden the initial concept, which he found too delimited in time and space. Observing profound changes in work organizations and taking inspiration from activity theories, he believes that it is now impossible to think of situations in which actors are coordinated with the classical frameworks, because activity and situations appear much more diluted. Knotworking therefore consists of the study of "activity nodes" and the articulation between them more than the analysis of individual action or of the structure as a crucible of actors and interaction. The vision is, therefore, intended to be resolutely dynamic, since it forces us to think about action by decorrelating it from the instituted organizational frameworks that are no longer operative in order to make explicit the diversity of situations and touch on the singularity of certain configurations.

The interest of knotworking also stems from its context of emergence and what it tells us about new configurations of action, particularly in the sphere of work. Engeström (2008) believes that knotworking is intrinsically linked to the new modalities of co-production of action. These interactions take place around a dual relationship, like the link between a client and a supplier, or a more complex relationship mobilizing more actors, for example a team of the SAMU in intervention. "Co-configuration" differs from the informal coordination of actors by producing meaning, responsibility, trust, etc. in a situation. Moreover, taking into account the role of technical objects and particularly digital technologies allows us to think of distribution in action nodes.

Knotworking, central in the perspective adopted by the team, acts as a two-way link in the development of the Calipso project. It provides a theoretical framework for thinking about complex, changing, and novel situations following the introduction of a technical device in a social sphere, but it is also a powerful way of affirming the need to follow an incremental path in methodology. Indeed, knotworking suggests a radical uncertainty of action. Insofar as situations are constantly co-constructing themselves, where meaning and coordination processes are located; it is, therefore, impossible to envisage what will actually happen: how can one be certain that a telemedicine device will be used according to the script of use (Akrich 1990) by its designers? This viewpoint is in line with the precepts of the Living Lab approach, which alternates the design process between test phases and user feedback. Knotworking is, therefore, mobilized both methodologically and theoretically to guide the launch of a technology qualified as experimental and to analyze the framework and its effects on the structuring of practices.

3.4. Identifying specific coordination problems to propose a general technological solution

3.4.1. *Building on problems identified in the field*

The birth of Calipso is based on a twofold issue problematized by health professionals. The first is the lack of link between city medicine and hospital medicine. This phenomenon is particularly apparent at two pivotal moments in the patient's journey: hospitalization, especially if it is an emergency, and discharge from a hospital. The procedures for transmitting information appear to be perfectible as they are so lacking, which pushes professionals on both sides to compensate by searching for information manually and laboriously through circuitous paths.

More generally, the two universes are not very porous, which causes dysfunctions due to a lack of information about the existence of certain programs, organizations, or jurisdictions. Whether entering or leaving the hospital, the Calispo tablet is designed to facilitate these steps by allowing a better link between information, for example by recording the follow-up sheet or by allowing hospital staff to access patient information (recent medical history, last prescription, contact persons, etc.).

The second area for improvement targets healthcare at home. Coordination procedures are relatively effective at an intra-professional level. However, the coexistence of several communication tools (different notebooks, for example) and the lack of formalization of these devices hinders an interprofessional collaborative dynamic, for example between the physician and the auxiliary.

Calipso is thus conceived as a channel for collecting and transmitting information between the different professions. The hypothesis of improved support stems from the use of a common vector to streamline the transfer of information and create a new collaboration tool. One of the singularities of the tablet is amalgamating medical and social information. Thus, the project partners are betting that the diversity of information contained in the digital liaison notebook is a means of taking the person into consideration in its plural dimensions.

3.4.2. *A design for experimentation, functionalities for the needs of professionals*

A touch tablet is chosen as it allows for a better grip than a smartphone and facilitates reading and writing. Each tablet resembles a notebook; all are nominative and designed to stay at home with each patient. This terminal responds to an ease of data processing within the framework of the experiment. Thus, the application is developed in a multiplatform manner[12].

The tablet is divided into five main tabs that structure the functionalities. The first is reserved for the "patient file", an information health profile that compiles essential information on the patient's health status. This information provides a synthetic vision of the main characteristics of the tablet holder. In addition, other information is indicated according to different categories: "environment, well-being", "safety, autonomy", and "food, hygiene". All of this information makes it possible to provide elements beyond the clinical indications.

The second functionality allows for tracing the patient's vital constants. The evolution of the indices appears in real time in the form of interactive histograms. This is one of the most frequently used functions of paper health records to document the patient's history, for example by calculating the correct dose of insulin for diabetic patients.

A third tab lists the patient's "equipment". The fourth tab is an information sheet that lists the most important information. Like a personalized directory, the "emergency card" lists the people to contact in case of need.

Finally, the fifth function is the "liaison notebook". The application's page looks like a Facebook "wall" where each user can leave a typed comment. Their identity appears as well as their status in relation to the patient. Several specific features exist, such as the possibility to specifically address a comment to someone and leave a comment in return. It is possible to categorize the messages (using the same labels described above) via color coding. Unlike other functions, the liaison notebook is accessible to everyone. The patient, who also has an account, can write comments.

12 The application can be used with Android or iOS devices.

3.4.3. *Through the projection of professional standards in the tool, misunderstanding of coordination and collaboration*

To access Calipso's features, you must first create an individual account in the application that grants different accesses depending on your status. Only the digital profile of healthcare professionals allows access to all the contents of the tablet and modification of medical information. The patient can consult everything, but does not have the right to modify his or her health data. Finally, family and friends only have access to the multidisciplinary liaison log.

This division into three categories generated considerable debate among team members. Two competing logics shaped the opposition: on the one hand, the desire for total openness of the system, where everyone would have complete freedom to write and modify the information (like a paper liaison notebook), and on the other, the desire to finely segment the levels of access according to the user's status. A compromise was reached, emphasizing the need to protect medical data and at the same time the collaborative virtues of the device. The application was, therefore, developed with simplified access according to three user categories.

Despite a shared ultimate goal of improving patient care, there are differing views on the value and use of the tablet. It seems necessary to dwell on what is played out through the antagonistic positions of the two camps and to show where the fault lines lie and how the technological device has been co-constructed in this context. The divergences concern in the first place the representations of the health system and the professional practices to be invented/modified.

The first division is illustrative of how the hospital operates. For its representative within the Calipso project, the tablet is a tool to increase the coordination of professionals, understood as the capacity of an organization to adjust its resources as well as possible by standardizing them and structuring the processes in order to achieve a desired objective. In other words, in order to "secure" the patient's pathway, it is necessary to reduce the choices of orientation possible by professionals. The railway metaphor is often used to compare the patient to a railway car, whose healthcare pathway must be judiciously directed in order to get the patient to the right organization, device or practitioner without taking the wrong route. The regional digital portal MyGHT is establishing itself as the information infrastructure with guiding figures that can be consulted by practitioners in the territory. The tablet, as a technical linking device, therefore becomes a normative tool to convert professionals to a common action repository. Such a functioning refers to several objectives, which include the rationalization of costs, the better coordination of the actors, or the possibility to evaluate the efficiency of care pathways that become comparable.

The tablet constitutes itself as a technical artifact that crystallizes the hospital culture in terms of standards of care and patient management. The professional ethos of hospital staff is in fact marked by a predominance of formal procedures for acts of care and a rigid hierarchical system. The initial desire to strictly compartmentalize the levels of access to the shelf according to status reflects the reproduction of the dominant professional culture of hospital institutions.

For its part, the association of independent professionals advocates an increasingly "collaborative and interprofessional" approach to healthcare, according to its representative in the project. This organization, initially created from the commitment of two practitioners (a nurse and a doctor), has gradually been structured by bringing together professionals who mainly work in the home (nurses, doctors, psychologists, pharmacists, etc.). In spite of their attachment to their independence, the association has been set up as a necessary framework for exchange in the care of patients. The aim of this bottom-up initiative was to structure the collaboration between professionals who previously did not know each other while the patients were shared. The association of volunteers allows the fluidity of information through the network of contacts. Trust is at the heart of this system, allowing professionals to anticipate delicate situations, for example a pharmacist who delivers medication to a nurse without waiting for a prescription from the attending physician in order to avoid the patient's treatment being interrupted. The association's dynamic, which has been working along these lines for several years, has foreshadowed several measures that are now emerging, such as the CPTS system (*communautés professionnelles territoriales de santé*, territorial professional health communities)[13] or the operation of multidisciplinary health centers, both of which aim to achieve greater cross-functionality between the various professions. The association's representative on the project team sees Calipso as an opportunity to transpose and generalize the collaborative functioning of its

13 https://solidarites-sante.gouv.fr/IMG/pdf/fiche_12.pdf.

organization to a broader framework. The technology is instrumented to reshape the links between professionals by allowing a better articulation around the patient.

3.4.4. *Technology, neutral ground for cooperation?*

The two partners of the Calipso project – representing the two sides of medicine (private and public hospitals) – are thus carrying contradictory representations on the work routines to be put forward. However, a general objective of convergence has solidified the relationships and allowed for a shared commitment; each of the caregivers agrees on a possible improvement in the fate of patients and on the fact that it is necessary to act in this direction. This "general interest" focus is broad enough to establish a consensus direction despite divergent professional ethos, but not so broad as to guarantee the functioning of the Calipso project. Convergence was, therefore, possible thanks to the dynamism generated around the collaborative design of the technology. Thus, professional actors invested a lot in the development of the technology: promotion to investors looking for a viable economic model, recruitment of professional colleagues, choice of patients to participate in an experiment, instructions to improve the usability of the device and the functionalities to be implemented, presentation of the expected benefits to institutions, etc.

Through these actions, many hopes have been engaged so that the conception of the device will lead to an adhesion beyond the members of the project. The commitment of Calipso's healthcare players was, therefore, less aimed directly at training in the technology than at transforming practices. Intrinsically, the Calipso tablets were used as a lever to transform existing practices: on the hospital side to formalize coordination practices, and on the independents' side to spread a more collaborative operation for healthcare at home workers.

Although they are expected to be the first users, the project's medical partners have not been at the forefront of tablet use, even standing at a distance, with one of them admitting, despite a relentless commitment to the project, that he was not interested in the technology and would rather write with a pencil on a paper notebook than be encumbered by a poorly designed tablet. This paradox can be explained, in our opinion, by the game of projection of uses in technology. Indeed, the Calipso tablet becomes the receptacle of hopes and as long as the device is not completely finalized (which means the end of the project), it allows a collective of actors to exist who project themselves towards a desirable horizon. As long as the functionalities have not been decided upon, it is necessary to continue the work of co-elaboration that gives the possibility of exchanges and projections. An unfinished technology, therefore, constitutes a support for the collaborative dynamic. The dynamics of the project, as a sociotechnical arrangement, channels into the Calipso tablet a dynamic work in progress sustained by a hope such as those in the pharmaceutical field (Angell 2000; Bubela and Caulfield 2004). One may, therefore, wonder whether coordination or collaboration are real goals or drivers that condition the horizon of the sociotechnical arrangement of the Calipso device.

In the case of the Calipso project, there is no real question of a design regime that would be meshed with techno-scientific promises (Audétat *et al.* 2015), even though there are many beliefs in the technical possibilities of digital technology. The implementation of a technical artifact can be understood as a pretext for enlisting professionals to realign organizational practices and to promote a shift towards more "collaborative" health. Technology is not only a pretext, it is also a means of recreating connections and is, therefore, seen as an intermediate object to bring together different actors (Vinck 2009) and influence practices and representations.

3.5. Methodological course of the tailor-made experimental device

A first version of the device is currently in the test phase. The experimentation consists of the launch of five tablets at five "pilot" users for a period of about two months. Prior to this, a mapping of the players involved made it possible to select patients with a variety of characteristics: a person at the end of life, disabled, chronically ill, etc. and a person with a chronic disease. The identification work was made possible thanks to the support of the project's healthcare professionals, who proved to be the necessary intermediaries with the field. The team endeavored to find "unconventional" case studies for experimentation in order to test the tablets.

In order to build an initial picture of the patient's situation, an ethnographic survey described the person's lifestyle, the type of care provided, their care habits, the structuring of their entourage, the use of liaison notebooks, etc. The results of the survey were used to build a picture of the patient's situation. It also involved mapping the medical actors and the patient's natural caregivers in order to contact them and include them in the experimentation. The professionals who spend the most time in the home (auxiliaries and nurses) were targeted as a priority, as well as close family members if necessary. A quick interview (individual or collective), often at the patient's home, made it possible to present the device and create digital accounts on the tablet to begin the experimentation. Once the tablets had been placed in the patients' homes, numerous home visits were necessary to accompany the users and ensure that there were no blocking elements hindering the use of the tablets. Participation in the experiment was on a voluntary basis. Negotiation work was necessary to enroll the participants and in particular the health professionals. Nevertheless, many were open to the idea of testing the tablet.

3.6. (Preliminary) results and conclusions

As the launch phase ended and the *in vivo* use of the tablets began for extended experimentation, some of the results of the survey were already significant. They are based on device presentations, laboratory use tests, and early role-playing to assess the relevance of the tablet tools. The preliminary results are mainly at three levels: a first on the relevance of the tool, a second, more macroscopic, on the dynamics of the project and the structuring elements of multidisciplinary research, and finally a third on the status of the technology as a frontier object (Star and Griesemer 1989).

An initial set of observations relates directly to the nested structuring of territorial projects one after the other. As detailed above, Calipso is indeed in line with other achievements that have forged its network of actors and, to a large extent, led to the definition of its expectations. However, this history did not prevent many approximations at the beginning of the project on the objectives, the practical modalities of co-design, and technology evaluation. These elements seem partly attributable to the significant discontinuities that exist between two projects. Indeed, despite the efforts of the historical actors to ensure transitions, many informal elements are lost and the collective memory is not completely shared. The resulting methodological trial and error can be seen as so many "short-term adjustments" (Matthieu and Louvel 2012) that sometimes penalize the possibility of constructing a research strategy on a larger scale. Thus, the cost of building the collective dynamic at the start of the project is necessarily greater. The phenomenon is amplified by its multidisciplinarity, which implies temporalities that do not overlap between partners, and project-based funding that has apparently become the general rule in academic research. To another extent, this fragmented research leads to a compression of spaces for reflection, which results in greater difficulties in creating reflexivity (Piponnier 2014).

Another series of observations results this time from the analysis of the configuration of actors mobilized during the launch of the tablets. To carry out this phase, a pair of researchers went to patients' homes to train professionals in the use of the tool. A separation of tasks made it possible to redistribute the roles: while one was in charge of explaining the usability and potential of the application, the second stood back to observe and avoid being entirely caught up in the action, which guaranteed a certain distance. However, the role of the first was indispensable to the launch, as his mission was that of a "handyman". Thus, like a car dealership, the seller is not necessarily the person who shows the buyer how a vehicle works. It is a special mission dedicated to a third party – a technician or a workshop preparer who knows the vehicle well – and therefore escapes the merchant relationship between the dealer (seller) and the user (buyer). The handover person has only the objective of bringing to the attention of the new owner the technical and usage specifications of the car to encourage its direct appropriation. The role of the handyman in the Calipso project has been successively taken on by several researchers in order to move back and forth between postures committed to action, with manipulations of the technical device in which the researcher became its spokesman, and a greater distance to assert a greater axiological neutrality. The alternation of these schematic postures and the reflexive discussions on practices have, in our opinion, made it possible to find a satisfactory distance to claim the label of action-oriented research without avoiding the production of more theoretical knowledge.

At the start of the Calipso project, the lack of a precise formalization of the role of each person in the launch necessitated a distribution of tasks along the way. Confronting the tablet with (potential) users allowed new issues related to the system to be identified. One of them directly concerns the methods of launch and use of the tablet in a more general context. When the tablet is deployed for a new patient, it is devoid of any information about the patient. Therefore, it seems essential to appoint a coordinating referent to ensure that the device is primed by entering at least the essential information from the patient's health profile and to train the other stakeholders in the use of the tool. Our ethnographic investigations prior to launch had highlighted the central role played by healthcare at home nurses. In fact, they combine several characteristics such as their status as health professionals, their proximity to the patients they visit regularly, and their often-close relationships with other professionals. As a result, they are expected to become key players in the implementation of the project on a larger scale. In other words, during the *in vivo* experimentation phase, several difficulties relating to the choice of actors for the launch led to a re-problematization of the stakes involved in framing and structuring the system within an institutional framework.

Other more expected results logically appear after the first half of the tablet's real-life situation. Thus, the time of adaptation and appropriation of the tool is strongly conditioned by age. Although designed for a wide audience and responding to universal design criteria, the tablet interface is not suitable for some users who are not used to digital technologies. Unsurprisingly, it is those in their forties and fifties that have been the most challenged. These obstructions often combine with a reluctance to spend time using a new tool which, although thought by its designers to "facilitate" existing situations, quickly becomes perceived as destructive of routine and cumbersome. All of these elements led to the development of "reinforced" training for future tablet coordinators and to imagine the device as a starting point for collective reflection to build a "healthcare strategy"[14] for the patient. In other words, the introduction of the tablet in a given environment raised questions about the collective and individual involvement of supervisors and partly prompted a collective rethinking of the methods of care.

The Calipso tablet and its realization led the project team to structure itself around a shared object despite the specific objectives. In the absence of technical stabilization of the application, the tablet became a border object, a basis for dialogue, and the driving force behind the projection of the various project partners. In spite of strong divergences on the project's goals and the expected modifications towards a more "multidisciplinary and collaborative" approach, the Calipso technology has solidified itself into a flexible tool thanks to the plurality of functionalities. During the launch, the tablet was

14 Medical term used by a doctor from the Calipso project.

constantly modified by early feedback and its final version was crystallized around a consensual and easily usable version for extended scenarios.

At this time, it remains unclear to what extent the tablet will play a role as a coordination aid or digital gateway between the city and the hospital. This will have to wait until the end of the experiment and the analysis of the semi-directive terminal interviews. However, it can be noted that the objectives of several groups of actors within the project remain, despite several months of collective sessions, at very unequal levels of expectation. Healthcare professionals have high hopes for the tool and see it directly as a vector for transforming the practices of other caregivers. In this logic, the tablet is envisaged as a means of duplicating the operation of a healthcare team already in place (association of self-employed professionals) or of imposing a new frame of reference for actions for those involved in the home (hospital medicine). For their part, the historical scientific actors of the project remain convinced that the Calipso system will not revolutionize patient care and that it will become one coordination instrument among others. For them, the tablet must become a form of support for processes between healthcare actors. The difference in the scope of the aims is explained by the remote issues depending on their environment. One could also evoke the motivations of the industrial partner who develops the tool with economic goals and an expected return on investment. However, dialogue remains possible between actors thanks to the importance of technology in the design process. Indeed, we have shown that it channels the actions of the different individuals who project their expectations.

At this stage of the survey, the concept of knotworking takes on its full meaning and illustrates the overcoming of a logic of coordination, whose definition in the project is not shared by the actors. It is through the launch of a frontier-object that professional oppositions were revealed. Thus, the term co-configuration corresponds better to the observed situation than to (sought-after) cases of coordination. The fields of observation highlight more a situation of production of meaning and of a set of collective activities than situations where a technology directly constructs the coordination of actors. We can thus hypothesize that co-configuration is a first effect of Calipso technology, an effect linked in particular to the status of experimentation, but which may lead in a second stage – and only in a second stage – to the creation of elements of coordination between actors.

3.7. References

Abou Amsha, K. and Lewkowicz, M. (2014). Observing the work practices of an inter-professional healthcare at home team: Supporting a dynamic approach for quality healthcare at home delivery. In *COOP 2014 – Proceedings of the 11th International Conference on the Design of Cooperative Systems*, Rossitto, C., Ciolfi, L., Martin, D., Conein, B. (eds). Springer, Cham.

Akrich, M. (1990). De la sociologie des techniques à une sociologie des usages : l'impossible intégration du magnétoscope dans les réseaux câblés de première génération. *Techniques et culture*, 83–110.

Almirall, E., Lee, M., Wareham, J. (2012). Mapping Living Labs in the landscape of innovation methodologies. *Technology Innovation Management Review*, September, 12–18 [Online]. Available at: http://www.timreview.ca.

Angell, M. (2000). The parmaceutical industry – To whom is it countable? *New England Journal of Medicine*, 342(5), 1902–1904.

Archer, N., Fevrier-Thomas, U., Lokker, C., McKibbon, K.A., Straus, S.E. (2011). Personal health records: A scoping review. *Journal of the American Medical Informatics Association*, 18(4), 515–522.

Aubry, R. (2007). Les fonctions de coordination dans le champ de la santé. *Santé Publique*, 19(special issue), 73–77.

Audétat, M. (ed.) (2015). *Pourquoi tant de promesses ? Sciences et technologies émergentes*. Hermann, Paris.

Bergvall-Kåreborn, B., Ihlström Eriksson, C., Ståhlbröst, A., Svensson, J. (2009). A milieu for innovation – Defining Living Labs. *2nd ISPIM Innovation Symposium*. New York, 6–9 December.

Berthou, V. and Gaglio, G. (2020). The differentiated enrolment of users in health and autonomy living labs in France. *Réseaux*, 4(4), 165–198 [Online]. Available at: https://doi.org/10.3917/res.222.0165.

Blanchard, N. (2004). Du réseau à la coordination gérontologique : un nouveau paradigme pour le secteur médicosocial ? *Retraite et société*, 43(3), 165–186.

Bubela, T.M. and Caulfield, T.A. (2004). Do the print media "hype" genetic research? A comparison of newspaper stories and peer-reviewed research papers. *CMAJ*, 170, 1399–1409.

Cardon, D. (1997). Les sciences sociales et les machines à coopérer. Une approche bibliographique du Computer Supported Cooperative Work (CSCW). *Réseaux*, 15(85), 13–51.

Castaldi, C. and Dosi, G. (2006). The grip of history and the scope for novelty: Some results and open questions on path dependence in economic processes. In *Understanding Change*, Wimmer, A., Kössler, R. (eds). Palgrave Macmillan, London.

Dubé, P., Sarrailh, J., Billebaud, C., Grillet, C., Zingraff, V., Kostecki, I. (2014). Qu'est-ce qu'un Living Lab ? Le livre blanc des Living Labs. *UMVELT*, 1st edition [Online]. Available at: http://www.montreal-invivo.com.

Elmarzouqi, N., Garcia, E., Lapayre, J.C. (2008). CSCW from coordination to collaboration. In *Computer Supported Cooperative Work in Design IV*, Shen, W., Yong, J., Yang, Y., Barthès, J.P.A., Luo, J. (eds). Springer, Berlin and Heidelberg.

Engeström, Y. (2008). Quand le centre se dérobe : la notion de *knotworking* et ses promesses. *Sociologie du travail*, 50(3), 303–330.

Eriksson, M., Niitamo, V.-P., Kulkki, S., Hribernik, K.A. (2006). Living Labs as a multi-contextual R&D methodology. *Proc. of 2006 IEEE International Technology Management Conference*, United States.

Fournier, P. (2002). La collaboration ville-hôpital, de la filière au réseau gérontologique : éviter une hospitalisation non justifiée ou réussir une sortie difficile. *Gérontologie et société*, 25/100(1), 131–147.

Herreros, G. (2009). *Pour une sociologie d'intervention*. Érès, Toulouse.

Leibing, A. and Tournay, V. (eds) (2010). *Les technologies de l'espoir. La fabrique d'une histoire à accomplir*. Presses de l'Université de Laval, Laval.

Liebowitz, S. and Margolis, S. (1995). Path dependence, lock-in, and history. *Journal of Law*, April, 205–226.

Marcus, E.G. (1998). *Ethnography Through Thick and Thin*. Princeton University Press, Princeton.

Mathieu-Fritz, A. and Esterle, L. (2013). Les médecins et le dossier santé informatisé communiquant : analyse d'une expérimentation du dossier médical personnel (DMP). *Réseaux*, 178–179(2), 223–255.

Mathieu-Fritz, A. and Gaglio, G. (2018). À la recherche des configurations sociotechniques de la télémédecine : revue de littérature des travaux de sciences sociales. *Réseaux*, 207(1), 27–63.

Matthieu, H. and Louvel, S. (2012). Le financement sur projet : quelles conséquences sur le travail des chercheurs ? *Mouvements*, 71(3), 13–24.

Nesti, G. (2018). Co-production for innovation: The urban Living Lab experience. *Policy and Society*, 37(3), 310–325.

Pérodeau, G. and Côté, D. (eds) (2002). *Le virage ambulatoire, défis et enjeux*. Presses de l'Université du Québec, Quebec.

Piponnier, A. (2014). Le projet dans les pratiques de recherche. Pour un retour réflexif et critique sur nos engagements. *Sciences de la société*, 93, 110–123.

Polomeni, P. and Larcher, P. (2001). *Les réseaux en santé. Objectifs et stratégie dans une collaboration ville-hôpital*. Masson, Paris.

Robelet, M., Serré, M., Bourgueil, Y. (2005). La coordination dans les réseaux de santé : entre logiques gestionnaires et dynamiques professionnelles. *Revue française des affaires sociales*, 231–260.

Schmidt, K. and Bannon, L. (1992). Taking CSCW seriously: Supporting articulation work. *Computer Supported Cooperative Work*, 1, 7–40.

Sentilhes-Monkam, A. (2005). Rétrospective de l'hospitalisation à domicile : l'histoire d'un paradoxe. *Revue française des affaires sociales*, 3, 157–182.

Shaw, S., Rosen, R., Rumbold, B. (2011). What is integrated care? Report, Nuffield Trust, London.

Star, S. and Griesemer, J. (1989). Institutional ecology, "translations" and boundary objects: Amateurs and professionals in Berkeley's Museum of Vertebrate Zoology, 1907–39. *Social Studies of Science*, 19(3), 387–420.

Suchman, L. (1997). Centers of coordination: a case and some themes. In *Discourse, Tools and Reasoning*, Resnick, L.B., Säljö, R., Pontecorvo, C., Burge, B. (eds). Springer, Berlin and Heidelberg.

Vezinat, N. (2019). *Vers une médecine collaborative. Politique des maisons de santé pluri-professionnelles en France*. PUF, Paris.

Vial, A. (2017). *Santé, le trésor menacé*. L'Atalante, Nantes.

Vinck, D. (2009). De l'objet intermédiaire à l'objet-frontière : vers la prise en compte du travail d'équipement. *Revue d'anthropologie des connaissances*, 3(1), 51–72.

PART 2

Digital Technology and Transformations in the Relationships between Professionals and Patients

Introduction to Part 2

Traditionally, the healthcare system places the user, the "patient", as an object of care provided by professionals, the "experts". The patient is often reduced to a passive role in the construction of his or her care pathway and has extremely little visibility on the use of his or her health data. In addition, the healthcare user currently has only a very limited panel of digital healthcare services compared to the uses that can be developed in other sectors. The digital shift in health, as defined by the WHO, must therefore have the essential objective of repositioning users as the primary beneficiary of digital health services by giving them the means to be real players in their own health, and thus meet their expectations.

While the use of artificial intelligence (AI) systems by the patient for well-being and medical purposes has given more responsibility and autonomy to the chronically ill patient, we will see how the strategy launched by the European Union some 15 years ago aims to modernize the organization that has characterized our healthcare systems until then. At the same time, on the side of healthcare professionals, how can the relationship between healthcare professionals and AI systems be improved for increased diagnostic performance? In this respect, how should the awareness and training of these healthcare professionals evolve to improve the complementarity of human-machine interfaces? And finally, in the face of the increasing technicization of healthcare, isn't the training and education of health professionals in the "humanities" and in particular in ethics crucial to the development of digital medicine that contributes to patient empowerment?

Introduction written by Roland RIZOULIÈRES.

An observation must be made regarding the fears that arise from the use of AI in the doctor-patient relationship. Faced with the power of human intelligence, the global AI, called "strong" AI – capable of understanding, learning by itself, inventing (or adapting), and being aware of itself – does not yet exist. And is not close to coming into existence! Yet, and even if it remains "weak" AI, its performance in some medical fields (medical imaging diagnostics, decision support, assisted surgery, augmented reality, etc.) are breathtaking and will only increase over time. These machines and all the technologies that surround them (nanotechnologies, genomics, sensors, 3D printing, etc.) are gradually leading us into a 4.0 world whose threats and deviances regarding medical ethics are unsuspected, not because of an autonomous AI that would enslave us, but because of the use that can be made of it by human beings themselves. Faced with the digitization of medicine, is the spirit of Hippocrates in danger? So, what are the real stakes for the doctor-patient relationship in the years to come? How can we identify and establish elements of an ethical charter presiding over technological evolutions? And, above all, how can we escape the protean risks presented by Medicine 4.0 if we do not succeed in this mutation in the best conditions?

Finally, the ethical dimension in the use of digital technology in health is explored in the specific context of the development and promotion of public health in West Africa, particularly with epidemics such as Ebola.

4

Use of AI Systems in the Care Relationship, Redefining Patient and Physician Roles

The vast majority of Western physicians are committed to respecting the Hippocratic Oath, the content of which has been integrated and modernized in various international legal instruments. The Declaration of Geneva, adopted by the World Medical Association in September 1948, is currently considered to be the modern version of the Hippocratic Oath. Its founding principles can also be found in the Principles of European Medical Ethics. In committing themselves to its content, physicians undertake, in particular, to respect "all persons, their autonomy and will, without any discrimination according to their condition or beliefs" and to maintain and perfect their skills in order to provide the best possible services.

While these guiding principles of medical ethics have not given way over time, the model of care in which they were originally applied has not. The traditional "paternalistic" model, in which the physician bore the full burden of responsibility for medical decision making, has gradually given way to an "alternative" model of care, in which responsibility for medical decision making is shared between physician and patient.

However, the use of artificial intelligence (AI) systems in the care relationship reinforces this desire to empower patients in the management of their health (section 4.1). As for healthcare professionals, the use of AI systems encourages the diversification of their skills (section 4.2).

Chapter written by Anthéa SÉRAFIN.

4.1. Progressive affirmation of individualized healthcare in the service of patient autonomy

In the long term, the European Commission's strategy for the digital transformation of health services aims to enable a global organizational evolution of the model of care. The idea is to gradually move away from a model centered around health professionals towards a model centered around the patient, supported by the medico-social sector. At present, the path is fragmented, based on reactive care, with an approach centered on the disease and the medical profession, dictated by the supply and with a passive patient. An integrated model of care is currently being developed, based on a logic of continuity of care, which would be more planned. The new approach, promoting the active role of the patient, is intended to be person-centered and demand-oriented.

A first step towards this evolution lies in the promotion of the responsibility of individuals (i.e. patients as well as healthy people) for its management (section 4.1.1). This empowerment movement also contributes to the achievement of the European Union's strategic priority: the development of personalized medicine (section 4.1.2).

4.1.1. *Reinforcing the patient's responsibility in the healthcare relationship*

Patient empowerment aims to develop health literacy, that is, the ability to responsibly acquire, understand, and use information to promote well-being or to stay healthy. Patient use of AI systems for wellness or medical purposes enables patients to become more involved in managing their health. Wellness-oriented AI systems, as connected objects or mobile applications, can provide personalized advice to those who use them to adopt a healthier lifestyle, which in turn can help prevent illness. Similarly, medical AI systems, when connected to a mobile object or application, can provide direct advice to patients on how to manage their illness.

The use of mobile health solutions, which provide individualized and directly accessible information, is therefore a vehicle for patient responsibility in managing their health (section 4.1.1.1). Illustrating this potential, a recent solution aimed at enabling self-management of various chronic diseases has recently emerged in Europe (section 4.1.1.2).

4.1.1.1. *Empowerment tantamount to patients' autonomy in managing their health*

In 2007, the European Commission published a white paper on the basis of the current Article 168 of the TFEU[1] (formerly Article 152 of the TEC)[2], entitled "*Ensemble pour la santé*". Its general objective was, over time, to increase the importance of health in all policies and actions of the community. It mentioned the fact that community health policy would consider the rights of citizens and patients as a starting point, specifically, patients' rights to receive the skills necessary for their well-being and the right to participate in decision-making. In other words, the new priority of the Community was already, at the time, to develop patient autonomy. This priority finds legitimacy in advice given by the renowned diagnostician at the end of the 19th century, W. Osler, "If you listen carefully to the patient, he will give you the diagnosis." Since then, this new dimension of the patient's role has become increasingly important. In 2018, the CNOM[3] noted that patients had become key players in healthcare, playing an active role in the evolution of physicians' knowledge.

However, the new solutions that have emerged thanks to the launch of the mobile health market, mainly smart devices and mobile wellness and health applications, are finding their rightful place in this strategy. Indeed, these tools constitute new vectors for health promotion, disease prevention, and monitoring. It is nevertheless very "important to ensure that these new technological solutions result in a real gain in autonomy for citizens and that they are not an additional factor of discrimination and economic determinism."

In general, health promotion and disease prevention enable citizens to acquire the knowledge necessary to improve their well-being. When it comes to disease monitoring, mobile health solutions coupled with AI systems open new perspectives. AI systems integrated into a smart device or mobile application allows for analyzing data collected about the patient, including information about the social, environmental, and dietary context surrounding

1 Treaty on the Functioning of the European Union.

2 Treaty establishing the European Community.

3 *Conseil national de l'Ordre des médecins*.

the patient or the patient's answers to regular questionnaires. Data can be collected either automatically, through portable, handheld, or implantable electronic devices, or with the active collaboration of the patient, through a smart device or mobile application. The cross-referencing of all these data, making the overall disease situation more legible, is a factor in improving the planning of the patient's care pathway. Indeed, as the European Commission (2008a) stated, "Once processed and transmitted to the healthcare professionals concerned, this information can be used to detect symptoms or abnormal physiological parameters earlier than during a routine or emergency consultation, making it possible to take measures to prevent the occurrence of serious complications."

Automated patient monitoring, therefore, makes it possible to avoid unnecessary consultations or hospitalizations (some medical acts could be performed remotely, or even by the patients themselves) and to optimize monitoring and treatment protocols. For the first time in 2017, a vascular and pulmonary cardiology department (that of the Centre Hospitalier Régional Universitaire de Lille) implanted a remote diagnostic device in the chest of a patient suffering from cardiac arrhythmia[4]. This device, connected via Bluetooth to a mobile application, is equipped with an AI system that is supposed to alert the patient *via* the application as soon as it detects that his heart rhythm is abnormal.

This new conception of the healthcare relationship, in which mobile applications are conceived as intermediaries between the doctor and the patient, implies that both are equally involved in the management of the disease and consequently in medical decision-making.

Many other chronic diseases particularly affect European citizens. A few figures verify this statement[5]; chronic pain (characterized when a person has been suffering continuously for more than three months) has an impact of 240 billion euros in the European Union, is the leading cause of accidental death, represents 31% of causes of suicide and leads to 88 million days of work stoppage. In the end, 150 million people in the European Union are affected and only 3% are properly cared for.

4 For more details: https://www.whatsupdoc-lemag.fr/article/smart-phone-lille-patients-et-cardiologues-sont-connectes.

5 For more details: http://mylittlesante.com/lucine-la-esante-santi-douleur/.

4.1.1.2. *Patient empowerment as a response to the European issue of chronic disease management*

In 2008, at the European Union's high-level conference on eHealth, Member State representatives stressed the urgency of deploying innovative ICT-based tools[6] for chronic disease management on a large scale. Currently, chronic pain is mainly treated with painkillers and psychotherapies. However, painkillers can lead to addiction, can have adverse effects, and represent a significant cost for variable effectiveness depending on the patient concerned. Ten years later, a study seems to show that the appeal from the member states has not had the desired effect; only a few chronic patients use mobile health applications or smart devices to manage their illness[7]. This result is all the more astonishing as it strongly contrasts with the growing development of these technologies in different sectors of the economy and industry.

What is the reason for this failure? The most likely origin of this observation seems to be the diversity of chronic diseases, and thus the lack of adaptability of some technological solutions to the different needs they create. It is, therefore more a problem of supply that is not yet sufficiently adapted to needs, than a problem of demand.

Indeed, the chronically ill who have the possibility of using mobile health solutions adapted to the needs generated by their illness perceive the beneficial effects of this use: "The different groups of users share the same point of view as regards the trust they have in their doctor, but the most connected feel more committed to the relationship." Aware that the care pathway now necessarily includes the home, health professionals and healthcare institutions are, for their part, now clearly committed to strategies for digital patient support. In fact, the use of mobile health applications and smart devices has consequences on the interactions of chronically ill patients with the medical and healthcare professionals, leading to a more positive perception of their ability to intervene in decisions concerning their health.

In other words, the use of mobile health solutions by people suffering from cancer strengthens their autonomy in the management of their disease; this is known as patient empowerment. In a study conducted in 2017, the Institut Mines-Télécom Business School specifies that this notion

6 Information and Communication Technologies.

7 The study sample consisted of 94% of people living with a chronic illness.

corresponds to a "process of personal transformation through which patients strengthen their ability to effectively take care of themselves and their health." This phenomenon helps to strengthen the patient's ability to act on the determinants of their health and their development and is, as such, strongly encouraged by the WHO[8].

Finally, the most important obstacle hindering the development of the mobile healthcare market for the chronically ill is the diversity of diseases grouped in this category. Very recently, an AI-based solution has been developed to reduce this obstacle; it is a solution created in 2017 by the Bordeaux-based start-up Lucine. By extending the mobile healthcare market to the growing number of chronically ill people in Europe, Lucine is typically the kind of solution that the European Union is seeking to stimulate through its AI and digital healthcare transformation strategies. It may, therefore, be interesting to study this case in more detail. It is a "digital therapy" adapted to the specific needs that differ according to the different chronic pathologies. According to founder Maryne Cotty-Eslous, the idea is to create one Lucine per pathology: "We are working on several topics in parallel: endometriosis, diabetes, burn-out and post-stroke[9] rigidities. But others are in the pipeline," particularly for pain related to multiple sclerosis or in the field of oncology. The application contains a system capable of measuring, analyzing, and relieving pain immediately, in a personalized manner. Concretely, the user can connect to a platform, accessible via his or her smartphone or tablet, and answer a questionnaire designed to reflect his or her personal history. In order to refine the elements highlighted by the answers to the questionnaires, the camera, used by the application, then uses various techniques to detect "external signs of pain": voice analysis, posture analysis, electroencephalogram (EEG) analysis, electrocardiogram (ECG) analysis, and pupil dilatation analysis. Thus, thanks to a database gathering all these subjective data relating to the patient and objective data relating to the specificities of the painful symptoms, the software detects the nature and functioning of the pain. It then determines a "pain score" and personalizes the treatment according to this result. The AI system then measures the effectiveness of the treatment results, in order to continuously adapt the treatment.

Medically, Lucine's treatments vary according to the intensity of the pain, the environment, and the emotional state. They may include multi-sensory

8 World Health Organization.

9 Cerebrovascular accident.

relaxation, a serious game, or an immersive virtual reality stimulation session. The placebo effect plays an important role in these treatments: "All you have to do is understand the brain and send it the right messages. In all, we have identified around forty different stimulations that will either divert the brain's attention, lower the level of cortisol (a hormone involved in stress management) by working on the patient's cardiac coherence, or provoke a cerebral orgasm, which will itself trigger the production of oxytocin and endorphin (two neuropeptides that act on well-being, known as happiness hormones)." Cotty-Eslous spoke of a "natural morphine shot"[10]. In other words, the application uses the placebo effect as well as visual and auditory stimuli that stimulate the brain to produce certain chemicals on its own to reduce the feeling of pain. Currently, Lucine's solutions are still in the experimental stage, but they are intended to be tested by large cohorts of patients.

Lucine's AI-based digital therapies, by enabling people with chronic pain to control their pain at home, illustrate the empowering potential of mobile health solutions. By offering solutions customized to each patient's profile, these solutions are also in line with the other international and European strategic priority in healthcare: the development of personalized medicine.

4.1.2. *Increasingly personalized medicine*

The high-level conference organized in 2015 on the theme "Making Access to Personalized Medicine a Reality for Patients" highlighted the need to promote a patient-centered approach to medicine at the European level. In the same year, the Council of the European Union (2015) noted that there was no commonly accepted definition of what "personalized medicine" is, but that it was nevertheless recognized that "it consists of a medical model that relies on the characterization of people's phenotypes and genotypes in order to propose the right therapeutic strategy to the right person at the right time and/or to establish the existence of a predisposition to a disease and/or to ensure timely and targeted prevention."

As seen previously, AI systems enable new approaches in the field of personalized and precision medicine. One of the most promising approaches is to use genomic data to drive AI systems. Currently, an AI system that

10 For more information: https://le-quotidien-du-patient.fr/invite/2018/11/06/soulager-douleur-cerveau-lucine/.

deals only with "classical" health data can only justify a situational match between two patients on the basis of elements in their medical records or analyses of the scientific literature. What would change with the integration of genomic data in such a system is that it could calculate a result by taking into account the entire genetic background of the patient, and thus provide hereditary justifications. This would, therefore, make it possible to offer each patient a more individualized healthcare pathway.

Another feat of deploying AI systems to improve the transition to personalized medicine is the advent of the "digital twin", of which several clinical applications are currently under development. Initially, this concept was born in the aeronautics, energy and automotive sectors. Thanks to recent advances in digital imaging, it has made its appearance in the healthcare sector, where it is assimilated to a virtual avatar of each patient. It is, therefore, a very faithful copy of the patient, "acquired by accumulating data on the patient, with the same risk factors and health problems. It enables treatments to be tested, the evolution of certain pathologies to be predicted and virtual operations to be performed"[11]. Several major advances are to be hoped for, in particular a reduction in *in vitro* and *in vivo* tests, compensated by an increase in *in silico* tests. Currently, "digital twins" are mainly used in the specific field of surgery[12].

If AI systems were integrated into such "digital twins", we could see the birth of "global" digital twins, whose data could be updated in real time. This would be possible by connecting a digital twin with a mobile application or a connected object, which can effectively collect data in real time. The main advance offered by "global" digital twins, thus connected to AI systems, concerns the quality of predictions about a patient's health. Indeed, they will allow to better know the statistical probabilities related to the evolution of a disease, life expectancy, and feasibility of surgery or chemotherapy. This mass of information, made available to each of us, would

11 For more details: https://www.whatsupdoc-lemag.fr/article/mon-medecin-mon-jumeau-numerique-et-moi.

12 https://www.pwc.fr/fr/decryptages/data/intelligence-artificielle-le-jumeau-numerique-une-promesse-pour-lentreprise-et-les.html. For the moment, digital twins are essentially used in the field of surgery with associated start-ups (neurosurgery for the placement of personalized stents (Sim&Cure), vascular surgery (Therenva), orthopedics for therapeutic planning and decision-making (Digital Orthopedics), etc.). At the same time, they are the subject of much research, particularly for the design of joint prostheses adapted to all types of morphology and for the modeling of synthetic organs.

constitute a real progress towards completely individualized care pathways and medical decisions.

It is, therefore, clear that healthcare solutions based on AI systems are really at the heart of the reorganization of all medical practices around the patient; they contribute to the transition towards new models of care in which patients become the main actors. This raises the question of the role to be played by healthcare personnel in the context of these new models of care.

4.2. Integration of digital and ethical concepts in the training of health personnel and in the education of citizens

Recently, the European Parliament asked the member states, as well as the European Commission, to determine whether training programs for medical and health personnel should be updated and harmonized at the European level with regard to the knowledge and use of the most advanced technological instruments. Pending their response, and with regard to the use of AI systems in the care relationship, it is appropriate to revisit the key competencies that should guide this potential harmonization. These had been defined as early as 2006 in a European Parliament recommendation that set out a common reference framework for all European Union member states (European Parliament and Council of the European Union 2006).

Indeed, for a digital, patient-centered model of care to succeed, healthcare staff must have the appropriate skills. However, before even thinking about adapting the higher education or continuing education pathways of health staff (section 4.2.2), a necessary prelude lies in the general development of citizens' digital skills (section 4.2.1).

4.2.1. *Global challenge of developing citizens' digital skills*

Internationally, there is a growing trend towards the need to rethink the traditional form of education in order to cope with the societal changes that AI will bring about: until now, the standard educational model has generally focused on the acquisition of a set of "key knowledge" and emphasized formal apprenticeships, such as reading, writing, and arithmetic. Today, information and knowledge have become ubiquitous, requiring data literacy (enabling students to read, analyze, and manage information) and AI literacy (enabling critical thinking).

As far as the territory of the European Union is concerned, in 2006 the European Union launched a strategy aimed at complementing the action of the member states in terms of the key skills to be developed for lifelong education and training. The context in which this reference framework took place was that of a digital divide, which had already established itself between the member states but also within them, this problem being accentuated by the fact that the first victims of these inequalities are the most vulnerable people.

However, this initial strategy was not enough to respond effectively to this challenge; in 2016, it was found that nearly half of the European Union's population lacked basic digital skills, and around 20% had none at all. This is an issue dear to UNESCO[13] which, through the various reports published by COMEST[14], has always stressed that the launch of AI systems on the international scene should be inclusive. This means that it should in no way lead to widening the existing digital divide, which is more marked at the international level than at the European level.

That same year, the strategy was, therefore, reaffirmed by the European Commission. The initiatives it proposes are in fact part of the wider context of the advent of the digital single market and reflect the urgent need to adapt the skills of European citizens to the needs created by the digital evolution of the labor market – the more skills that are adapted, the more competitive European citizens will be. Although the content of teaching and the organization of education systems is the responsibility of the member states, the European Commission believes that only concerted efforts will lead to sustainable results.

In order to carry out this cooperation, it has set common strategic objectives for the European Union, including the development of digital skills. It has also committed itself to bringing together both member states and stakeholders (including social partners) to facilitate communication between relevant actors at EU level. The aim is for them to commit themselves to action, in particular by identifying and sharing good practices,

13 United Nations Educational, Scientific and Cultural Organization.

14 World Commission on the Ethics of Scientific Knowledge and Technology.

so that these can be more easily replicated and scaled up. It is even envisaged that the OECD will assist member states in drawing up their national action plans.

Nevertheless, it seems that this arsenal of cooperative measures has not been sufficient to advance at the pace desired by the Commission. Arguing the importance of cooperation between stakeholders in building a European identity based on common values and cultures, the Commission has, therefore, recently adopted a Digital Literacy Action Plan. This time, it uses a firmer vocabulary:

> There is a need to go "wide" as all citizens need to have an understanding, at different levels, of the different aspects of digital competence, and there is a need to go "deep" for more specialized skills in informatics required in the ICT profession.[15]

More specifically, with regard to citizens' knowledge of AI, the European strategy emphasizes that ICT education and ethics should be integrated into all curricula, including non-technical studies, so as to equip the workforce with the knowledge needed to evolve in a digital work environment. Indeed, it is first and foremost the responsibility of education systems to anticipate the changes brought about by the development of new technologies in order to enable future generations to ensure their prosperity. In addition to the integration of ICT knowledge into educational programs, bottom-up projects enabling citizens to successfully make their voices heard should be implemented, like participative platforms on AI. Second, it is equally important to anticipate the supply of new job profiles that will generally result from the launch of AI systems, especially in the area of developing self-learning algorithms.

To this end, the European Commission has launched the Digital Opportunity Traineeships project, which enables Erasmus students to carry out internships to acquire advanced digital skills. In parallel to this project, all actors in AI (states, companies, and individuals) are strongly encouraged to develop learning opportunities in the workplace, particularly by investing more in digital skills training. Thirdly and finally, the European Commission affirms its willingness to offer assistance to workers whose jobs are likely to undergo the most transformations due to the launch of AI systems.

15 https://eur-lex.europa.eu/legal-content/EN/TXT/PDF/?uri=CELEX:52018DC0022&from=EN.

It is understandable that the European strategic approach takes a global approach to the issue of skills in that it contains an economic component (relating to the adaptation of education systems and lifelong learning) and a social component (relating to the support offered to workers particularly affected by the launch of AI systems). Moreover, it should be recalled here that this is not a minor, adjunct, or peripheral strategy, but a strategy whose implementation is crucial to ensure a better adaptation of the supply to the demand on the European labor market. This crucial character is confirmed by the magnitude of European funding dedicated to its implementation for the 2014–2020 period, amounting to 27 billion euros.

Across all occupational sectors, the launch of AI systems substantially changes the skills currently required to perform existing jobs. Indeed, it makes it possible to carry out tasks that were previously impossible to perform because they were too tedious or economically unprofitable, to automate tasks previously performed by humans, and even to provide decision-making assistance. As the health sector is no exception to these benefits, it must be recognized that the launch of AI systems requires a review of the skills to be emphasized in graduate and continuing education programs for health sector personnel.

4.2.2. *Issues specific to the training of healthcare professionals*

As early as 2008, the European Commission encouraged member states to take measures to promote the use of ICT in healthcare institutions and to make greater use of European structural funds to adapt the initial and continuing training of healthcare professionals and the sector's infrastructure, as well as to improve their working conditions. Some professions are, more than others, currently required to "collaborate" with AI systems: medical imaging, cardiology, general medicine, and the nursing community. For other trades, such as oncology or palliative care, many projects are at the experimental stage.

A report, written by the Institut Montaigne in January 2019, informs us that the launch of AI systems in the health sector will have important consequences to which healthcare institutions and the conditions of practice of healthcare professionals will have to adapt. According to the same report (Institut Montaigne 2019), it would seem that today such consequences would mainly concern the most innovative institutions with sufficient critical mass in terms of medical, technological, and financial capacity. This observation somewhat contradicts that of D. Gruson (2018), who believes that "health solutions integrating AI systems will first find their place in countries without efficient health systems or in regions of developed countries characterized by a medical demographic problem or an inability of health institutions to engage, through the classic processes of change management, in relevant recomposition of the healthcare offer". Finally, this contradiction shows that there is no consensus on the precisely expected impact of deploying AI systems in healthcare institutions. For this to happen, we must wait for a precise study listing the tasks that can be fully "automated", those that can benefit from the simple support of AI systems and those that can only be performed by a human brain.

Despite these uncertainties, there seems to be general agreement that the main threat to the use of AI systems by healthcare professionals is an over-reliance on automation, leading to an impoverishment of their skills. In this sense, the European Parliament stressed the importance of providing health personnel with appropriate education, training and preparation to ensure that they are equipped with the highest possible level of competence. According to the CNOM, whose terms are very clear, "the current challenge is to establish the best possible alliance between human and machine and to 'increase' the potential of medicine through the use of technology. AI has the capacity to work considerably faster on immeasurably higher volumes of data, but on a very precise, well-delimited task, while the human brain retains its supremacy when it comes to reasoning, analyzing its environment, communicating."

In the healthcare sector, AI systems must, therefore, be deployed to provide assistance to professionals, consisting of reducing the risk of human error. A study included in the same CNOM report supports this statement, while providing some details. Researchers have analyzed the reliability of diagnoses made by physicians alone, by AI systems alone and by physician-AI system duos. This study found that physicians, compared to AI systems, predict twice as many good diagnoses on the first try. However, the detailed results show that this gap is reduced in the presence of common pathologies, while it increases in favor of physicians in the presence of uncommon symptoms. The researchers concluded that healthcare professionals would perform better by using an AI system to complement their own skills. In the context of the healthcare relationship, the fruits of this complementarity can only be reaped by stimulating certain skills in the training of healthcare personnel.

As seen in section 4.2.1, the acquisition of e-skills has been a priority for the European Union since 2006. According to the European Parliament, such skills aim to enable "the safe and critical use of Information Society Technologies (IST)". The aim is, therefore, to introduce mastery of ICTs into the training curricula of healthcare personnel, so as to place them in a position to search for, collect and process information in order to use it critically, that is, by assessing its relevance. Concerning the use of AI systems, the idea is to place professionals in a position to supervise their operation.

Reforms on this subject are gradually beginning to be implemented at the national level. In France, for example, the Conference of Deans of Faculties of Medicine is committed to including the issues of algorithmic medicine in the curricula of all medical students, the objective being to raise awareness of the key concepts of AI, and this first step should then gradually be extended to all health professions. More specifically, concerning surgeons who use surgical robots to operate on a patient, the European Parliament suggests the creation of a kind of license. This would guarantee that surgeons are competent to supervise the robot, that is that the initial programming and choices of the robot remain within their decision-making sphere.

Other skills that need to be emphasized in the context of the care relationship are those related to ethics. As with the training of those who create AI systems, the training of health professionals who use AI systems must, therefore, evolve towards greater consideration of ethical concepts in the exercise of their activity. This confirms the fact that ethics is indeed the essential corollary of the development, launch, and use of AI systems.

In this perspective, the CNOM draws attention to the fact that "more than ever, the ethical approach and the expression of an accompanying medical deontology will have to be associated with the scientific teaching of medicine based on evidence: training in the humanities, deontology and ethics, and human relations, must be strengthened in a world that is becoming increasingly technical" (Conseil national de l'Ordre des médecins 2018). The European Parliament recommended, more broadly:

> An attitude of critical appreciation and curiosity, an interest in ethical issues and respect for both safety and sustainability, in particular as regards scientific and technological progress in

> relation to oneself, family, community and global issues.[16] (European Parliament and the Council of the European Union 2006).

Moreover, a worrying phenomenon reinforces the indispensable nature of the integration of ethics in the training of personnel intervening in a care relationship. Even though many studies attest to the positive effects of empathy on patients, it has been shown that natural empathy diminishes during the course of a doctor's or nurse's training[17]. To prevent this phenomenon from persisting, the acquisition of social skills by healthcare personnel should be revalued. According to a definition of the European Parliament, social competences include

> personal, interpersonal and intercultural competence and cover all forms of behaviour that equip individuals [...]. Social competence is linked to personal and social well-being which requires an understanding of how individuals can ensure optimum physical and mental health, including as a resource for oneself and one's family and one's immediate social environment, and knowledge of how a healthy lifestyle can contribute to this. [...] it is essential to understand the codes of conduct and manners generally accepted in different societies and environments (e.g. at work). It is equally important to be aware of basic concepts relating to individuals, groups, work organisations, gender equality and non-discrimination, society and culture. The core skills of this competence include the ability to communicate constructively in different environments, to show tolerance, express and understand different viewpoints, to negotiate with the ability to create confidence, and to feel empathy.[18]

Thus, the health professional would play more of an advisory and coordinating role in the healthcare relationship, which could go hand in hand with closer collaboration with social sector staff.

---

16 https://eur-lex.europa.eu/legal-content/EN/TXT/HTML/?uri=CELEX:32006H0962&from=EN.

17 Speech by Professor S. Lelorrain at the SimforHealth Conference, April 27, 2017, cited in (Conseil national de l'Ordre des médecins 2018).

18 https://eur-lex.europa.eu/legal-content/EN/TXT/HTML/?uri=CELEX:32006H0962&from=EN.

Finally, these developments lead to the realization that the use of AI systems, whether by the patient or the physician, is a practice that promotes patient self-care. This practice offers the patient the possibility of being more involved in the management of his or her health, while benefiting from the advice of the healthcare professional. However, this autonomy in the management of one's health can only be truly beneficial if the risks to one's private life and to the preservation of one's free will are properly controlled.

4.3. References

Conseil national de l'Ordre des médecins (2018). Analyses et recommandations : médecins et patients dans le monde des data, des algorithmes et de l'intelligence artificielle. White book, Conseil national de l'Ordre des médecins, Paris.

Council of the European Union (2015). Médecine personnalisée pour les patients. Communication JOC421, Conseil de l'Union européenne, Brussels.

Espace éthique d'Île-de-France (2015). Big Data et pratiques biomédicales : implications éthiques et sociétales dans la recherche, les traitements et le soin. *Les cahiers de l'espace éthique*, Paris.

European Commission (2008a). La télémédecine au service des patients, des systèmes de soins de santé et de la société. Communication (2008)689, Commission européenne, Brussels.

European Commission (2008b). Livre vert relatif au personnel de santé. Communication (2008)725, Commission européenne, Brussels.

European Commission (2014). Livre vert sur la santé mobile. Communication (2014)219, Commission européenne, Brussels.

European Commission (2016). Une nouvelle stratégie en matière de compétences pour l'Europe : travailler ensemble pour renforcer le capital humain et améliorer l'employabilité et la compétitivité. Communication (2016)381, Commission européenne, Brussels.

European Commission (2018a). Plan d'action en matière d'éducation numérique. Communication (2018)22, Commission européenne, Brussels.

European Commission (2018b). Permettre la transformation numérique des services de santé et de soins dans le marché unique numérique ; donner aux citoyens les moyens d'agir et construire une société plus saine. Communication (2018)233, Commission européenne, Brussels.

European Commission (2018c). Un plan coordonné dans le domaine de l'intelligence artificielle. Communication (2018)795, Commission européenne, Brussels.

European Economic and Social Council (2018). Avis sur la transformation numérique des services de santé et de soins dans le marché unique numérique. Communication, Conseil économique et social européen, Brussels.

European Parliament (2019). Une politique industrielle européenne globale sur l'intelligence artificielle et la robotique. Résolution 2018/2088 (INI), Parlement européen, Brussels.

European Parliament and the Council of the European Union (2006). Les compétences clés pour l'éducation et la formation tout au long de la vie. Recommandation JOC962, Parlement européen, Brussels.

France Stratégie (2018). Intelligence artificielle et travail. Report, Rapport à la Ministre du Travail et au secrétaire d'État chargé du numérique auprès du Premier Ministre, France Stratégie, Paris.

Gruson, D. (2018). *La Machine, le médecin et moi*. Éditions de l'Observatoire, Paris.

Institut Mines-Télécom Business School (2017). Impact des nouvelles technologies sur la santé et la qualité de vie des personnes vivant avec une maladie chronique. Study, Institut Mines-Télécom Business School, Évry-Courcouronnes.

Institut Montaigne (2019). Intelligence artificielle et emploi en santé : quoi de neuf docteur ? Note, Institut Montaigne, Paris.

World Commission on the Ethics of Scientific Knowledge and Technology (COMEST) (2019). Étude préliminaire sur les aspects techniques et juridiques liés à l'opportunité d'un instrument normatif sur l'éthique de l'intelligence artificielle. Communication, UNESCO, Paris.

5

Artificial Intelligence Ethics in Medicine

5.1. Artificial intelligence in question

The concept of artificial intelligence (AI) dates back to 1955, just 10 years after Turing invented the machine that deciphered the Enigma, the message coding system invented by the German army, and after von Neumann modeled the principles of what a computer could be. That is to say, AI was introduced very early in what became the computer science we know. Medicine was quickly invested by computer scientists as a field of experimentation, notably with Mycin in 1972, an expert system for the diagnosis of infectious diseases. In the aftermath, especially with the increase in computing power due to transistors and electronic chips, many AI techniques were born. Connective systems, of which the current deep learning[1] is one example, could only emerge when the computing power was sufficient, that is, around the 2000s. During these 50 years of slow growth in the computing capacities of the machines determined by Moore's law, symbolic systems based not on data but on logic emerged. Because of some of their limitations, notably for inference engines, these systems have lost interest in favor of the connectionist systems that will be described in section 5.3. We now know, in a more or less consensual way, that it is from the convergence, or even fusion of these two thoughts, that an advanced AI will emerge.

Chapter written by Loïc ÉTIENNE.

1 Deep learning is a type of artificial intelligence capable of learning through a neural network system and under human supervision.

Because, let's face it, AI (in the sense of global intelligence) does not exist anywhere in the world! What we know how to do with algorithms and data processing remains "weak artificial intelligence". The term "artificial intelligence" is overused, and we put just about anything and everything in it. What the media are feeding us with as algorithms, Big Data, machine learning, expert systems, etc. are just flags flying in the wind of communication without really knowing what it means or what it refers to.

AI works with algorithms, which are nothing more than hard procedures: "If... and if... then." Any reflection leading to a decision is based on this principle: "If the door is open, then I pass through." But, "if the door is closed and there is a tiger behind it, I don't pass through." It's just common sense. But the machine must be informed that a tiger has escaped from the zoo next door and is behind the door because it is hungry! Every single one of our household objects uses algorithms to work. Does that qualify them as "intelligent"? The answer is in the question.

Regardless of the computing power and algorithm capabilities, we remain in the field of low AI. "Strong" artificial intelligence, that of a human being, or even of advanced animals such as octopus or mice, is not for everyone. Human intelligence is by essence not definable by humans, because to study a system, one should be able to extract oneself from it (simplification of Gödel's[2] incompleteness theorem).

We cannot, therefore, understand our own intelligence, but we can perfectly evaluate its capacities (calculation, memorization, invention, arts, emotions, etc.), evaluate its actions and define its behaviors. To think that the machine as it is designed in 2019 will be able to match human intelligence is a delusion. An intelligent being is capable of learning (what machines are beginning to know how to do), but also of understanding (what it does not know how to do), inventing (thus adapting), and above all being aware of itself! On these last three points, it is clear that the most evolved of the machines is very far from having the intelligence of the smallest mouse, since it does not understand what it does, it invents only by random tests and not by intuitive construction, and it has strictly no conscience of itself, by the simple fact that it did not pass by the millions of years of evolution that living beings had to undergo.

2 Kurt Gödel, an Austrian mathematician born in 1906, who established that a theory sufficient to demonstrate basic theorems of arithmetic is necessarily incomplete.

Thus, the fears that we have in face of the myth of HAL 9000 in *2001: A Space Odyssey*[3], this computer that takes its autonomy in front of the human being, remain of the order of the fantasy. In fact, this irrational fear in the face of AI is the tree that hides the forest and which prevents us from thinking about the real danger which threatens us, that of the world of the Internet of Things (IoT), that is to say, the world of sensors. I will come back to this in section 5.3.

These fears have infiltrated the doctor-patient relationship, and this has been the case ever since the actual implementation of these fears in France in the 1980s. At that time, Minitel made it possible, for the first time in the world, to connect any telephone subscriber to a server capable of providing information and collecting data about them. In 1987, I started offering medical advice and answers to patients' questions by creating the *3615 Écran santé*[4] with other doctors from SOS Médecins[5]. Even though it was only a summary, this service already had the embryo of an expert system that we were going to perfect later on docteurclic.com that I created in 2001. To this day, the MedVir expert system[6] that we have developed has more than 10 years of experience and has been able to treat millions of patients.

This application and many others, first on Minitel and then on the Internet, in particular Doctissimo[7] in France and Google for the whole world, have been strongly introduced into the doctor-patient relationship. We are at the point where patients, before and after the consultation, go on the Internet where they learn the worst and the best. There is no value judgment here, but the simple observation that the relationship is now triangular thanks to the Internet: the patient, the doctor, and the machine. This World 3.0[8] is now a

3 Film by Stanley Kubrick released in 1968 where the computer HAL 9000 takes control of a spaceship.

4 Minitel service created in 1987 with the support of Gan, which carried out the first teleconsultations in the world and has provided nearly 450,000 in 13 years.

5 SOS Médecins is a group practice created in 1966, which was the first in the world to organize emergency home visits 24 hours a day, 7 days a week.

6 Artificial intelligence system for diagnosis and decision support for patients and healthcare professionals.

7 Website created in 1998 that has set up forums allowing patients to dialog with each other.

8 The concept of World 3.0 is a relational architecture between two individuals or two groups of individuals and the computer. Thus, Medicine 3.0, by connecting the doctor, the patient, and the machine, creates a 3.0 kind of architecture.

reality, and it is clear that apart from a few collateral effects, this access to health information and AI tools has considerably changed the doctor-patient relationship. It is on this very precise stage, which is the very foundation of all medicine, that we can examine the AI issue as well as everything that surrounds it: sensors, advances in the biological and human sciences (especially neurosciences), new materials, and the evolution of expert systems. These four pillars constitute the foundation of this Medicine 3.0 where patients as well as doctors should be able to pursue their relationship in a peaceful and intelligent way. What are the real challenges for the doctor-patient relationship in the coming years? How can we establish elements of an ethical charter governing technological developments? And above all, how can we escape the risks presented by Medicine 4.0[9] if we do not succeed in this mutation?

It is not on theoretical considerations that I will develop my reflection, but on the fruit of my work for 32 years centered on my real job as an emergency doctor and on my virtual job of designing a medical artificial intelligence.

5.2. The doctor-patient relationship

The patient consults the doctor for a complaint that he or she expresses in his or her own words, and with the elements of culture that he or she may have gathered from personal experience or through the Internet. The physician's role will be to listen to this complaint and to give it a status; these are the "symptoms", which the physician must test for validity in order to bring them into a diagnostic process. This presupposes a spirit of analysis that is both objective and subjective as well as a capacity for negotiation, where the doctor's art in Canguilhem's way is revealed. As much as the machine is in the process of being able to analyze the objective nature of the complaint (natural language, creation of clusters, clearing out synonymies, evaluation of meaning, etc.), it is and will be totally powerless as long as it does not require its own experience, which will come from reliable and qualified Big Data, the "Smart Data". These words have a precise meaning. "Big Data" means the mass of data collected by any computer tool, while "Smart Data" means a set of filtered and hierarchical Big Data. "Small Data"

9 In the continuity of 3.0, Medicine 4.0 adds a fourth actor: sensors or other machines. Thus, thanks to interoperability and interpersonal exchange, machines would be able to do without humans and impose their decisions on the doctor-patient couple.

means digital data, generally coming from connected objects, which will be examined in section 5.3. The current quest for Big Data focuses on the mass of data at the expense of its meaning (Smart Data) and its objective digital measurement. At the very primitive stage of the doctor-patient relationship and in this privileged moment when patients entrust their health to their doctor, we can see that all this data is indeed, in relation to patients and their individuality – weak data, so far away from the reality on the ground. In spite of the considerable progress made over the last 20 years and recently with multi-agent systems, the machine is far from having the subjective analysis capabilities that doctors must use in their relationship with patients.

Once the symptom(s) that is/are considered acceptable have been isolated, doctors will include them in the complex process of diagnosis. To do this, they have three tools at their disposal: firstly, the survey, also known as the "anamnesis", which consists of asking patients relevant questions; secondly, the clinical examination, which allows them to examine the patient directly with their five senses and indirectly with objects (stethoscope, blood pressure monitor, temperature, etc.), and thirdly, a clinical examination, which allows them to examine the patient directly with their five senses and indirectly with objects (stethoscope, blood pressure monitor, temperature, etc.). Finally, complementary non-invasive (ultrasound, electrocardiogram, CT scan, MRI[10], etc.) or invasive (blood tests, biopsies, exploratory surgical procedures, etc.) examinations. It is thanks to the synthesis of the information obtained by these three tools that physicians are able to make a "diagnosis", and very often a "non-diagnosis", and to assess the seriousness of the patient's situation. Here again, this stage of the diagnosis requires skills in which physicians' art must operate; they must convince their patient of the need for examinations, therefore negotiate, identify in the answers to their questions what seems true, false, or questionable, and above all guess what patients have not told them. Just as the machine is already adapted to ask pertinent questions (expert systems), to interpret digital examinations (deep learning), and even to perform invasive procedures (surgical robots and interpretation software), it is also difficult, despite multi-agent systems, to understand and imagine what is behind the patient's complaint and what is behind what patients have not said. Another limitation is the data of the clinical examination, because the five senses of physicians are still irreplaceable today. But we can safely think that thanks to intelligent

10 Magnetic resonance imaging: images produced by subjecting the patient to a strong magnetic field. It is now an essential imaging test.

sensors, the clinical examination of doctors will be completely useless within five years, even dangerous because the examinations might be less efficient, especially since the teaching of medicine for 30 years has unfortunately abandoned the clinical examination and semiology in favor of diagnostic protocols and the prescription of examinations. Without a deep reform of medical studies and selection criteria, our future doctors will gradually become deaf, blind, and unfit for clinical examination, while the sensors assisted by AI will gain in reliability. But whatever these performances in this field, the machine will always lack this essential component of the clinical examination, which is the human contact, which deeply ties the relationship and which will always remain irreplaceable.

Once the diagnosis has been established, doctors must convince their patient with objective arguments, and it is clear to what extent the Internet plays a role that can strengthen doctors' opinion or, on the contrary, diminish or even annihilate it. There is here, if not a negotiation, at least a need for conviction and explanations that are essential for the patient to accept the diagnosis. And this point is fundamental, because the treatment, its good compliance, and even its effectiveness (increased by the placebo effect[11], and decreased by the nocebo effect[12]), depend on the success of this step. It is clear that doctors' listening to the complaint, their consideration of a patient's body through the clinical examination and their humanity in announcing the diagnosis are essential to the establishment of trust, which in turn is essential for the next step, which is the path to recovery. Where the machine has an undeniable asset is its infinite memory, particularly in terms of therapeutic databases and protocolization. It is a considerable aid for physicians in the field of medicine as well as in surgery and endoscopy techniques, where augmented reality will play an increasing role. It is undoubtedly in this field that physicians are the readiest to accept the machine, because it does not question their intelligence, it only makes up for their natural physical and memory limits.

Doctors' objective is the cure, or at least the stabilization of the disease, and their nightmare is the error, the *status quo* of the patient's condition, or even conflict, which can sometimes go as far as litigation. This path to

11 Positive therapeutic effect caused on the patient by the confidence he or she feels in his or her doctor and/or in the proposed treatment.

12 Inverse effect of the placebo effect, where distrust diminishes the positive effects or even causes negative therapeutic effects.

recovery is narrow, uncertain, fraught with pitfalls due to complications, side effects of treatments, intercurrent events, nosocomial diseases, in short, a set of factors that are most often barely or not predictable. The very concept of healing is subject to discussion, as patients and doctors do not necessarily have the same satisfaction index, and both have different criteria for estimating it. And here, apart from the factual elements of protocolized monitoring during follow-up, it is only, and truly only, a question of the human relationship between doctors and patients, the machine being simply there as an impartial witness.

Finally, within 10 years, AI and all that constitutes the ecosystem around it will be able to do as well as, if not better than, the doctor in different areas: analysis of patients' complaint, investigation of the history of the disease (anamnesis), clinical examination, interpretation of complementary tests, diagnosis, and therapeutic follow-up. But where the machine will never be able to replace doctors is on what makes all the negotiation aspects of the complaint, the diagnosis, and the cure. For it is no longer just a question of dissecting what our body machine sends us back, but of everything that makes up the specificity of the human species, its spirit, its intelligence, and everything that is beyond us.

At this point in the discourse a question of importance emerges: what will be left to us doctors, once we have been dispossessed of what was our specificity (diagnosis, treatment) and our instrument of power? This is what we will see in section 5.4. Without deflating the subject, the future of the physician is far from being so bleak.

5.3. Digital medicine ecosystem

Currently, Medicine 3.0 (i.e. the doctor-patient relationship in the ecosystem where the machine is ubiquitous) is based on four pillars: expert systems of all kinds, connected sensors under the IoT (Internet of Things), biological sciences, and new materials. This interrelation between these four pillars is the foundation of Medicine 3.0, where the doctor-patient relationship is embedded.

The expert systems, which we call "artificial intelligence" by abuse of language, are either of a connectionist nature (deep learning), being in fact "artificial recognition", as a company like CGTR does for radiology, or of a symbolic nature (inference engines, fuzzy logic[13], etc.), coming under the heading of "artificial reasoning". And then there is what could be called "artificial knowledge", syntactic and semantic search engines like the IBM Watson for cancerology, whose role is to analyze unstructured texts in order to transform them into structured data that can be understood by all machines. For machines to be interoperable, that is, able to exchange data, they must share the same repositories (ontologies). The question of ontologies is absolutely central, and there is still a long way to go to make ontologies as diverse as Loinc, Snomed CT, ICD 11, etc. coincide. All these expert systems produce data that are very heterogeneous (human, environmental, epidemiological, digital, etc.) and in the absence of harmonization, interoperability does not yet seem to be a possibility.

IoT tools, which could be called the "world of connected sensors", are highly specialized objects for collecting specific data. Currently, constants (blood pressure, temperature, blood glucose, etc.) are based on very old measurements that are included in the diagnosis and monitoring of many diseases. However, as we will see in this same chapter about new materials, it is likely that within five years, new constants will appear and shed new light. In the meantime, sensors are increasingly reliable, they see their data via the Internet, they are miniaturizing, can sometimes be installed, use energy recharged in a renewable way, with a very long lifespan, and can deliver their data through very slow networks covering the entire territory (the electrical network for example). These data can be univocally and reliably linked to any individual, in real time, with geolocation, and transferred to computers capable of handling them. We expect a lot from these Big Data, forgetting that taken out of their context, they lose their meaning and, therefore, their value. A young person who has a blood pressure reading of 120/80 and a pulse of 50 beats per minute is *a priori* perfectly in the norm. But an elderly person who has the same numbers and who has a pacemaker should call for medical help immediately, because this means that the pacemaker is probably broken. Therefore, the data only makes sense in relation to a clinical condition, a personal file and a medical history. This shows the close link between expert systems and IoTs. One can think that on the five-year horizon, new sensors will appear: intelligent tissues, objects measuring certain metabolites continuously in tears, sweat, saliva,

13 Symbolic artificial intelligence system making it possible to make diagnoses and decisions in incomplete and uncertain universes (unlike the diagnosis of a car breakdown, where the observed universe is totally known and controlled).

urine, which are very refined fluids, sensors with pressure feedback allowing for palpation, artificial noses able to detect odors in small quantities, accelerometers coupled with muscle activity measurements measuring physical activity, etc. In the same vein, cameras with facial recognition already make it possible to follow any person moving around in places that are equipped with them. There are 170 million facial recognition cameras in China, and eventually there will be one camera for every three Chinese people. There is no need to be a visionary to imagine what all these sensors will be able to provide as cross data and the use that could be made of them. In the field of health, all biological or imaging data or data from physical sensors will be able to provide an AI with a vision of our body and our behaviors in real time and continuously.

The biological sciences are also booming: immunology, neurosciences, genetics, manufacturing of new molecules, etc. Research itself is changing in this field, with silos gradually replacing a transversal and collaborative vision. Not a day goes by without new discoveries being made or new applications appearing in fields as varied as genomics, genetic engineering, the understanding of the intimate mechanisms of the cell, fine intercellular relations, the multiplicity of chemical and hormonal mediators. Thanks to exchanges on the Internet, the phenomena of transversality and inter-professionalization will allow specialties that were previously very distant and disjointed to communicate and exchange on common problems. 4P medicine (predictive, preventive, personalized, and participatory) is on the move, with a strong link between these biological sciences and the fourth pillar of Medicine 3.0, which is the development of new materials.

These new materials are, for example, the result of nanotechnologies that enable the design of tissues, fluids, solids, and even biological structures. Microchips are capable of continuously measuring blood sugar levels in saliva or through patches placed on the skin, which considerably improves the monitoring of type 1 diabetes. Bioprinters will be able to make organs as complex as the pancreas or kidney from any person's stem cells, revolutionizing the possibilities of transplantation. Not to mention considerable progress in the field of robotics and augmented reality. It is impossible to go into details here, or even to list the areas where the technology will intervene. All this fundamental research will interact with the three previous pillars: quantum computers, biological computers, implantable and interlinked sensors, bio-electronic interfaces, etc.

The strong interactions between these four pillars of Medicine 3.0 allow and will continue to allow for the multiplying applications that will gradually transform the human being into a bionic human, which will revolutionize the diagnosis, treatment, monitoring, and prediction of diseases. The transhumanist vision of augmented humans, pushing them even further away from the frontiers of death, raises real questions from which we cannot free ourselves. Ethical reflection is then no longer a simple debate of ideas between philosophers, sociologists, politicians, religious leaders, doctors, etc. but a real imperative as we will see in section 5.5.

5.4. Medicine 4.0

The knowledge that will emerge from all these structured data, obtained through applications, interconnected sensors, and expert systems, will participate in the construction of an intermediate AI between the current weak AI and a strong asymptotic AI. Our world will thus evolve in a very short time from a Medicine 3.0, where the human being still has a free will, to a Medicine 4.0, where data from sensors connected to over-powered central computers will be able to do without the human decision. To give an image, the doctor-patient relationship is likely to evolve in the same way as the client-banker relationship. The human relationship we used to have with our bank advisor has gradually evolved into a client-banker-computer relationship. It is the computer program, according to the rules that have been provided to it, that will, in case of overdraft, refuse your checks, introduce bank charges, or even transmit your file to the banking interdiction service. And when you call your advisor, she takes a contrite look to tell you that she can't do anything about it, because it is the machine that has decided.

Within 10 years, dispossessed of everything that constituted their profession, and somehow their power, doctors will prove powerless in the face of the machine's decisions, because its knowledge and the data it will manipulate in its neural networks, which are currently totally opaque, will be much more powerful than what the doctor will be able to argue. Why is this? Because the doctor-patient relationship is now totally subject to economics. Currently in France, there is no age limit, for example, for hip prostheses, stents, or coronary angiography, because our healthcare system is supportive and benevolent. One may wonder how far this benevolence will go when calculations prove that these examinations or treatments are of no effectiveness beyond a certain age, and especially that they are economically unreasonable. We will then have passed into an Orwellian world[14] where the doctor-patient relationship as well as the insurer-patient relationship and the government-citizen relationship, will be stripped of all free will. That is the risk, and it is not that far from us. Not because of the risk presented by AI itself, but by the use it will make of the data provided in continuous flow by the sensors. Indeed, if we consider that all data is time-stamped, geolocalized, and brought back to a person, and that all these data can be examined by a weak AI devoid of any ethical reflection, the least of our acts will be tracked within the framework of a healthcare pathway that is benevolent today, but which can be less and less benevolent. Currently in China, facial recognition cameras coupled with data collected on smartphones (journeys, purchases, etc.) make it possible to highlight non-citizen-like behavior or behavior deemed deviant, with direct consequences: refusal of housing loans, prohibited or forced travel. The techniques exist; they are operational and are an attack on our freedom that we would consider intolerable in the West. What would it be like if, following the same processes in the health field, we crossed sensor data, analysis results and X-rays, patient file data, and all the digitized elements of our lives? The risk would not be AI per se, but the unethical use that would be made of our data.

5.5. Question of ethics

The question of ethics is central, even crucial, and constitutes the last bulwark of humanity against the power of machines. Ethics is contingent on the morality of society. What was unethical at one time may become ethical at another because society's moral rules have shifted. The levers of morality are not so numerous; they are essentially the technical advances that make possible today what was not possible yesterday as well as the human relationships within society and the economic factors. These three variables weigh heavily on what defines the norms, rights, and duties that the law tries to guarantee and which constitute "deontology". I say "tries" because ethical reflection is generally retrospective (jurisprudence is established once harm has occurred) and not prospective (rules are anticipated to avoid harm). Ethics is defined by four values: beneficence, non-maleficence, justice, and autonomy. These values can be measured by answering questions: is a particular action

14 Reference to George Orwell, the famous writer and author of *1984*, a novel in which after a nuclear war, society is under total police control and whose expression of this totalitarian surveillance is symbolized by the famous Big Brother that has become commonplace.

ethical, and why? Without doubt, this is the first step to be taken for an evaluation of the ethical behavior of machines and information systems.

In the field of e-health, and thus of AI which is part of it, it is rather difficult to propose a simple model of what ethics is. If we compare e-health to a moving car, the wheels would be on one side the patients and on the other the health professionals, with a strong and structured interaction that is the doctor-patient relationship. For this vehicle to move forward, it needs an engine: information systems, algorithms, and practices. The engine cannot function without gasoline, which is health data here. But it needs oxygen, that is to say finances, which are investments and income linked to use. The engine generates energy that drives the car and also produces data (Small, Big, and Smart). The goal is the destination, therefore the objective – diagnosis, decision, treatment, prevention, which are all issues in the doctor-patient relationship. In the end, ethics is the road the car takes to get there.

If we take this modeling, which is admittedly very imperfect, but which allows us to fix ideas, a few salient elements emerge: health data are elements of patients' real life (the history of their disease and symptoms, their "constant", their analysis and imaging results, the treatments they have followed, and the follow-up that has been carried out). All of these health data may be inaccurate, incomplete, or subject to variation. These are real-life data. They are clearly distinguishable from the notion of data. What we call data is real-life data that has been digitized by an information system and put into boxes allowing various machines to exchange information about patients. It is this data that feeds other machines that will classify, prioritize, and structure it. It is this data that allows the car engine to adapt, learn, and better understand the ecosystem. But between the "real data" and the "data stored in the database", there is a process that could be called "computer digestion", which introduces its share of error and oversimplification.

I'll take the following simple example of a patient's complaint: "I have a migraine." Does this mean that the person has been diagnosed as having a migraine and this is a new episode? Or does it mean that the person has a headache right now, and is blaming it on a migraine that has already been diagnosed? Or is it because of what he/she thinks is a migraine? Or simply because migraine is the synonym he/she used to say he/she has a headache? This simple example shows that without a health professional or a strong AI, this data cannot be qualified, and that if the machine transforms by simplification this "input information" into the "database", it will manufacture nonsense. Therefore, Big Data are, from my point of view, a machine to make nonsense. And the question that immediately arises is whether it is ethical. Indeed, in terms of justice and autonomy, we can consider that the machine's approach is ethical, both in terms of goodness (helping the person) and non-maleficence (not to be mistaken about the meaning of the word migraine); this approach is not ethical.

If I limit myself to this single example, which is the daily life of health professionals in their relationship with their patient, it is clear that if the machine does not understand the "meaning of the patient's complaint", its approach is unethical. In order for it to do so, it must understand the patient's vocabulary in all its diversity, and link it to an ontology of symptoms. The question of ontologies is absolutely essential, because if the information conveyed is tainted by errors or approximations, the machine will not have sufficient intelligence to restore the meaning of the data.

Another example: you take a blood test in a laboratory in Montpellier, and the same blood test in Paris one month later. Between these two blood tests, there is a variability that is not only due to variations in your state of health, but to the simple calibration of machines whose standards are quite fluctuating. Therefore, we cannot judge the exact value of a data item if there is no common reference system (collection conditions, calibration of machines, analysis models, etc.). Therefore, variability induces biases and a difficulty in giving the data a certain status. Is it ethical to provide uncalibrated data that cannot be compared from one laboratory to another?

Let's go back to the anamnesis: when the doctor asks a question about a patient's ethnic origins, it is because the answer to this question will direct the doctor towards certain diagnoses rather than others and she will be able to justify the reason for this question perfectly. But if it is a machine that asks this question, it must be able to justify the reason for it in the same way. Machines do not understand what they are doing. Is it, therefore, ethical to put into circulation a machine that has no argumentative or at least explanatory logic?

5.6. What lessons can be learned?

If we summarize the important points, it is first clear that the current AI is far from being a true global and strong AI. Only the addition to symbolic systems of a layer of deep learning and a beginning of explanatory logic can reasonably make weak AI evolve towards an intermediate AI. On the other hand, it is on technological developments, especially in biomaterials and biological sciences, that the most disruptive advances will be made. And it is on the applications of this disruption, especially on biosensors and real-time monitoring systems that we will have to be vigilant, because they will be the bridge between the current Medicine 3.0 and the Medicine 4.0 to come.

Another point that I share with several people, including Jérôme Béranger, is the need to introduce ethical comments in the source code. Any action or procedure included in the source code of an application should include, if not answers, at least questions about the ethical consequences of what this procedure indicates. For example, is it ethical to ask a question about religious or ethnic background to guide or refine a diagnostic hypothesis, and if so, how will it be used?

On the user side, it is urgent to think about what the rights, duties, and protection of the "digital citizen" should be, in other words, the virtual double that the digitization of the human being will entail. Our virtual image is gradually slipping away from us and sinking into an unfathomable black hole whose depth and effects we know nothing about. It is clear that, as Gabriel Ganascia points out, AI is likely to profoundly change our human values, raising fundamental ethical questions about our human condition.

It is also necessary to be able to explain how the algorithm works. For example, in the case of expert systems, just as a doctor can explain why a machine asks such and such a question, so are the machines themselves incapable of doing so. This explanatory capacity is part of an ethical approach, because it allows us to justify our actions and explain their purpose. It will also be the means to provide the machine with the beginnings of a capacity to understand its own actions, an indispensable capacity to evolve towards an intermediate AI. This is what we are doing with the CNRS team[15] in Toulouse to provide MedVir with a beginning of argumentative logic.

The few examples above show that in medicine, the ethical question is central, and that in e-health or e-medicine, our ethical reflection is very late, if only because the medical code of deontology is no longer adapted to the

15 *Centre national de la recherche scientifique.*

world of e-health. I built a mental map of the code of deontology from a simple commercial software (FreeMind). This analysis revealed that nearly two-thirds of the articles of the code of deontology need to be revised to be adapted to the e-health ecosystem. The creation of an e-deontology code, which I have been calling for since 2016, is becoming an absolute necessity.

It is also vital for medicine that medical studies and their teaching be thoroughly reviewed, in particular with a return to semiology (the study of signs), a compulsory learning of the history of medicine, an in-depth training on the doctor-patient relationship, the introduction of notions of health economics, and the sensitization of young doctors to the economic implications of their prescriptions. Perhaps then it will be necessary to consider separating doctors into two categories: on the one hand, the caregivers in charge of the intimate relationship with the patient, and on the other hand, the technicians in charge of dialoguing and accompanying the machines, both of them communicating through a kind of Balint e-groups[16] allowing them to control the evolution of the machine in a World 4.0.

Finally, none of this can work without investment and, therefore, return on investment. Data is an important source of revenue, and the ROI[17] is legitimate for the industrialists and researchers who have contributed to its development and use. But this cannot happen without a true "ethical monetization of knowledge", which raises questions that go far beyond the GDPR[18] and the ownership of health data.

5.7. Real benefits of artificial intelligence

I finally come back to this question that I left unanswered: what will be left to doctors who, because of the performance of the machine and AI, will have lost everything that contributed to their power and therefore part of their legitimacy? And as a corollary, how will patients be able to keep this trust which is theirs? I think that doctors – and this is why the rehumanization of medical studies is vital – will have no choice but to reinvest in the

16 Michael Balint, a British physician, who founded in 1930 a group of physicians' discussion groups to reflect on the presentation of a clinical case in which the caregiver-patient relationship was a problem. The e-groups would be an extension of these groups by electronic means.

17 Return On Investment.

18 General Data Protection Regulations.

relationship with their patients, relieved that they will be contingencies that currently worry them by seeing their knowledge and decision-making power diminish.

Regaining the power of empathy and active listening is the future of medicine. We have five years to make the machine an ally and not a future enemy.

5.8. References

Béranger, J. (2018). *The Algorithmic Code of Ethics: Ethics at the Bedside of the Digital Revolution*. ISTE Ltd, London, and John Wiley & Sons, New York.

Canguilhem, G. (1966). *Le normal et le pathologique*. PUF, Paris.

Chapouthier, G. and Kaplan, F. (2011). *L'Homme, l'animal et la machine*. CNRS Éditions, Paris.

Domingos, P. (2015). *How the Quest for the Ultimate Learning Machine Will Remake Our World*. Basic Books, New York.

Étienne, L. (2020). *Les Sorciers du futur*. Marabout, Paris.

Ganascia, J.G. (2017). *Le Mythe de la singularité*. Le Seuil, Paris.

Lachaux, B. and Lemoine, P. (1998). *Placebo, un médicament qui cherche sa vérité*. Medsi/MacGraw-Hill, New York.

6

Digital and Public Health in West Africa

6.1. Introduction

In Africa and West Africa in particular, the issues of availability and equitable access to quality healthcare and services towards universal health coverage are acute; disparities are noted between countries, between rural and urban areas, or between social strata within the same country and those who are vulnerable pay a heavy price. Digital technology has come to bridge the gap in the challenge of real-time information and communication as well as to lighten unnecessary burdens and optimize choices in the light of exchanges between all stakeholders.

As a result, digital technology, our indispensable daily companion, guarantees access to rights and informed choices. Today, the means exist and are used for this purpose everywhere. Clearly, global and sustainable development by all depends fundamentally on it. Healthcare and related services and data management rely on technologies to prevent, detect, manage, and monitor health events (ACBF 2011).

Thus, the contextualization, appropriation, monitoring, and evaluation of the ethical use of digital technology for global health are essential. Similarly, to develop capacities to promote public health using digital technology with a holistic approach towards the shared vision of universal health coverage in West Africa, the sharing of responsibilities towards innovations is crucial.

Chapter written by Alpha Ahmadou DIALLO.

From the perspective of CSU (*couverture santé universelle*, universal health coverage), digital technology will contribute effectively to reducing the burden of disease: an environment favorable to the integration of prevention, surveillance, and health promotion services with the participation of beneficiaries. It is also the basis for the emergence of good practices for individual and collective health and for the reduction of treatment times. Moreover, it is a precursor to the conduct of future research and opportunities for sustainable change.

It is being used in nutrition programs in Côte d'Ivoire, in the surveillance of maternal deaths and diseases with epidemic potential in Guinea or Liberia, in input supply and immunization, but the challenges are daunting. While digital technology is now an opportunity to prevent disease risks or restore health, it also represents a threat to the right to health: cybercrime, the use of platforms for human trafficking (sale and purchase of domestic servants in some countries), gender-based violence, competition, the issue of equity in access to healthcare, human rights issues related to the confidentiality of personal data and their ethical use, etc.

Technological change provides new tools to make advances that reduce the effects of fragile health systems. It touches on the mass data of innovative learning, satellite imagery, artificial intelligence, and many others. Most importantly, digital change is influencing policies, programs, society, and behaviors. This is worthy of close study, both from a sustainability perspective and from a human development and ethical perspective (Atun 2012). Together with technologies, the requirement lies in the need for a new governance model for health systems in the context of the digital revolution in the face of isolation and mobility (WHO 2016b).

6.2. Context and questions

From 2013 to 2016, West Africa (Guinea, Liberia, and Sierra Leone) faced the first outbreak of Ebola disease. Over the past four decades of Ebola history, the scale of the outbreak has been unprecedented in terms of the areas and social strata affected, the widespread astonishment at the risk of rapid spread in the region and elsewhere, and the consequences. In the three countries most affected by the disease, the number of cases has been estimated at *28,616* with *11,310* deaths and more than *17,000* survivors. In Guinea, 2,544 deaths were recorded out of a total of 3,814 cases, representing a fatality of 67%, and 1,270 survivors (WHO 2016b). Ebola survivors represent a research interest: understanding the nature, timing, and prevalence of post-Ebola sequelae is still a major challenge, as are the consequences and responses to emerging viral infections. The Ebola epidemic illustrates the impact of zoonotic transmission of the virus in the context of the simultaneous presence of other factors facilitating the expansion of the disease (Piot *et al.* 2014). The severe health crisis caused by Ebola has shown the extent to which affected countries are vulnerable to epidemics with pandemic risk.

This sad synoptic picture of the context can be attributed, in part, to the poor performance of the health system, whose fragility has been exposed. This state of affairs has been aggravated above all by the deficit and the way in which communication is ensured in the face of rumors, the lack of knowledge of the disease, and the reluctance to take preventive measures, particularly with regard to funeral rites. The state of severe road degradation does not facilitate access to healthcare for mothers and children, and illiterate and poor households are exposed to other difficulties.

Community-based epidemiological surveillance and prevention through digital health remain essential for early detection, public health action, control of outbreaks with epidemic potential, and management of chronic diseases. They improve relationships between communities and structures and increase the sensitivity of detection of targeted diseases (WHO 2018b). Ebola control and the resilience of the post-Ebola healthcare system have required close collaboration between all actors directly or indirectly involved in the promotion and preservation of human and animal health, biosecurity and biosafety, and environmental protection. With this in mind, Guinea, with the support of its partners, has committed to developing the One Health strategy. This is an integrated approach to developing priority interventions by emphasizing digital health within the framework of pooling resources and multidisciplinary experiences in order to promote, in an inclusive process, the improvement of health and health security. SMS, messaging, and data-sharing platforms have accelerated the process towards an integrated system for data collection, decision-making, and action.

The One Health approach is a multi-stakeholder platform for the effective management of public health events through surveillance, prevention, detection, and rapid response to public health threats. It facilitates the achievement of the objectives of the International Health Regulations

(RSI, 2005), the Veterinary Services Performance (*Performance des services vétérinaires*, PVS) and the Global Health Security Agenda (GHSA) through health monitoring by sharing information and data for better anticipation and responsiveness of the system. In light of this and to apply the IHR, a joint decree referenced No. A/2017/3337/MS/MEPA/MEEF/SGG was issued on the creation, organization, and operation of the One Health national platform was signed by the Ministers of Health, Livestock, and Environment on July 31, 2017, reflecting the political commitment to develop the approach. The platform's mission is to coordinate with a multisectoral and multidisciplinary approach all health and health-related interventions to prevent, detect, and respond to emerging and re-emerging diseases with epidemic and pandemic potential that pose a public health threat, based on digital engagement and sharing.

In a structured system such as the health system, learning, sharing, and cultivating the culture of evidence-based decision making is essential. And for communication to provide the necessary real-time insight, it is imperative that learning materials for concepts and best practices are recognized, shared, and used (Brainard and Hunter 2016). Today, *applications* that offer instantaneous services, like those related to maternal, neonatal, and child health, epidemiological surveillance or field surveys using smartphones and tablets, are fairly widespread in the countries of the Economic Community of West African States (ECOWAS) area, which are low-income countries.

This is a significant step towards the delivery of digital public *health interventions*, meaning that appropriate technological functionality to achieve the objectives of public health policy, programs, or services is a reality. Technologies enable interoperable platforms to facilitate simultaneous exchanges by various stakeholders on data of common interest and increasingly broad impact. As a result, the rapidity of exchanges through a dynamic and sustained process increases trust, performance, and sustainability (WHO 2018c).

In addition, as part of the DHIS2 platform flexible mechanisms are developed for communication via SMS, email, and consultation of the platform itself. This allows information to more quickly reach key decision-makers and actors for action, sometimes even anticipation, as necessary. Already, the input supply system has been significantly improved; the same is true for certain laboratory, imaging, or functional exploration tests. Digital technology offers enormous opportunities both in the search for healthcare and in the areas of prevention, drug supply, programming of advanced vaccination strategies, or synchronization between several sites, some of which are intercountry. Another advantage is that the completeness and quality of the information is increasingly the promptness of monthly health statistics reports are good; even better, the data collected are of good quality through cross-referencing and instant feedback (GSM Association 2019).

The analytical focus between the demand for health services and the capacity of the health system to provide adequate responses in terms of resources, policies, organization, and medical practices raises the imperative need for technological innovation. Thus, it is underpinned by the fact that the review encourages us to transcend barriers in order to translate the commitments expressed by political will into concrete action. This is due to the fact that innovation-related issues are complex and must be supported by public policies, in line with the vision of health system transformation and the constraints inherent in the appropriation of both technological and institutional innovations with strong local leadership as well as also in terms of ethical practices and relationships of trust between all stakeholders.

Thus, in a context marked by high rates of poverty, illiteracy, and serious and recurrent epidemics with a fragile healthcare system, innovation in public health to profoundly transform the healthcare system is among the concerns shared by decision-makers, healthcare providers, beneficiaries, researchers and partners in the field.

The current situation in public health innovation highlights the paradox that resources are scarce; those that are available are distributed inequitably with less monitoring or accountability, and the need for quality and equitably accessible healthcare services is ever increasing. The flawed referral and counter-referral system for emergency obstetric care, inadequate surveillance, and management of chronic and emerging diseases make it imperative to accelerate healthcare innovations. Hence the interest in revisiting the quality of evidence contribution through digital media in medical policy and practice, particularly to encourage and strengthen innovation in the complex field of public health, and to do so in a sustainable manner. Clearly, in healthcare pathways, implementation research is an area where benefits in prevention, health promotion, and healthcare are decisive. However, the current situation reveals organizational dysfunctions, poor performance of human resources, and dissatisfaction with healthcare services, sometimes due to a lack of medication, reagents, pooling of resources and expertise, or exploitation of existing potential (Brainard and Hunter 2016). Concrete examples supporting the choices, actions, and challenges are not lacking. But how can innovation be accelerated?

Undeniably, the benefits of digital health in terms of innovation and facilitation are immense, and the potential is vast. Nevertheless, experiences show that digital healthcare raises issues related to the governance of the system, the availability and quality of healthcare services for human development, such as the digital right versus the right to healthcare and the ethics of healthcare, including health emergencies. The World Economic Forum has described the digital revolution as the fourth industrial revolution, with potentially far-reaching consequences for all aspects of life in society, including health. Digital data and digital health have been identified as one of the seven accelerators of the Global Action Plan for Healthy Living and Well-Being for All, with a view to achieving sustainable development goals.

Appropriately implemented digital health interventions can improve the quality, availability, and equitable access to health services. At the same time, the use of health-related applications and mobile devices is evolving worldwide, beyond high-income areas, and more and more people are seeking some form of online health information (Atun 2012).

Digital healthcare highlights its scope in the areas of frontline health assistance, particularly as a tool for clinical decision support, data collection, and communication. In Guinea, through digital health, significant progress is being made in the field of maternal mortality reduction and the monitoring of health events, especially within the framework of the One Health approach. Health is certainly a fundamental right recognized in national and international laws and guidelines. But between the spirit of the texts and everyday practices, the pitfalls are enormous and in many respects border on the violation of sacred human rights through negligence and other inappropriate behaviors.

The readings, interpretations, and expectations of decision-makers, actors, and service beneficiaries influence the methodological tools promoted in the framework of innovation. The levels of complexity and the implications of innovation for public health on political and normative changes, medical practices, and networking make it necessary to work together to ensure the sustainability of what has been achieved for the health security and well-being of all.

In order to do this, it is essential to ask key questions, three of which stand out as priorities:

– How to improve the involvement of telephone operators and other technologies to guarantee digital health?

– What technical and operational capacities for innovation of digital healthcare are needed, with the potential for impact on the transformation of healthcare systems that facilitate synergies between public healthcare policies, programs, and actors in healthcare development, as well as the beneficiaries of services?

– What prospects and opportunities can be found in the African context for sustainable capacity building in digital healthcare, including harmonization of efforts and integration or pooling of resources in the African space?

6.3. Theoretical framework of analysis and associated concepts

The process of conceptualizing the framework for the development of the study's theoretical model is schematically inspired by the health system transformation of the World Health Organization (WHO). Thus, from the causal analysis of the coherent construction of the health system's building blocks, the emphasis is placed by triangulation on the place of the digital in the performance of the healthcare system in relation to the needs, requirements, and rights of patients and communities. The choice was thus made to organize the study around values, responsiveness, and exclusivity, and is being carried out in three phases. Firstly, the analysis of the situation, especially during and after Ebola, involving academics, administrators, service providers, and civil society organizations and partners, was essential, as it drew on the experiences and testimonies of all those involved. Secondly, the priorities for action were defined. Thirdly, the framework for good collaboration between all stakeholders with clearly described roles and responsibilities, combined where necessary, and a mechanism for monitoring and evaluating progress and needs for capitalization and sustainability was defined.

In this chapter, it was possible to identify the realities of healthcare surveillance and information systems through the literature review and key informant interviews; Health Information System (HIS) implementation staff currently use DHIS2 (District Health Information System 2) to collect and generate indicators. This platform made it possible to present the current configuration of health information systems and the availability of resources, as well as to identify opportunities for using digital technology for innovations. The knowledge generated in this case study can inform choices regarding the role of health data and information systems as facilitators of synergies between public healthcare programs and modes of alerting about failures and deficiencies in the healthcare system that respect standards and human dignity.

The analysis of innovation in public health reveals that thanks to technological and digital advances, the ability to provide local services is increasing. This highlights the importance of digital technology today and also the fact that several factors interact and the actors' spheres of influence vary from one context to another in the process of continuous improvement of public health, especially in low-income countries and in health emergencies. There is a convergence of views to point out that West Africa is a region plagued by recurrent social and political crises with weak healthcare systems and policies as a corollary. Healthcare systems are faced with the double burden of emerging/re-emerging epidemics and deadly endemic diseases such as malaria, tuberculosis, HIV/AIDS, etc., hence the need for a paradigm shift, healthcare system governance, and tools for innovation, anticipation, and better responsiveness.

Public health governance is guided by values, standards, and procedures to produce and maintain evidence-based health outcomes towards universal health coverage. To do this, transformations are needed to address the critical and complex challenges to be met by taking advantage of the inspirations, experiences, and opportunities for innovation adapted to the context and aspirations of users. The scientific literature contributes to the discernment of the link established between the relevance of the nature or urgency of public health action, policy, and digital technology towards reforms and good practices. The fruit of creative genius and combined efforts, digital healthcare is a systemic and innovative process. It is the culmination of a prioritization program with new tools and a coherent methodological approach to induce change in favor of continuity and quality of services, while respecting the right to health and also personal data. This necessarily involves a strategy to promote digital technology in the field of prevention and management of health problems during and outside public health emergencies.

Public health innovation is an iterative process of co-construction (pilot project, modeling, scaling up, and capitalizing on lessons learned for readjustments) desired and supported by policies and partners that respect the principles of the public health system alignment with national strategic directions. This desire is reflected in a clear commitment, itself built and consolidated through documentation, sharing of knowledge, experiences and/or benefits, and advocacy. Consequently, innovation for digital healthcare in Africa is based on the results of the systemic analysis of public health issues: study of needs, context, and opportunities for the development of the integrated approach. Similarly, it underpins the materialization of digital modeling into essential interventions with new methodological tools adapted to the context in order to generate convincing results that induce change. As such, the focus is on prioritization, synergy of action, appropriation/internalization of the theory of change, and the responsible engagement of stakeholders: decision-makers, healthcare providers, researchers, beneficiaries, and communities. This hypothesis highlights both the digital healthcare policy and the sphere of influence of various actors, as well as the human and technical means for innovation and sustainability.

It is naturally accepted that in order to influence policy and practice, multi-stakeholder efforts, evidence, and technology can help achieve universal health coverage (CSU) by 2030. In sum, knowledge, innovations and "working together" with a shared vision and strategies will sustainably boost public health in West Africa, a region marked by poverty, low levels of community education on health and ecosystem imbalances conducive to climate change, and the emergence of dangerous pathogens at the human-animal interface. In such an environment, digital technology is eminently useful. Therefore, digital health policy is a crucial need. Already, the WHO is promoting the report "mHealth, New Horizons for Health through Mobile Technologies" (WHO 2011). Thus, an mHealth policy is essential. "For a project to really take off, it needs to grow and be integrated into the health system," says Jill Fortuin of the University of Cape Town, South Africa.

Indeed, in a spirit of solidarity and a new start based on an inductive, multidisciplinary, and complementary approach towards the ultimate goal of improving the health and well-being of populations, particularly mothers and children, digital technology is essential. It is an organized, focused, and rapid approach to take action to save lives and mitigate the adverse effects of inequity in access to quality healthcare and services. The impact of digital technology highlights the ability to overcome obstacles, to revisit practices, to adapt the standards and mechanisms required in the face of new underlying requirements in relation to the new organizational and managerial scheme in a given context, and also a necessary leadership. Already, it is clear that innovation is influencing medical policy and practice in the face of current challenges. Thus, only multi-stakeholder efforts based on evidence can accelerate the achievement of Sustainable Development Goals (SDGs). This implies that the determinants of success in the innovation process include: monitoring, respect for human rights, equity, gender, responsible participation, and ownership (Piot *et al.* 2014).

The right to health versus the transformation of a healthcare system capable of responding to the needs of care and services requires innovation to improve availability, quality, equity in access, use of services, and citizen participation over the long term. Sustainable human development depends on it. This underscores the ability to harness the potential for healthcare innovation in sustainability by taking into account the context and strategic directions.

As part of the response to epidemics, significant research work has been conducted in Guinea and the sub-region. The use of some of this research work and other more recent research has made it possible to *analyze the theoretical framework* of digital healthcare innovation with theoretical references. The approach used consisted of a combination of literature review, data collection, and analysis and interpretation of results through triangulation and comparison. Concrete examples are given in the dynamics of the integrated fight against recurrent and serious epidemics (including measles, cholera, tuberculosis, HIV, Ebola, Lassa fever, etc.), chronic or frequent diseases such as malaria, family planning, surveillance, and notification of maternal deaths at the community level.

6.4. Practical illustrations

Digital technology is being used to reduce the burden of disease, to build on the failure of the healthcare system, and to drive decision making and action to solve problems and even innovate.

Health information systems are one of the six building blocks of a country's health system and play a critical public health function. They are, therefore, important for the CSU. Electronic health information systems offer many possibilities for the use of data, especially for public health surveillance.

The lessons learned from the health crisis related to the Ebola virus epidemic (2013–2016) have led to a good commitment in Guinea by the State and its development partners to strengthen the resilience of health systems in West Africa. Thus, a new National Health Policy (*Politique Nationale de Santé*, PNS) in 2015 and a Health Development Plan (*Plan de Développement Sanitaire*, PNDS 2015–2024) have been developed. The post-Ebola health policy has the vision of "a Guinea where all populations are healthy, economically and socially productive, benefiting from universal access to quality health services and care with their full participation." This vision has been translated into a 10-year PNDS plan (2015–2024) and reduced into a three-year plan for the recovery and resilience of the health system (PRRSS 2015–2017), developed to address the epidemic of Ebola virus disease and post-epidemic challenges through annual operational action plans by level and entity of management of health services (MS/Gui, PNDS 2015).

The implementation of the strategies defined in the above documents is guided by guiding principles that underpin a coherent and harmonized approach to achieving universal health coverage (CSU) outcomes: (1) program efficiency, effectiveness, and innovation; (2) people-centered care and integrated services; and (3) partnership. Digital technology plays an essential role in this.

A joint review was carried out in 2018 on the main theme "Guinea's Progress Towards Universal Health Coverage", focusing on indicators and targets. It focused (WHO 2018d) on the major concerns to be addressed during the analysis of problems, gaps in progress, and solutions to the problems identified that need to be addressed to improve results through policy dialog for action and digitalization towards health system performance. The review is based on reports from the health districts and regions as well as health programs and studies such as SARA, EDS, MICS, CNS, etc. It reports on the performance of the health system by highlighting the contribution of digital technology on adherence to commitments and efforts in favor of equitable access to services, efficiency, and local partnership for healthcare development (UNICEF 2017).

In most ECOWAS countries, Orange Money is a means of mobilizing funds for healthcare and paying fees. In Cameroon, telemedicine is a reality that improves exchanges between providers in order to qualify the service and relieve patients often received in emergencies and in remote locations. In Togo, a learning platform for secondary schools has enabled a clear innovation towards the excellence of teachers and students. In addition, SMS messages are used to negotiate appointments or share views and information without disrupting a meeting (USAID 2019).

In view of the burden of disease in West Africa, there are emerging systems of health insurance; epidemiological surveillance; and prevention, detection, and health promotion services that are more adapted thanks to digital technology. With the ever-increasing demand for quality health services by a young population, the epidemiological transition, and low incomes, health systems are increasingly torn between *priorities*. Digital healthcare is increasingly contributing to the equitable provision of essential and quality service packages (WHO 2016b).

Countries such as South Africa, Kenya, and Ghana are already developing their technical and institutional capacities for Health Technology Assessment (HTA). Globally, French-speaking African countries, which are marked by communicable and chronic diseases, climate change, and globalization, are still lagging behind with disparities in terms of progress in digital healthcare (WHO 2012).

In Guinea, SMS, messaging, and data-sharing platforms accelerated the process toward an instantaneous and institutionalized mechanism for real-time data collection, processing, and action needed to close the gaps. For example, in Guinea, the interoperability of the SAP database used for epidemiological surveillance (*Agence nationale de sécurité sanitaire*, National Health Security Agency), DHIS2 (SNIS), and Ihris for health human resources management has improved data and responsiveness. Similarly, data on malaria, HIV, immunization, tuberculosis, community-based systems (CBS), and reproductive health (RH) cease to be collected according to donor wishes. The trend is to move towards the integration of data management systems of public healthcare programs and projects using digital technology without overlooking the ethical dimensions (Keusch and MacAdam 2017).

Also, hospital management platforms are used to improve responsiveness in terms of clinical decision-making processes and transparency. Specialized databases are important sources. Social networks are also used to facilitate exchanges on health: stakes, reality, and challenges of dissatisfaction. These spontaneous exchanges are in many cases relayed by the press and individuals. These subjects are even invited in the debates of the deputies of the health commission of the National Assembly. It is now common to organize calls for applications for large-scale collaborative projects, sometimes focused on sensitive health issues, or online teleconferences. This opportunity is exploited for projects or other initiatives to be developed for health innovations. Similarly, the publication of online articles is progressing, especially in English-speaking countries. Digital technology also makes it possible to reduce indirect costs: transport of the patient and accompanying persons, unnecessary travel in search of healthcare, missed work opportunities, etc.

Digital technology promotes equity in access to healthcare, including in remote areas (telemedicine), in a context where the availability of healthcare personnel is often to the detriment of these areas, with a high probability of sustainability of local healthcare structures thanks to digital technology.

Despite the potential of digital healthcare to act as a facilitator for enhancing synergies, the path forward for the digital transformation of global health presents many challenges (Nuffield Council of Bioethics 2016). In the future, important concerns should be recognized and addressed, including the possible exacerbation of inequalities and the need for better and optimal regulation to ensure data privacy and security. Many digital healthcare interventions are marred by siloed implementations, often donor-funded and based on vertical programs, which raise issues of interoperability and data sharing. Resource constraints in many contexts prevent the exploitation of many of the exciting opportunities offered by the digitization of procedures and standards (WHO 2011).

It is obvious that increasingly digital technology for healthcare is part of our daily lives, everywhere. Already, digital technology is contributing to in-depth transformations of health systems. Nowadays, digital technology is at the service of health development through innovation in the collection and sharing of information for action to guarantee equitable access to services and rights for all, and to ensure that all people have access to the same services and rights, and the benefits of the care pathway and the terms and conditions of the provision of services are known. However, it also serves to reveal the dysfunction of healthcare services: availability, organization, quality or satisfaction, constraints/difficulties of professionals, etc. to take ownership of technological innovation in the often-difficult relationships between care providers and patients. Digital technology also makes it possible to transcend the complexity of health policies, programs, and the synergy of actors to transform the healthcare system towards resilience: epidemiological surveillance, management of endemic or chronic diseases, palliative care that is necessary in a context of poverty, lack of community involvement due to weak political dialog, etc.

Digital technology has made it possible to make progress while encouraging social dynamics in the epidemiological surveillance of diseases with epidemic or zoonotic potential, as well as in the management of data on births, maternal, and neonatal mortality at the village level, relying on the services of community health workers (trained, equipped, and supervised to carry out their duties) around the health center. Among the components of the equipment for the community health worker is a telephone. It should be noted that the community health worker works under the supervision of the head of the health center. The health center manager compiles and controls the surveillance and routine data and transmits them via telephone or DHIS2 (Internet).

Since the end of the Ebola epidemic (2016), all health centers and hospitals in the country are equipped with computers with a kit for connectivity to the Internet. With interactive platforms, the dialogue for healthcare between professionals, between them and decision-makers or communities, and the possibilities of improving access to services that meet expectations are multiplying. Increasingly, stakeholders in the health system and associated reforms are integrating the dimensions of public health, health emergencies, good practices, and the need for documentation for decision-making and action. This bodes well for the best prospects for public health programming towards the CSU. Another encouraging aspect is based on the awareness of social responsibilities.

The participation of users, citizens, and other protagonists of health services and policies has become a leitmotiv for the co-construction of post-Ebola health systems. Moreover, the challenges of public health governance underline the major contribution of community participatory digital innovation schemes to the coordination, identification, and resolution of even complex health problems (WHO 2018a). Undoubtedly, the promotion of a co-construction of health policies and services coexists with the strengthening of capacities for health monitoring, framing stakeholder participation and action. It is, therefore, judicious to ask whether digital innovation can flourish, spread, capitalize, and be sustainable in a context marked by the low level of resources allocated to health and the possible sophistication of digital instruments and their ethical framework in the implementation and evaluation of public health action.

In short, it is a question of looking at the paradoxes of digital innovation in the field of health, understood in the broad spectrum of the field including prevention and health promotion, and also medico-social assistance and public-private partnerships. Digital innovation, which is sometimes complex (technologies, organization, interaction, and financing) and where the capacities of the healthcare offer and prevention or promotion programs are weak, is nevertheless a necessity, since it conditions the sustainability of the healthcare system in a context of strong demographic growth, weak economy, high prevalence of chronic and infectious diseases, development of ambulatory healthcare services, and e-health below expectations, as well as weak community commitment to health. At the same time, communities' financial possibilities are reduced, the alignment of partnerships with health development vision and strategies is weak, contractualization is almost non-existent, and public-private partnership is weak, while significant changes are expected both in improving the coverage of essential inventions and in improving the quality of delivery and equity of access for all, especially for those most in need regardless of their social, economic, faith, or disability status.

As a result, digital technology in itself provides enormous benefits in real time but cannot solve all the coordination/piloting problems that are acute today in a system that is required to adapt to transformation in order to meet the health needs of especially vulnerable and disadvantaged populations in an environment characterized by limited resources or poor roads, as is the case in Guinea and many African countries. Most importantly, it is important to critically review the paradox that digital technology offers for health in terms of the benefits and opportunities for healthcare system transformation and the effects likely to emerge in terms of altered relationships between care providers and between providers and patients, or respect for human rights in the management of data (Upshur and Fuller 2016).

A recent report highlights three areas: (1) frontline health assistance through clinical decision support tools; (2) public-private partnership, as the private sector tends to play an important role in the digital health landscape, both in terms of health systems and patient experience (e.g. offering community-based health services and private health insurance online or informing people about types of services and free care can quickly change the understanding and use of health services); (3) community engagement, which can motivate the implementation of a health intervention more easily and in a short time frame.

These few examples of digital health have the potential to redefine the vision, choices, priorities/interests, and purpose of public health in Africa, which is plagued by recurring epidemics, disasters, and conflicts. Moreover, universal health coverage, health promotion, and health security, especially in terms of synergy of action, are closely linked to digital health. They could provide promising avenues for investigation in the near future.

6.5. Challenges and capitalization of experiences and potential for transformation

The analysis raises issues related to interests, agendas, and priorities that are not always shared. Informed public health decision making is critically dependent on the availability of reliable, real-time information. The role of health information and/or epidemiological surveillance systems is to produce, analyze, and disseminate data. In practice, systems do not function properly as the result of coherent action by various stakeholders interacting at different stages of the information production process; they are complex and fragmented and often do not meet the needs of public health programs.

The priorities identified are based on the following actions: strengthening the responsiveness of the HIS to produce current and reliable data; improving the quality and availability of health data and using it as a reference for action and innovation; and producing indicators that make it possible to evaluate the effectiveness and impact of public health policies.

Digital healthcare interventions such as maternal and child health, early detection activation system, notification and communication of cases of disease under surveillance, prevention, promotion, and public health accuracy offer a high transformative impact potential for global health in West Africa.

The challenges posed by digital technology to transform the healthcare system, medical practices, professions, and the care provider-patient relationship are numerous. Moreover, in view of the scope of digital technology and the associated ethical aspects, an in-depth analysis of the benefit-cost ratio and the institutional and legal mechanisms to be put in place is necessary to promote a policy of innovation for health through digital technology in the context of limited resources.

In order to meet the challenges, the combined efforts of each and every one of us are indispensable. According to consistent sources, efforts are being made to address the challenges simultaneously. The principles of donor alignment for digital healthcare were launched in recognition of the need to strengthen country ownership, minimize fragmentation, and promote coordination of global digital healthcare financing.

Many countries have put in place national strategies to harmonize digital health interventions in their healthcare systems and are in the process of implementing some form of data privacy regulation. However, there is no consensus on the best process for equitably developing digital health and harmonizing global health efforts. An inclusive approach is needed in West Africa.

6.6. Conclusion and lessons learned

The assessment of the introduction and quality of public health innovation has been built around the following values and requirements: validity, relevance, effectiveness, efficiency, responsible stakeholder participation and commitment, and sustainability. The following tools are also at the heart of the process: platforms for exchange, networks for sharing, promoting the use of data and knowledge in a continuous way towards problem solving, and ownership and consolidated local partnership.

Results and gaps are analyzed to understand the factors of progress and inhibition as well as the roles and responsibilities of stakeholders, including beneficiaries/communities, in the process of developing interfaces of exchange in mutual trust. The lessons learned include the value of facilitating the innovation advances to closely identify what worked well and what did not work to identify areas for reorientation/adjustments needed and new elements to be integrated to accelerate the momentum towards better results from innovations with positive impacts.

In an environment marked by precarious hygiene measures, an ecosystem conducive to the emergence of serious diseases, food insecurity, degraded roads, a poorly performing health information system, and the trivialization of risk, advances in technology and their ethical use are of crucial interest. In addition, where road and transport conditions are catastrophic, digital technology offers definite advantages.

At the current stage of the development and promotion of digital public health in West Africa, which is often marked by conflicts, epidemics, and disasters, exchanges on and for health are understood, transcended, and managed on a daily basis with degrees of trust, respect for human rights, and public utility: added value of exchanges, profits made, constitution and ethical management of data banks, scaling up of good practices, and sustainability/perpetuation.

6.7. References

ACBF (2011). Rapport sur les indicateurs de capacités en Afrique 2011 – le renforcement des capacités dans les États fragiles. Report, ACBF, Harare.

Atun, R. (2012). Health systems, systems thinking and innovation. *Health Policy and Planning*, 27(4), iv4–iv8.

Brainard, J. and Hunter, P.R. (2015). Do complexity-informed health interventions work? A scoping review. *Implementation Science*, 11, 127.

Diallo, A.A. (2019). Development of epidemiological surveillance in post-Ebola community based in two health districts in Guinea interventions, challenges and prospects, PHPP. *Allied Journals*, 18, 2637.

Doussau, A. and Grady, C. (2016). Deciphering assumptions about stepped wedge designs: The case of Ebola vaccine research. *Med. Ethics*, 42, 797–804.

GSM Association (2019). The mobile economy Sub-Saharan Africa 2018 [Online]. Available at: https://www.gsma.com/mobileeconomy/sub-saharan-africa/.

Keusch, G.T. and MacAdam, K.P.W.J. (2017). Clinical trials during epidemics. *Lancet*, 389, 2455–2457.

Ministère de la Santé de Guinée (2015). Plan national de développement sanitaire (2015–2024). Report, Conakry.

Ministère de la Santé de Guinée and the Coordination nationale de lutte contre Ebola (2016). Stratégie de riposte contre Ebola. Report, Conakry, April.

Nuffield Council of Bioethics (2016). Conducting research and innovation in the context of global health emergencies: What are the ethical challenges? [Online]. Available at: http://nuffieldbioethics.org/wp-content/uploads/Global-health-emergencies-short-note.pdf.

WHO (2011). mHealth: New horizons for health through mobile technologies [Online]. Available at: https://www.who.int/goe/publications/goe_mhealth_web.pdf.

WHO (2012). National eHealth Strategy Toolkit. World Health Organization and International Telecommunications Union [Online]. Available at: https://www.who.int/ehealth/publications/overview.pdf.

WHO (2016a). Guidance for managing ethical issues in infectious disease outbreaks [Online]. Available at: https://www.who.int/ethics/publications/infectious-disease-outbreaks/en.

WHO (2016b). Relèvement des systèmes de santé après Ebola : priorités et approches techniques [Online]. Available at: http://www.who.int/csr/disease/ebola/health-systems-recovery/early-recovery/fr/.

WHO (2018a). The principles of donor alignment for digital health, Digital Investment Principles [Online]. Available at: https://digitalinvestmentprinciples.org/.

WHO (2018b). Global Action Plan for health lives and well-being for all. Accelerator 6. Data and digital health [Online]. Available at: https://www.who.int/sdg/global-action-plan.

WHO (2018c). Classification of digital health interventions [Online]. Available at: https://www.who.int/reproductivehealth/publications/mhealth/classification-digital-health-interventions/en/.

WHO (2018d). Suivi, évaluation et revue des stratégies sanitaires mondiale – plateforme de pays pour l'information et la redevabilité. Report, WHO, Geneva.

Piot, P., Muyembe, J.-J., Edmunds, W.J. (2014). Impact de l'épidémie d'Ebola sur la transmission zoonotique du virus dans le contexte de la présence simultanée d'autres facteurs. *L'Institut de veille sanitaire*.

Unicef (2017). Situation analysis of children and women in Kenya 2017 [Online]. Available at: https://www.unicef.org/kenya/Situation_Analysis_of_Children_and_Women_in_Kenya_2017(1).pdf.

Upshur, R. and Fuller, J. (2016). Randomized controlled trials in the west African Ebola virus outbreak. *Clinical Trials*, 13(1), 10–12.

USAID (2019). Artificial intelligence in global health: Defining a collective path forward [Online]. Available at: https://www.usaid.gov/cii/ai-in-global-health.

PART 3

Supporting Digital Healthcare

Introduction to Part 3

With the advent of ICT focused on Big Data and their algorithmic processing, it appears difficult to find a balance between the availability of medical data, their confidentiality, and their protection. From now on, a "data intelligence" seems to be the strategic answer for the management of data use and data deviance. AI is becoming an essential evolution in the processing of digital information. It holds great promise, but also brings with it great anxieties, hazards, and dangers that need to be corrected or even eliminated in order to guarantee its launch in accordance with the legal framework, moral values, ethical principles, and the common good. The conflicts in question can be very varied. Such a revolution, therefore, entails ethical risks around data with personal characteristics such as integrity, reliability, security, respect for privacy and individual freedoms, reputation, regulation, etc.

Therefore, the whole purpose of this section is to shed light on the nature of the support needed for digital health so that it is both benevolent and effective for the citizen. In this context, it becomes essential to establish an ethical and legal reflection, in particular on the processes of sourcing, control, processing, and supervision of these ICTs in order to maintain a predominant place for confidentiality and trust among digital actors, and thus contribute to a certain control of risks and deviances. Thus, even if today, ethical recommendations have little impact on the functional scope of an AI and introduce an additional level of complexity in the design of self-learning systems, it becomes essential, in the future, to design and integrate ethical criteria around digital healthcare projects related to AI.

Introduction written by Jérôme BÉRANGER

Ethics cannot constitute an absolute answer; it is not an exact science that, through theorems and axioms, would lead to a universal truth. It can only hope to tend towards it in order to establish a relationship of trust between companies using digital data and society. Its aim is to provide orientations that do not seek consensus, but reveal existing antagonisms. Thus, the differences of opinion illustrate the difficulties that digital professionals and society as a whole will have to face. Therefore, it is necessary to bring meaning to data, algorithms, and their uses in order to create real added value to digital medicine. This necessarily involves the elaboration, construction, and development of an algorithmic ethic. Because, in our opinion, writing and thinking about the future of algorithmic ethics is simply making it possible!

Finally, a brief look at the launch of digital technology in Europe immediately leads to the conclusion that the speed of development is not the same as in the Americas. The reason for this is certainly cultural, but it may also be linked to the legal framework that European countries have chosen to adopt. The purpose of this contribution is to provide an explanatory overview of the legal framework for applications in France. It emerges that, in terms of telehealth, the French concept is unique compared to that of our European neighbors, whereas in terms of data processing and use, it is the European states that, together, have opted for a unique framework compared to that implemented in the United States.

7

Designing and Innovating in Digital Healthcare: Co-design for Taking Patients' Needs into Account

7.1. Introduction

Digital healthcare is developing thanks to technological advances in digital technology, artificial intelligence, and Big Data: a small pill dispenser to monitor medication intake and avoid unnecessary handling, a smart glass to anticipate the risk of dehydration in the elderly or infirm, patient-centric information feedback systems to facilitate decision-making by healthcare professionals, surgical robots that facilitate or even replace the specialist's actions, applications to support patients in complying with their treatment, and data-sharing systems to facilitate tele-consultation or the coordination of remote teams around the patient.

There is currently an acceleration of innovative solutions, due to the technological progress driven by rich and dynamic ecosystems of start-ups and research laboratories, and the need to reorganize the healthcare system as well as to deliver interventions in a different way, new services to users, etc.

However, many of the testimonials in the previous chapters, as well as the feedbacks from experience, reveal the extent to which limiting our understanding of digital healthcare to this technological aspect alone does not take into account the challenges as well as the specific conditions that

---

Chapter written by Corinne GRENIER, Rym IBRAHIM and Susana PAIXÃO-BARRADAS.

can transform technological advances into solutions that meet the needs of users and professionals; similarly, many innovative solutions struggle to emerge from a phase of experimentation to be appropriated in broader contexts, just as they struggle to truly transform relationships or the organization of healthcare interventions.

Indeed, we consider digital healthcare not only as a technological breakthrough, but as a paradigmatic shift that transforms the relationships between patients and professionals, as well as professional practices and the organization of structures delivering care and support. Thus, for example, digital healthcare is based on or presupposes a self-quantified[1] empowerment of the patient[2] to take charge of his or her own health; applications that facilitate remote and "off-site" work for organizations like an EHPAD[3], a hospital, or a specialized establishment for the disabled are based on a profound transformation of the representation that one makes of the "expert and legitimate place" where the care is delivered. On the other hand, by taking an interest in the design phase of innovations, an explanation lies, in particular, in the use of classic, so-called closed approaches, which consist of developing a solution without involving the stakeholders who will have to use it as soon as possible, and in particular professionals as well as patients and users.

Moreover, these classic approaches to innovation, often top-down, are imposed on those who are meant to use them, without their involvement, which explains why these innovations do not make sense, or why these actors find it difficult to integrate them into their practices. Finally, designers tend to develop solutions based on typical users who resemble them (Mayère 2018).

Finally, these healthcare technologies are based on new modes of co-determination between actors, which, if they are not properly supported, come up against the siloed work habits that characterize the healthcare field (Bommert 2010). These silos, as well as the new models for thinking about healthcare, make it difficult to cross the boundaries between the different

1 Self-quantified: refers to the production of data (health, life situation) that patients "produce" themselves and on themselves, through the use of devices such as smartphone, smartwatch, etc.

2 Empowerment: refers to the development of the patient's (or health user's) power to act.

3 Residential facility for dependent elderly people or medicalized retirement home.

segments of the healthcare field and the different categories of actors, and limit the ability to innovate radically or to embrace new issues (Bommert 2010).

This is why many authors call for new approaches to innovation in the public sectors (Nambisan 2008), and in particular for innovation approaches that are open to new actors and are collaborative, which consist of mobilizing the resources, expertise, and knowledge of a variety of actors to discover, develop, and implement new ideas (Castro Gonçalves 2015). The quality of innovation is then potentially enriched (Nambisan 2008) by the participation of this variety of actors (see Example 7.1).

7.1.1. *New approaches to healthcare innovation*

EXAMPLE 7.1 – Innovation at Sainte-Justine Hospital, Montreal, Canada[4].

Montreal is reputed to be a creative city and this dynamic has entered the Sainte-Justine Hospital (mother and child care hospital), eager to reinvent its reception and assistance methods, its care spaces for patients and their families, and the places where professionals practice. The establishment is exploring collaborative projects with the SAT (*Société des arts technologiques*, Society for Technological Arts, a transdisciplinary center for research, creation, and dissemination of digital culture) and many other players. Inspired by Montreal's Hacking Health, the Coopérathon is a marathon of cooperation to stimulate exchanges and the creation of innovative solutions with a social impact in the field of health. In 2018, the theme was "digital intelligence at the service of people and communities", focusing on new technologies such as artificial intelligence, smart devices, and new processes. And to better support the players involved, the hospital has created an innovation platform, to facilitate and accelerate innovative solutions at the heart of healthcare and services, teaching and research, health promotion, and management activities.

EXAMPLE 7.2. – Smart devices for remote home monitoring for the elderly (Picard 2018, p. 134).

The starting point is to provide elderly people living at home with smart devices to monitor their behavior and avoid or prevent incidents such as

4 www.chusj.org/fr/a-propos/L-innovation-au-CHU-Sainte-Justine/Hackathon-Cooperathon.

falls, running away, etc. "The aim of the device is to warn the user about his or her 'bad behavior'. But this kind of experience does not go well. Many people involved in this type of experience have stopped quickly. If a sensor lights up, for example, the person feels as if they are being watched" (Picard 2018, p. 134). A participatory design approach was conducted to overcome these barriers, starting with interviews aimed at understanding the relationships and representations that these people had of devices, and then of their needs. The designers thus uncovered two entry points for designing these smart monitoring devices: what is acceptable/accepted, and the emotions associated with the devices. An initial simple device was prototyped, to encourage early use. In a second step, more complex devices were designed, offering more functionalities; and its acceptability was made possible by working on its image, that is, of a "companion" that takes care.

A large part of the literature focuses on the management of such a collective of actors, from a partnership perspective, to encourage companies to go beyond their competitive situation, in favor of the collective creation of added value for all (Le Roy *et al.* 2013). These actors can be mobilized from the start of the innovation process, or identified and enlisted during it, depending on emerging strategic issues (Maurer and Ebers 2006), or additional knowledge needs.

In this chapter, we focus our attention on the mobilization of patients or users in innovation processes, not only as recipients of certain innovations, but also as co-producers of them. Like other stakeholders, they are considered as "actors" rather than as a "human factor" (Kanstrup *et al.* 2014). And we are particularly interested in the approaches carried by co-design[5], considered as a methodological approach of an experiential nature allowing for co-design in a collaborative way, by embracing the patient experience, and facilitating the appropriation of the devices thus conceived. This methodological approach based on design has recently been developed in the field of healthcare (Ostlund *et al.* 2015), particularly in Living Labs specialized in this field of intervention (see section 7.2.2).

5 Co-design or design thinking is an innovative design management approach, inspired by the practices of designers, developed in the 1980s at Stanford University by Rolf Faste, and popularized by Tim Brown (through the agency IDEO) in the second half of the 2000s.

7.2. Methodological approach of co-design in healthcare

After having presented the co-design, we propose to organize our reading of this approach around a grid that makes it possible for us to present the main concepts used and to provide a framework for the analysis of some cases that we show in section 7.3. The aim is thus to examine the conditions that make it possible to decompartmentalize modes of thought and to break out of the usual professional or institutional logics in the healthcare sector, which make it compartmentalized and difficult to transform (Grenier and Denis 2017).

7.2.1. *Co-design in healthcare*

Steen *et al.* (2013) define co-design as a collective, collaborative, and open innovation process that engages the end-user in the development of innovation. This new form of innovation design promotes the integration of people with divergent points of view and interests, gathered around a common shareable goal. Sanders and Stappers (2008) place at the heart of co-design the creativity of designers and non-designers working together in the design development process. It is considered that it can improve cooperation between people from different disciplines and thus strengthen innovation practices (Steen *et al.* 2013). In recent years, providers of care and medical and social support activities have been adopting collaborative approaches from service design (Pellerin and Coirié 2017; Grosjean *et al.* 2019). For example, the research work conducted by the Care Design Lab of the École de design Nantes Atlantique is part of this ecosystem context by associating health and design practitioners, patients and caregivers, and researchers and design students. The projects carried out between 2014 and 2016 have identified a growing interest among healthcare professionals in design and its positive impact on the evolution of their practices related to the integration of diabetes treatment in the daily life of the patient and the ambulatory pathway of patients in a private healthcare institution (Guilloux and Le Bœuf 2017).

The co-design of services within multidisciplinary collectives of stakeholders is characterized by a human-centered approach and by the use of conceptually designed methods and tools to acquire contextual knowledge, bring actors together, and create and visualize new ideas for solutions (Pirinen 2016). Moreover, co-design is based on a strong hypothesis, derived from design methods to develop innovations: that of the complementarity between convergent and divergent thinking. Divergent thinking is understood as a person's capacity to produce a large number of answers to a given question (fluidity), which are outside the cognitive and normative frameworks usually mobilized by this person. In contrast, convergent thinking is understood as the ability to find the best answer to a given problem.

Service co-design is based on inspiring visual methods and tools, including three frequently used tools: brainstorming (Osborn 1974), a method that encourages the generation of original ideas, practiced in a collective manner, emphasizing the quantity of ideas, and without any criticism or judgment (Mongeau and Morr 1999); the persona, defined as the typical profile of people (Cooper 2003) interested in the uses of innovation (made up of images, photos, or drawings illustrating this profile in terms of age, gender, size, social and professional environment, etc.) and giving a sense of empathy between the designer and the user (Kumar 2012); the storyboard, as a representation technique (illustrated in the form of comic strips, photos, drawings, or video) of the innovative project, allowing the passage from an abstract idea to a concrete device or service (Ball and Christensen 2009) by scripting the actions of the user using the future innovation. These tools facilitate knowledge sharing between participants (including the user), negotiation of differences, generation of new solutions, and rapid experimentation. Participants are appointed "experts in their field" and play an important role in the development of knowledge, the generation of ideas, and the development of concepts. The principle is that everyone is creative.

7.2.2. A grid for analyzing the processes of co-design in healthcare

We propose to present service co-design approaches around three important steps: provoking the entry into a co-design approach (section 7.2.2.1); immersing the actors in a space favorable to imagination and co-design work (section 7.2.2.2); and encouraging design iterations to develop projects (section 7.2.2.3).

7.2.2.1. *First step: provoking a co-creation process through co-design*

Our research is taking place in new approaches to promote spaces that are favorable to innovation, that is, creating complementarities and specific arrangements aimed at creating and then developing new ideas or products (Fabbri and Charue-Duboc 2016).

The purpose of these spaces is to allow actors to break away (more or less strongly) from their usual ways of thinking and behaving (Grenier and Denis 2017), which stem from their entrenchment in institutionalized environments, and then to be able to imagine something new, which we elaborate on in section 7.3.1.

However, entering into an innovation process remains difficult, due to the paradox of entrenchment, which explains the difficulty of changing or adopting new ways of doing things when the prevailing routines give legitimacy to the dominant players (Hargrave and Van de Ven 2006), and makes it difficult to mobilize certain players to participate in innovation processes (Edmondson and Bohmer 2001; Obstfeld 2011). Some studies focus on the roles of peripheral actors, or even actors outside the field concerned, in their capacity to bring about change. Some authors question how to encourage entrepreneurs to innovate through collective dynamics, when they are reputed to be locked in the belief in their own capacities alone (Bandura 2007), any external idea being perceived more as a threat than an opportunity (Cooper and Saral 2013). Finally, we are interested in the identification of "jolts" (Munir 2005) that would be at the origin of an entry into a process of transformation. This jolt may be of a political, regulatory, cognitive, or relational nature, for example, a sudden event, such as the urgency to respond to a new business competition, an injunction to transform an organization following an external evaluation highlighting poor performance in a quality of service, or on financial indicators, and regulatory or technological changes. This jolt can also result from an awareness of the need to innovate in a context of slow but inexorable changes in the healthcare landscape.

7.2.2.2. *Second step: immersing oneself in a space that is conducive to innovation*

Fabs Labs, third party venues (Grenier *et al.* 2020), and more generally any space set up to foster creative exchange (see example in section 7.2.2.1), provide an innovative and collaborative environment where new knowledge is exchanged and ideas are developed.

7.2.2.2.1. Service co-design for healthcare innovation: an example of the role of Living Labs

The Living Labs are meeting and design spaces that bring together public and private actors, companies, professionals, financiers, users, or their associations with the aim of designing, experimenting, and collectively evaluating innovative solutions in technology, organization, and services, and offering new answers for structures, individuals, and society. In France, the Living Labs Santé et Autonomie (LLSA)[6] were created by Robert Picard and Antoine Vial. The working mode is based on the principles of co-design and co-construction of these solutions and makes it possible for them to be tested in (almost) real-life situations. Let's take a look at some examples:

– Autonom'Lab[7] (Limousin): Autonom'Lab is an innovation center for uses in "homecare services and autonomy", financed by the Limousin region and Europe since January 1, 2011, and which brings together very different actors such as local authorities (ARS[8], Caisse des dépôts, Limousin expansion), health organizations (CHU[9], Bourganeuf hospital), end users, competitiveness clusters, universities, and companies (Legrand, Sirmad). To certify the respect of the individual in its projects, Autonom'Lab has adopted a deontological and ethical charter signed by all members. Some achievements include adapted housing for elderly people who no longer want to stay at home but do not wish to enter the EHPAD (in partnership with the Mutualité française, one of the main French Mutual Insurance Institution);

– Lusage[10] (Broca Hospital, Paris): this laboratory for the use of technologies for and by the elderly is involved in the field of cognitive disorders, in particular Alzheimer's disease, in order to promote non-medicinal interventions and gerontology. It develops solutions by bringing together engineers specializing in disability technologies, a sociologist and

---

6 www.forumllsa.org.

7 www.autonom-lab.com.

8 ARS: *Agence Régionale de Santé*; i.e. Regional Health Agency.

9 CHU: *Centre Hospitalier Universitaire*; University Hospital, generally the main hospital in its regional territory.

10 www.lusage.org.

doctors specializing in geriatrics, as well as memory care consultants from the Paris region, local information and coordination centers (CLIC), daycare centers, health networks, patient associations, etc.;

– Laboratoire de Recherche en Imagerie et Orthopédie[11] (LIO, Montreal, Canada): this laboratory is associated with the École de Technologie Supérieure and the Research Center of the Hospital of Montreal University. The LIO's mission is to participate in the advancement of knowledge and the development of methods for the biometrology, imaging, modeling, and morphofunctional and physical evaluation of biological systems in humans and animals as well as in the development of medical devices. The participative approach of the LIO Living Lab has made it possible to promote the transfer to an industrial partner of a new technology for the functional evaluation of the knee, KneeKG, which is now being developed worldwide. The challenge of the initial research had been to be able to collect movement data revealing the 3D functioning of the knee during the gait cycle in a precise, repeatable, and sensitive way. This research produced the KneeKG: an anatomical harness that allows motion sensors to be attached almost rigidly to the knee bones, to identify and quantify mechanical biomarkers to aid diagnosis, personalization of the care trajectory, and follow-up for various pathologies (osteoarthritis, patellofemoral pain syndrome, ligament injuries, etc.). The work then continued to help users better interpret the data generated by the technology. Based on the data collected, a "KneeKG Report" is automatically produced, which makes the interpretation of the examination results, which are essential for the use of the product, immediately readable.

These spaces, which generally bring together experts in the fields of innovation, users, companies, or professionals who will use the innovation, as well as institutional players and financiers, promote an immersion as close as possible to the uses to be invented (IDEO 2015), through learning and experiential techniques (Hall *et al.* 2019), which promote innovation through an original combination of knowledge (Kolb 2015).

What makes such a space (that is, the characteristics conducive to innovation) has been studied in different directions. For example, Bucher and Langley (2016) distinguished reflexive spaces, where actors will seize upon new ideas and knowledge to re-evaluate their established routines from

11 www.etsmtl.ca/Unites-de-recherche/lio/accueil and www.forumllsa.org/membre/laboratoire-de-recherche-en-imagerie-et-orthopedie-lio.

experimental spaces where routines (new or re-articulated) are validated and used in projects. Boiteau and Baret (2017) proposed translation spaces in which actors can cross interpretive boundaries and overcome controversies about work situations. Recent work focuses on third places, understood as "a space in which temporary proximities are constructed (Torre 2008) and in which specific relational assets are produced" (Suire and Vicente 2015, p. 17). There is a set of dimensions that enable these spaces to be places conducive to innovation: the variety of actors acting there, the alternative animation and socialization practices, the socio-materiality of this third place, the community life, around a common project, the co-construction of knowledge, and the micro-systems of governance (Grenier *et al.* 2020).

7.2.2.3. *Step three: encouraging design iterations and project development*

The creation of an innovative solution to a complex issue, relating to the health and the well-being of human beings in their social living environment, never emerges suddenly. On the contrary, it is the result of many iterations of ideas, interactions, prototypes, and tests, according to a cycle that repeats itself several times, that ultimately users and professionals find satisfaction in such a solution. The iterative design process is thus at the heart of the service design process. These iterations are based on three criteria that together serve to evaluate what is produced at each stage of the design process: the feasibility of the development and the use of the innovative solution, its desirability by the various users and its economic viability (Brown 2009; Leavy 2012). Therefore, following the example of Hargadon and Douglas (2001), "whether it is ultimately institutional or social, a 'good' innovation starts with 'good design'" (Ibrahim 2018, p. 183). For other authors, co-design makes it possible to increase the affordability of an innovation device, that is the capacity of an object to suggest its own use, as long as, during its design, stakeholders have integrated into it the way future users want to use it, the representations they make of its use (see example in section 7.2.2.3.1).

7.2.2.3.1. Example: smart pill dispenser

The smart pill dispenser is a medical device, according to French regulations. Being connected gives it a new use/value: to make taking medicine easier and more controlled (through the programming of a schedule, with audible alarm, which can be managed by SMS); to avoid unnecessary handling of medication; to facilitate the renewal of prescriptions. It is presented in the form of a weekly box with four cells/day. Its development was financed by a FUI (*Fonds uniques interministériels*, inter-ministerial one-off fund). It was developed in the LLSA Kyomed[12] (based in Montpellier in southern France). During the design workshops, prototypes were developed for each use of the identified main users (affordance): patients, pharmacists, doctors, nurses, caregivers, other healthcare professionals (96 people). Each was mobilized for one to two hours; but to compensate for this short time, a film was used to represent long-term use. Evaluations were carried out iteratively, as the first prototype was enriched: evaluations relating to the product itself (shape, material, functionalities) to identify possible obstacles to its use, as well as the use of the platform for relaying information to monitor drug compliance; evaluations of medical and economic benefits (Picard 2018, p. 121).

An important dimension of these iterative processes relates to the diversity of the actors who are involved in the co-design and innovation processes. This diversity brings together professionals (and users) from various organizations and fields of activity (e.g. health, the digital sphere). It is recognized that the diversity of these points of view and knowledge is a source of innovation (Levitt and March 1988), particularly by making innovation possible at the frontiers of different worlds.

Conflicts or divergences are also considered as resources in the design process. However, it is still necessary to know how to manage them, because diversity can be just as much a source of disturbance, misunderstanding, or even blockage (Porac and Mishina 2002). In particular, attention must be paid to giving a place to patients and users, who constitute one of the interesting facets of these co-design approaches, and more generally of these collaborative design spaces. When we examine a number of healthcare innovation approaches, it is clear that the role of these users has long been marginalized. In fact, these new methodological experiments, which directly involve patients and sometimes their families (Bouchard 2006), are based on the acceptance of these actors as active rather than passive patients, on a new distribution of roles between patients and practitioners, and more broadly on the concepts of empowerment and patient experiences. Yet, it is a strong attention to this principle of inclusion of users in the design process that is constantly called for. Conversely, while one association had mobilized a service design approach to develop a new type of housing (see example in section 7.3.1), the user (future resident) was absent from the design workshops. A major argument of the

12 www.kyomedinnov.com/fr.

promoter was to preserve his word from the symbolic "weight" of the professionals, who were more accustomed to interacting and discussing in these work contexts (Grenier *et al.* 2020) (see section 7.3.1 for alternative solutions developed to give the user back his word).

7.3. Illustrations

We are using our analytical grid to explore two innovative projects in the field of healthcare. Each project allows us to illustrate one or more of the steps we have just proposed.

7.3.1. *Service design workshops to envision collective and smart housing for the elderly*

The "*Habitat collectif et connecté pour les seniors*" (HCC) project, a collective and smart housing project for seniors, was carried out in 2015 by the PSP PACA[13]. The PSP PACA was then tasked by the Regional Council to support home services providers in their HR skills development and in the identification of strategic directions for job growth in the region. At the time of the project, the PSP PACA had nearly 120 members. By joining the cluster, all of them claimed to be committed to the values of ethical care for people and social and environmental responsibility.

Through the HCC project, the main aim of the PSP PACA was to stimulate collective reflection, leading to the specifications of a new form of housing, as a demonstrator of the distinctive skills of the cluster's member service operators, integrating both technological and social innovations. The specifications were then to serve as a basis for a call for tenders submitted by the Region.

In an innovative way with respect to its habits, the PSP has chosen to rely on an innovation approach centered on uses and involving a multiplicity of actors integrated in the territory. The collective and smart housing project presented an ideal opportunity to get off the beaten track and experiment with new methods, while remaining true to its values. The PSP team chose to call upon a service designer specializing in eco-design.

13 PSP PACA: *Pole Service à la Personne de la région PACA* ; i.e. "personal services division", homecare providers of the PACA Region (southern France).

7.3.1.1. *Project structuring*

The collective and smart housing project took place over a year, from the launch of the first service design workshops to the final drafting of the housing specifications. The project schedule included several specific stages: (1) service design workshops with professional actors (5 months), (2) service design workshops with users (4 months) and, at the same time, (3) consultation of the users on the basis of initial sketches, online and via paper questionnaires (4 months), (4) writing and formalization of the specifications by the PSP team and the designer, and in parallel (5) search for project leaders (2 months).

7.3.1.2. *Selection of participants and house designer*

The participants in the first wave of workshops with professionals were initially selected on a voluntary basis. The PSP then solicited in its network and beyond the actors of the territory, with multiple skills and perspectives, likely to have a relevance on the design of such a housing project: departmental councils (local authorities in charge of social and medico-social action), municipal innovation poles and healthcare Living Labs, local business clusters (sustainable buildings, secure communicating solutions, biomedical), an association of occupational therapists, the Regional Health Agency (a decentralized state administration), and third-sector financiers.

The designer was chosen on the basis of his territorial anchorage and on his portfolio of projects, which are quite oriented towards public innovation and participatory democracy. For the PSP team, it was imperative that it share the values promoted by the cluster and its members.

7.3.1.3. *Conduct of service design workshops*

All members who declared themselves as volunteers were invited to take part in the workshops offered by the cluster. There were five such workshops, held approximately every three weeks, on topics previously defined according to the requirements of the project specifications and schedule: (1) the users and their house, (2) the house and its environment, (3) services and care, (4) zoning and development, and (5) the economic model. In total, about 30 different entities were represented at least one co-design workshop, with an average of 10 participants per workshop.

During the first workshop, which was the longest in terms of duration (a whole day), the co-design cycle was introduced by a reminder of intentions on the part of the director of the PSP, and through a presentation by the designer of the design process. The aim was to begin the acculturation of the participants to co-design and the principles of applied circular economy. The director of the PSP and the project leader reminded the participants of the importance of an "interdisciplinary" approach, guaranteed by the diversity of the participants present (and as many different points of view). The participants were also invited to take advantage of all that could have been produced collectively, to enrich the projects of their own structures.

The workshops were facilitated by the designer (with the support of the PSP team, ensuring group cohesion), according to a process alternating phases of work in small groups and phases of restitution and collective reflection in full groups. To this end, the designer was led to make use of a range of *ad hoc* exercises and tools, aiming to allow participants to share their knowledge, display it through the construction of shared mental maps, project themselves in the users' pathway, and work in a contributory way on physical materializations such as maps and models.

During the workshops, the exchanges were marked by conviviality and were rather uninhibited . The first workshop was particularly marked by the debate and in-depth reflection moment that it generated. Several parts of the workshop led to lively discussions and exchanges between participants, in particular the presentation of the approach (which did not include workshops with the users at the beginning, to the surprise of some participants), or again, the inventory of the dimensions to be taken into account in the design of the house (the different orientations taken in the choice of its dimensions having been strongly commented and discussed).

These debates, initiated by somewhat subversive participants, but mediated by the designer, PSP members, and other more conciliatory participants, and enriched by the expert insights of participants with a more institutional profile, highlighted a number of tensions that arose in the design of the house:

– the place of professionals versus users in design;

– the cursor to be placed between home and establishment;

– the social action logic or the healthcare logic;

– technological surveillance versus preservation of social ties.

While the positioning of housing in relation to the existing offer also gave rise to slightly more technical debates, this on the other hand federated the participants around their expertise in the complexity of the field of care for the elderly, and against a common scarecrow (but not represented among the participants): the model of the EHPAD-type establishment.

Through the different dimensions addressed during the five workshops, the concept of collective and smart housing was gradually shaped and refined. The questions that the designer had deliberately left open during the discussions were practically resolved "on their own" as the participants projected themselves in a very practical way into the life of the house to be designed, and gave the concept a meaning compatible with the values they held.

At the end of these first five workshops, the designer and the PSP team produced an initial synthesis and graphic formalization of the collective and smart housing, which was presented during an intermediate restitution session to all the participants, project funders, and institutional bodies. A consultation of the users, members of the network of the cluster having volunteered, was then launched on a digital medium (supplemented by a paper medium). A new series of workshops, this time with users, was organized. These workshops, co-facilitated by the designer and members of the PSP team, were organized at the level of the five types of territories covered by the PACA region (rural, urban poor and affluent, coastal, mountainous), and very different in terms of their geographical and socio-economic characteristics. These workshops consisted of conceiving with the users the elements that were not dealt with by the professionals, in refining certain aspects of the housing, in validating or invalidating the ideas put forward, and in ranking the identified use values. These workshops enabled the PSP to produce a final version of the specifications, which were distributed when it was released in 2016.

7.3.1.4. *Appropriation of the specifications and artifacts produced during the workshops*

At the end of the project, four project leaders (three of whom had not participated in the workshops) had taken up the specifications formalized by the PSP: a municipality mayor and three departmental federations of rural associations for home help and care. However, among these three federations belonging to the same national network, varying degrees of ownership could be observed:

– the first, which was itself based on a different set of specifications which it had helped to draw up, had adopted the HCC specifications for comparative purposes only, taking up certain elements without modifying the bases of its own project already initiated;

– the second was based on the HCC's specifications as inspiration for some of the dimensions of the housing (particularly the smart dimension) and also to take up the principle of user consultation, whose specifications had demonstrated the diversity of points of view, depending on the specific characteristics of the land;

– the third relied on the entire specifications to carry out its housing construction project.

As for the workshop participants, even if they did not necessarily become project leaders, certain elements of the design process were taken up. For example, the association of occupational therapists (a profession with a philosophy close to that of designers) was inspired by certain tools used by the designer to enrich his own design tools. Similarly, a deputy director of a Department Council particularly appreciated the work on mapping and promised to take it over so that he could co-develop the strategic roadmaps of his Department. Similarly, some elements of speeches constructed in workshops were taken up by various participants, including members of the PSP team. Certain metaphors or sense of humor that emerged in the resolution of tensions (mentioned above) were used in the form of humorous vignettes in the specifications. Generally speaking, like the designer's tools, these discursive elements were considered to be significant by the participants, even though they had not yet read the specifications.

The year 2019 finally saw a happy outcome despite a marked political alternation at the level of the Region (and an uncertainty that lasted nearly 3 years), namely the official publication of a regional call for tenders based on the specifications.

7.3.2. *Designing digital tools to improve the performance of athletes by taking their emotions into account*

A design project was conducted within the Kedge Business School's design school in a postgraduate course, in collaboration with a start-up, Curiosity, created by two psychologists and specializing in the healthcare and well-being of high-level athletes. Curiosity's request was to develop a device that could be used by athletes in therapeutic sessions led by psychologists, through immersion in virtual situations, to learn how to manage emotional blockages, such as fear, anger, stress, etc. which they often feel in competition or training situations. Curiosity's goal is to improve the performance and emotional intelligence of athletes. It wanted to enrich itself with the pedagogy of design and its methodology to transform their idea into practice.

The objective of the course is to immerse students in a professional design context. More specifically, the person in charge of the course (Susana Paixão-Barradas) oriented the students' work towards taking into account emotions in the process of designing an innovative solution. The pedagogical team was composed of a pro-faculty and a design researcher experienced in emotional design, and mobilized an ecosystem of actors and stakeholders that integrates the company: a researcher in computer science from the University of Toulon (southern France), 12 design students, and 14 sports and non-sports citizens.

The project lasted one month (April 2018). It began with a theoretical contribution in emotional design and cognitive psychology. Then, the Curiosity psychologist administered a questionnaire to the students called The Herrmann Brain Dominance Instrument (HBDI[14]) to help them better understand their choices, their way of working, learning, managing a group, and communicating. Based on the results of the questionnaire, the psychologist set up four work teams, each composed of varied and opposing profiles to stimulate dialog and the collective intelligence of the groups.

The project was carried out following a three-step iterative process: immersion, iteration, and prototype creation.

---

14 The Herrmann Brain Dominance Instrument (HBDI), developed by William "Ned" Herrmann, is a system for measuring and describing people's brain preferences. It is a type of cognitive style measure and model, often compared to psychological assessments such as the Myers-Briggs type indicator, the Learning Orientation Questionnaire, or the DISC assessment.

7.3.2.1. *First step: immersion*

Immersion is a step that has two objectives: to acclimatize to the new ecosystem (the start-up, virtual reality, psychology, etc.) and to immerse oneself in unknown fields, such as sports, emotions, and emotional design. It is all the more facilitated when students can develop an empathy with the subject they will be working on. This is why the course leader invited the students to live different experiences, related to sports and non-sports situations, through virtual reality and being "in the field".

For the virtual reality experiments, the students had at their disposal, for one month, a room fully equipped with appropriate devices (headphones, a large screen, speakers, and a computer with several games and virtual reality programs). These devices were tested on the first day with the start-up, arousing the students' interest in experimenting, observing, and analyzing emotions. An atmosphere of collective work and a good team spirit emerged among the students and, even in the absence of classes, they went to the experimentation room to play with and test the equipment.

The field immersion was done in groups, with each group representing an emotion (joy, sadness, anger, and fear), an emotion attributed according to the results of the HBDI brain preference questionnaire. They experienced emotions related to the practice of sports through direct observation (behaviors towards devices, gestures, attitudes, moods) and participant observation; they also conducted non-directive and semi-directive interviews with all the actors and stakeholders (coaches, trainers, families, and sportswomen) concerned by the project area.

Figure 7.1. *Virtual reality immersion and exposure of field data collection results*

The method for analyzing the data collected during the interviews and observation phases was based on the principles of "Grounded Theory" (Glaser and Strauss, 1967). Thanks to this analysis, the students were able to bring out certain design issues from the data, which were then discussed during the design of the solution. At this stage of the process, the students focused their attention on how emotions are felt and how they can be detected during sports practice (swimming, rugby, soccer, or dance).

The analysis of all this empirical material and the design issues that emerged were presented to the various actors and stakeholders of the project (the professor, the designer, the IT, and the start-up) for pooling and discussion. The discussions made it possible to formulate "problems" that the design process had to solve, such as: "If, in a context of competition, fear provokes disgust and anxiety in front of the opponent, how is it possible to represent this emotion and its manifestation in a virtual reality device?"

7.3.2.2. *Second step: iterations*

After this first phase, the students returned to the field to obtain validations from the different athletes and to continue data collection.

They analyzed how to represent these emotions with appropriate shapes, colors, gestures, and movements using different design tools: images, collages, videos, and drawings. This search for representation resulted in the creation of a persona and storyboard (Figure 7.2) that depicts athletes and their emotions (fear, anger, sadness, and joy) in the context of a typical day of swimming competition.

The results obtained during this phase of interaction between the field, the students, the professor, and the start-up were used to create a video device, which will be presented first to the same previous actors, then to the athletes.

7.3.2.3. *Third stage: creation of the device and tests*

The students then returned to the field to resume the evaluation cycle and continue data collection. This new phase allowed the filming of a video, representing the development of the solution.

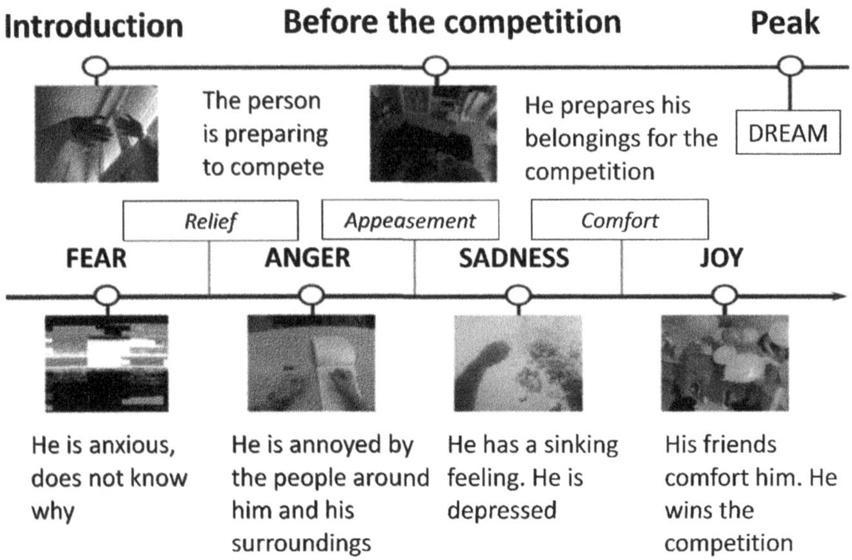

Figure 7.2. *Storyboard presentation of the created persona*

This video represents a typical day of competition for an athlete. It is composed of five different scenes:

– first scene: the day before the competition, we see the athlete being coached before going to bed;

– second scene: during his rest, the athlete has a nightmare (emotion of fear);

– third scene: the next day, on the day of the competition, the athlete is in his usual environment; he feels anger in reaction to different behaviors and attitudes that annoy him;

– fourth scene: the athlete tries to "disconnect" and feels sadness;

– fifth scene: the athlete is now on the starting line, totally focused on his competition, which he wins, feeling joy.

The video was watched with volunteers (14 participants, sports, and non-sports), selected to compose a diverse sample (age, gender, sports practice) in order to refine this first version and validate the prototype.

For this purpose, during the viewing, participants were equipped with electroencephalograms (EEG). The help of a computer researcher, who works with video slides, the creation of virtual environments, and the analysis of emotions, was essential at this stage. He analyzed the emotional impacts captured by the EEG sensors using a camera that recorded participants' facial expressions as they viewed the video (see Figure 7.3). These expressions were related to interest, engagement, stress, relaxation, and excitement. An individual questionnaire was also administered after viewing the video. Subsequently, all of these data were analyzed to verify the impact of this device on the emotional state of the participants.

Analysis of data from the encephalogram sensors revealed that all participants reacted with body reactions (movements, grimaces, etc.) to the five scenes in the video. This result validated the ability to provoke reactions to first-level emotions, that is, at the visceral level, which is an irrational and unconscious reaction to an unknown situation (Norman 2004).

Figure 7.3. *Data collection by EEG sensors, video, and a form*

The individual questionnaire makes it possible for us to understand the emotions felt by the participants at other levels: the behavioral level, related to memory and the conditions of experimentation with the video (for example, sensory immersion, especially through sound), and the reflexive level, corresponding to the image that each person has of themselves and their own experiences and references.

Finally, this video was used as a prototype for the development of a device in 360° format that will be used in a context of virtual reality immersion by the company Curiosity.

7.4. Conclusion

In this chapter, we have explored the link between co-design strategies and the appropriation of elements by participants in innovation workshops, focusing in particular on the contribution of service design. This approach is gaining in "popularity" in the healthcare field, and seems powerful enough to extract those who use it from daily routines, which enshrine some characteristics that are not conducive to innovation: institutional and professional compartmentalization, weak recognition of patients' so-called secular knowledge, difficulties in extracting themselves from cognitive and regulatory frameworks to embrace new issues. It is only by deploying collective, collaborative, and open approaches that innovation can be both social and technological and increase its appropriation in daily life (professional or otherwise).

To continue these testimonials, the link between appropriation and the development of entrepreneurial capacities of participants in co-design workshops should be highlighted as well. The elements (concepts, objects, tools, methods) appropriated by the participants of co-design activities are indeed likely to be integrated into their "personal toolbox", their stock of knowledge or resource repertoire, in what can be considered a constructive activity (Rabardel 2005). For the outputs of a co-design activity to be appropriable, it must, therefore, be able to draw heavily on the knowledge, ideas, and know-how held by the participants, and then enrich and recombine them during the creative process (Ibrahim and Desmoulins 2019). Conversely, the arguments mobilized by participants in co-design workshops, in collective discussions (political and technical) aimed at delineating problems and solutions and linking them together (Zittoun 2009, 2014), are also likely to enrich their repertoire of resources. Leaving room for debate, during dedicated time throughout the creative process, can therefore be a source of added value, insofar as, if this process is well facilitated and animated, participants will be able to collectively delimit the problem they wish to solve, the orientation they wish to give to the solution they are building.

Whether on a cognitive or political level, it is indeed by interacting and negotiating on the basis of their interpretation of lived situations that participants will gradually be led to share "mental models" (Weick *et al.* 2005) – that is, a common vision of the world – on the basis of which they can be led to make collective choices and decisions. As such, co-design approaches inspired by design can be particularly relevant in that they alternate phases of divergence and convergence of ideas and are based on shared experiences. The collective enrichment or transformation of mental models and the appropriation of socio-material artifacts (objects, concepts, methods, tools, arguments) thus contribute to providing individuals with new resources relevant to the accomplishment of their "entrepreneurial" projects (Ibrahim 2018), that is, in our understanding they are likely to give rise to concrete innovations.

7.5. References

Ball, L.J. and Christensen, B.T. (2009). Analogical reasoning and mental simulation in design: Two strategies linked to uncertainly resolution. *Design Studies*, 30(2), 169–186.

Bandura, A. (2007). *Self-efficacy: The Exercise of Control*. W.H. Freeman, New York.

Boiteau, K. and Baret, C. (2017). La conduite du changement en hôpital psychiatrique : le rôle des centres de traduction dans la valorisation des innovations lors d'un projet de promotion du bien-être au travail. *Politiques et management public*, 34(3–4), 231–246.

Bommert, B. (2010). Collaborative innovation in the public sector. *International Public Management Review*, 11(1).

Bouchard, M.J. (2006). De l'expérimentation à l'institutionnalisation positive, l'innovation sociale dans le logement communautaire au Québec. *Annales de l'économie publique, sociale et coopérative*, 77(2), 139–165.

Bucher, S. and Langley, A. (2016). The interplay of reflective and experimental spaces in interrupting and reorienting routine dynamics. *Organization Science*, 27(3), 594–613.

Castro Gonçalves, L. (2015). Strategizing across boundaries: Revisiting knowledge brokering activities in French innovation clusters. *Journal of Knowledge Management*, 19(5), 1048–1068.

Cooper, A. (2003). The origin of personas. *Cooper Journal of Design* [Online]. Available at: http://www.cooper.com/insights/journalofdesign/articles/theoriginofpersonas1.html.

Cooper, D.J. and Saral, K.J. (2013). Entrepreneurship and team participation: An experimental study. *European Economic Review*, 59, 126–140.

Edmondson, A.C. and Bohmer, R.M. (2001). Disrupted routines: Team learning and new technology implementation in hospitals. *Administrative Science Quarterly*, 46, 685–716.

Fabbri, J. and Charrue-Duboc, F. (2016). Les espaces de coworking : nouveaux intermédiaires de l'innovation ouverte ? *Revue française de gestion*, 254, 163–180.

Glaser, B.G. and Strauss, A. (1967). *The Discovery of Grounded Theory: Strategies for Qualitative Research*. Aldine, Chicago.

Grenier, C. and Denis, J.L. (2017). S'organiser pour innover : espaces d'innovation et transformation des organisations et du champ de l'intervention publique. *Revue politiques et management public*, 34(3–4), 191–206.

Grenier, C., Ibrahim, R., Duprat, L. (2020). Comment organiser un tiers-lieu éphémère pour favoriser l'émergence d'innovations institutionnelles ? Le cas d'un pôle d'opérateurs de services à domicile. *Innovations*, 66(1), 89–115.

Grosjean, S., Bonneville, L., Marrast, P. (2019). Innovation en santé conduite par les médecins et infirmières : l'approche du design participatif à l'hôpital. *Innovations*, 3(60), 69–92.

Guilloux, G. and Le Bœuf, J. (2017). Design et territoires de pratiques en santé : enjeux pour la recherche et la formation. *Sciences du design*, 7(2), 25–37.

Hall, K.W., Bradley, A.J., Hinrichs, U., Huron, S., Collins, J.W.C., Carpendale, S. (2019). Design by immersion: A transdisciplinary approach to problem-driven visualizations. *IEEE Transactions on Visualization and Computer Graphics*, 26(1), 109–118.

Hargadon, A.B. and Douglas, Y. (2001). When innovations meet institutions: Edison and the design of the electric light. *Administrative Science Quarterly*, 46(3), 476.

Hargrave, T. and Van de Ven, H. (2006). A collective action model of institutional innovation. *Academy of Management Review*, 31(4), 864–888.

Ibrahim, R. (2018). Soutenir l'innovation par l'organisation d'actions collectives... Ou comment nourrir les capacités d'agir entrepreneuriales de dirigeants d'entreprises. Le cas des opérateurs de services à domicile en région PACA. PhD thesis, Aix-Marseille Université, Aix-en-Provence, France.

Ibrahim, R. and Desmoulins, C. (2019). Émergence de compétences collectives et élaboration stratégique lors d'une activité créative. *10ème Journées du GT Innovations AIMS : "De la créativité à l'innovation"*. AIMS, Université Grenoble-Alpes, Grenoble.

IDEO (2015). The fields guide to Human-Centered Design: Design Kit. Document, IDEO.

Kolb, D.A. (2015). *Experiential Learning: Experience as the Source of Learning and Development*, 2nd edition. Pearson Education, London.

Kranstrup, A.M., Bertelsen, P., Nohr, C. (2014). Patient innovation: An analysis of patient designs of digital technology support for everyday living with diabetes. *Health Information Management Journal*, 2–9.

Kumar, V. (2012). *101 Design Methods: A Structured Approach for Driving Innovation in Your Organization*. John Wiley and Sons, Hoboken.

Le Roy, F., Robert, M., Lasch, F. (2013). Coopérer avec ses amis ou avec ses ennemis. *Revue française de gestion*, 39(232), 81–100.

Leavy, B. (2012). Collaborative innovation as the new imperative – Design thinking, value co-creation and the power of "pull". *Strategy & Leadership*, 40(2), 25–34.

Levitt, B. and March, J. (1988). Organizational learning. *Annual Review of Sociology*, 14, 319–334.

Maurer, I. and Ebers, M. (2006). Dynamics of social capital and their performance implications: Lessons from biotechnology start-ups. *Administrative Sciences Quartely*, 51(2), 262–292.

Mayère, A. (2018). Patients projetés et patients en pratique dans un dispositif de suivi à distance. *Réseaux*, 207, 197–225.

Mongeau, P.A. and Morr, M.C. (1999). Reconsidering brainstorming, group facilitation. *A Research & Applications Journal*, 1(1), 14–21.

Munir, K. (2005). The social construction of events: A study of institutional change in the photographic field. *Organization Studies*, 26(1), 93–112.

Nambisan, S. (2008). Transforming Government through Collaborative Innovation. Document, IBM Center for the Business of Government, Washington, D.C.

Norman, D. (2004). *Emotional Design: Why We Love (or Hate) Everyday Things*. Basic Books, New York.

Obstfeld, D. (2011). Creative projects: A less-routine approach towards getting new things done. *Organization Science*, 23(6), 1571–1592.

Osborn, A.F. (1974). *L'imagination constructive : créativité et brainstorming*. Dunod, Paris.

Ostlund, B., Olander, E., Jonsson, O., Frennert, S. (2015). STS-inspired design to meet the challenges of modern aging: Welfare technology as a tool to promote user-driven innovations or another way to keep older users hostage? *Technological Forecasting and Social Change*, 93, 82–90.

Pellerin, D. and Coirié, M. (2017). Design et hospitalité : quand le lieu donne leur valeur aux soins de santé. *Sciences du design*, 2(6), 40–53.

Picard, R. (2018). *Connected Healthcare for the Citizen*, ISTE Ltd, London, and John Wiley & Sons, New York.

Picard, R. (2018). *Connected Healthcare for the Citizen*. ISTE Press, London and Elsevier, Oxford.

Pirinen, A. (2016). The barriers and enablers of co-design for services. *International Journal of Design*, 10(3), 27–42.

Porac, J. and Mishina, Y. (2002). Interorganizational cognition and interpretation. In *The Blackwell Companion to Organization*, Braum, J. (ed.). Blackwell, Oxford.

Rabardel, P. (2005). Instrument, activité et développement du pouvoir d'agir. In *Entre connaissance et organisation : l'activité collective*, Lorino, P., Teulier, R. (eds). La Découverte, Paris.

Sanders, E.B. and Stappers, P.J. (2008). Co-creation and the news landscapes of design. *CoDesign*, 4(1), 5–18.

Steen, M., Arendsen, J., Cremers, A., de Jong, A., de Koning, N. (2013). Using interactive model stimulations in co-design: An experiment in urban design. *CoDesign*, 9(1), 2–16.

Suire, R. and Vicente, J. (2015). Récents enseignements de la théorie des réseaux en faveur de la politique et du management des clusters. *Revue d'économie industrielle*, 152, 91–119.

Weick, K.E., Sutcliffe, K.M., Obstfeld, D. (2005). Organizing and the process of sensemaking. *Organization Science*, 16(4), 409–421.

Zittoun, P. (2009). Policy change as discursive approach. *Journal of Comparative Policy Analysis*, 11(1), 65–82.

Zittoun, P. (2014). *The Political Process of Policymaking: A Pragmatic Approach to Public Policy*. Palgrave MacMillan, London.

8

Ethical Governance and Responsibility in Digital Medicine: The Case of Artificial Intelligence

8.1. Introduction

From autonomous cars to facial or voice recognition, artificial intelligence (AI) has developed and structured itself in a spectacular way over the last five years and is now part of our daily life and close environment. The widespread use of intelligent algorithmic applications feeds our hypnotized imaginations with the promise of a better world, where the computing power of machines could reduce or even eliminate disease, accidents or crime. Parallel to this, a growing doubt about AI is beginning to develop, portraying the technology and its exponential progression as a potential danger to the survival of humanity. We need to keep in mind that the computer without information will not be able to learn or automate human action. AI stores the information that humans choose to give it. As a result, the acquisition, storage, consumption, and management of Big Data (gigantic volumes of data) constitute four decisive demands for any contemporary society, and in particular in the field of medicine where data has a high level of sensitivity because it is associated with the integrity of the person. Contemporary medicine has now become almost inconceivable

---

Chapter written by Jérôme BÉRANGER.

without the use of new technologies associated with digital technology. This emergence of the computerization of medical data today raises both hope and mistrust among health professionals and users.

To what extent can algorithms and those who design them be left in control of medical decisions? How can we guarantee the confidentiality of our private lives from the growing appetite of machines powered by the collection of personal data? How can we prepare for the upheavals and consequences that AI will bring about in the medical sector and in particular in the doctor-patient relationship? Will doctors retain their free will in the face of the autonomous expert system of medical decision support? Does the development of AI in the health field make doctors fear that they will be replaced in the long term? All these questions will be the subject of reflections on the moral stakes and risks of AI in medicine and will lead to the enunciation and implementation of essential ethical principles and recommendations, as well as an algorithmic responsibility for a new digital medicine.

8.2. Artificial intelligence applied to the world of healthcare

The idea of developing autonomous machines probably dates back to Greek antiquity with the automata built by Hephaestus, as recounted in particular in *The Iliad* (Marcinkowski and Wilgaux 2004). These automata were mechanical, such as the Vaucanson duck, designed by Jacques de Vaucanson in 1738, and exhibited at the Palais Royal in 1744, which was undeniably one of the first robots (Colloc 2018). It was in 1956 that John McCarthy, computer scientist and nominal father of AI, first used the term artificial intelligence at a conference at Dartmouth College. For Brian Krzanich, President and CEO of Intel (the world's leading microprocessor manufacturer), AI is not just the next tidal wave in computing, it is the next major shift in human history. AI is not a classic computer program. It is not just about programming; it is also about education. It is part of a very wide and varied field of technologies that rely on autonomous and cognitive functionalities. It must be noted that the case against AI has mixed fantasy, science fiction, and long-term futurology, forgetting even the basic definitions of the latter.

The concept of AI[1] is to develop computer programs capable of performing tasks normally performed by humans that require learning, memory organization, and reasoning. The objective is to provide notions of rationality, reasoning, and perception (e.g. visual) functions to control a robot in an unfamiliar environment. The machine is programmed to "learn how to learn". Using algorithmic feedback loops, the machine can modify its internal parameters and variables used to manage the representation of each stratum from the representation of the previous stratum. These layers of functionality are learned by the machine itself and not by humans.

From this postulate, we can say that the machine becomes autonomous and intelligent, constructing its own structures of "computation" and relying on axiomatic decisions. Just as human functioning analyzes a situation before changing its behavior, AI allows the machine to learn from its own results to modify its programming. This NICT (new information and communication technology) already exists in many applications, like on our smartphones; it likely will soon be extended to all areas of daily life. AI applications are now invading all sectors of activity and professional spheres of society, particularly the healthcare sector. Algorithmic uses are multiplying tirelessly every day a little more. Operational uses are diversifying: predictive or precision medicine, diagnostic or treatment support tools, assisted surgery, epidemic anticipation. In each case, AI can be used to promote human nature and its performance, creating real opportunities that must be seized and properly used, particularly in the context of the doctor-patient relationship (see Box 8.1).

In the health sector, AI can be used for:

– better individual and community/public healthcare: detection and treatment (particularly in medical imaging, internal medicine, dermatology, ophthalmology, and cardiology);

– harmonizing care processes and supporting doctors in their consultations and medical decisions;

– generating alerts and calls to healthcare professionals and/or patients (better fluidity of the patient circuit and primary-secondary healthcare networks);

– optimizing therapy and healthcare management planning;

1 ISO 2382-28:1995 defines artificial intelligence as "The capability of a *functional unit* to perform functions that are generally associated with human intelligence such as *reasoning* and *learning*."

– recognizing medical images and interpreting them (especially in nuclear medicine, radiology, ophthalmology, and dermatology);

– assisting in paramedical care (paramedical humanoid robot);

– establishing an earlier, more precise, and personalized diagnosis;

– assisting in medical decision making and establishing predictive analyses via a diagnostic assistant;

– enabling communication interfaces between patients and healthcare professionals through a chatbot-type conversational agent[2] (e.g. in conversational oncology);

– following patients in real time and make adjustments to their treatment according to their individual situation (personalized and proximity medicine);

– improving access to new scientific and medical knowledge in a timely manner.

Box 8.1. *Cases of AI use in the healthcare sector*

8.3. Problems and ethical risks specific to digital technology

Ever faster, ever lighter, and more varied, information has an exponential growth rate that seems to double every two years. This is why the new information and communication technologies (NICT) are investing in the different fields of society and must allow for both qualitative and economic optimization of all industrial and civil processes while adapting to the regulatory and legislative framework or making it evolve. Calculating statistics from these data has enormous potential value for our society, but these advantages come with significant risks, particularly for the privacy of the "owners" of these data. The creation, maintenance, storage, distribution, and use of Big Data in healthcare are, therefore, becoming a major challenge. Individuals are constantly torn between hoping for a beneficial advance and worrying about a personal nuisance. This feeling of fear and mistrust is amplified as soon as it concerns personal medical data, because its nature is directly associated with the privacy of the individual. The

2 Chatbots are software robots with AI that can communicate with a human being in natural language or written chat. They can play the role of actual stewards. They can be referred to as proactive intellectual assistants. They are systems capable of perceiving, deciding, acting and learning, and endowed with independence. They are found in particular in relationship marketing (helpdesk) because they provide advice and information to customers (e-helpdesk).

algorithm can tend towards discriminations, which can be carried out on the one hand by simple cross-checking of data sets, and on the other hand by the reintroduction of profiling without the obligation of prior identification. For example, it has been shown that in the United States, algorithms that calculate the risk of recidivism of prisoners and that decide on their conditional release or continued imprisonment maintain discrimination. The data used are biased from the outset, reflecting the fact that the machine does not go beyond human subjectivity but industrializes it.

To this, we can add the risk of Internet users being locked away because of using personalized services based on their behaviors, habits, and attitudes. Such a phenomenon goes against the free will and empowerment of the individual, and contributes to a reductive homogenization of information. One of the risks that surrounds the digitization of the public sphere also concerns the fact that people are judged not on their actual act or on a fact, but on their propensity to carry out a behavior that their personal data lends them according to their relationships, desires, needs, and habits. This would be tantamount to reducing human potentiality to statistics and probabilities controlled by algorithms. The misuse of algorithms also contributes to amplifying the risk of overconfidence in the choices advocated by the machine's calculations, based on potentially erroneous or random assumptions, but likely to influence people's choices without them being really aware of it. From a more macroscopic point of view, we are entitled to ask ourselves the question of the "solutionist" risk of a society that systematically turns to an algorithmic approach that partially masks the complexity of the socio-ethical-economic issues that require other types of intervention. Some algorithmic systems have a significant social impact; for example, they can massively influence political behavior through "filtering and enclosing bubbles"[3]. Finally, algorithms can have "black box" effects due to the opacity and lack of transparency of the algorithmic system. Healthcare professionals as well as patients have no information and explanation on how AI works.

In addition, one of the important ethical issues of Big Data technologies is their apparent objectivity in illustrating social reality with scientific authority and technical rigor. However, there is a certain obscurantism (even

3 The algorithms of social networks like Facebook create an informational "bubble" of filtering and confinement, limiting access and exchange with people of different opinions.

a lack of transparency) in the algorithms used. To this, one can associate results that are likely to be distorted by multiple methodological biases. Indeed, the algorithm simply and "stupidly" learns what it is asked to learn, and replicates stereotypes if they are not sorted and classified. For example, the data available and used may be biased through their construction, or the nature or choice of questions to obtain them. Vigilance must, therefore, be exercised with regard to the identification, reporting, and traceability (sourcing) of this digital data. The algorithm itself, through its functioning and purposes, may reflect the biases of its designer, his or her commercial interests, political opinions, or even introduce discriminations or exclusions prohibited by law.

In addition, for several years now, we have been seeing the massive diffusion of fake news via algorithms, particularly from social networks. In 2017, the study report "Fake News Machine" (Gu *et al.* 2017) asserted that today, we can influence or even manipulate an election with 400,000 dollars, by setting up a device for the massive transmission of false information on social networks (Balagué 2018).

At the same time, scientists have to fight against problems of obsolescence of the methodology used to obtain results and may need to start from the data initially collected for reanalysis. It should be noted that storage costs cannot be borne by individual teams and must be taken into account by research structures, which must, therefore, record data over time and make them accessible over a long period of time.

Moreover, some people denounce the negative consequences that can result from this information view – illustrated by Big Data – if it is reserved for a few predominant operators. Others point out the risks of discrimination (in access to employment, insurance, access to services, the pricing of products and services) or censorship that individuals could be the target of because of the algorithmic processing of their digital data, aimed at offering personalized services with dynamic pricing that could deprive them of autonomy and freedom of choice. To this can be added the concerns, even fantasies, about a "dictatorship" of data and predictive algorithms requiring a definition of a "calculated human" that would challenge the principle of self-determination, a principle that is, in our opinion, the very nature of every human being (Zolynski 2015).

The use of an expert decision-support system presents the risk of making the patient's place in the medical decision-making process disappear. Therefore, it seems essential to preserve patient participation by reinforcing the obligation to inform the patients and obtain their consent in the presence of a predictive computer tool (Hervé and Stanton-Jean 2018). The power and relevance of decision-support processes could profoundly distort the decision-making process and call into question the role of the user doctor, who could end up feeling replaced by an intelligent machine that is more efficient than him or her and infallible. As a result, AI could lead to a disengagement of the clinician from the decision-making system. However, as the performance of these intelligent agents can make people forget their limits, it is essential to ensure that healthcare professionals retain a major role in the decision-making process. In spite of this situation of principle, the fact remains that the question of their medical responsibility arises when they refuse to rely on medical decision support software or oppose the result obtained. Moreover, as strangers to the solution provided by the predictive computer system, they may feel liberated from their responsibility in their therapeutic choices. A source of relief, the result generated by the machine could, however, have the consequence of opening the way to a denial of responsibility by clinicians, which is all the more problematic since they could then be convinced that, since the decision is made by the decision-support tool, they would be legally exonerated from it (Hervé and Stanton-Jean 2018).

In addition, AI raises specific ethical issues. Indeed, learning algorithms, which learn from many examples, lack transparency and traceability tools to explain their results. Hence the expression "black box", often used to qualify the opacity of some intelligent systems and agents. Epistemic opacity poses major limits to the ability of a clinician to give patients meaningful explanations about how AIs work and how they reach conclusions about individual patients (Hervé and Stanton-Jean 2018). A question naturally arises: Does this technical barrier compromise the ethical and professional obligations of physicians to provide sufficient levels of information to their patients? Indeed, how will healthcare professionals be able to explain to their patients why they take a medical decision from an expert system, when the designer of this AI no longer knows how the machine conceives this decision?

Finally, there is a risk of reproducing injustices or discrimination in machine learning. This is why supervision of machine learning is particularly important. Some developers set up evaluation processes specifically dedicated to the issue of neutrality in learning, reserving test phases before operational launch.

On the other hand, the same people who are worried also retain an important hope towards the opportunities that these NICTs can bring. In this context, a climate of hot and cold has set in, alternating between infatuation and suspicion towards digital technology. As a result, the relationship of trust between the players in the health sector (Terry 2014) has become more fragile in an increasingly digital ecosystem. Indeed, this issue of trust is becoming crucial for the individual, which is concerned about its fundamental freedoms, as well as for companies, both in terms of brand image and reputation, and in establishing a lasting and healthy relationship with its stakeholders (Nye 2008).

Thus, in a context of disorientation of minds and concern about the digitization of our world, it seems fundamental to us to return to the fundamentals of ethics. What are our human and moral values? How can they be inscribed and applied in this digitalized ecosystem? In any case, a balance must be established between protection and innovation, which requires a framework for the use of AI and the Big Data associated with it. From this observation, we are led to think that one of the ethical challenges of the digital world would be to eliminate the existing gaps between the initial human intention linked to openness, sociability, co-production of values for NICTs, and their possible drifts and reversals of meaning that we observe through the practices that are carried out.

8.4. Ethical and moral questions related to AI

This digital revolution – illustrated in particular by the growing emergence of decisions made by algorithms contained in platforms, machines, or technological objects – raises a whole series of ethical questions centered on the protection of individuals against the disclosure and exploitation of their personal data, and on a possible "over-mathematization" of society. Indeed, consumers often lose all control involving the dissemination of their data. Who uses and exploits digital data? For what purpose? What is the free will of data users? Where is it stored? How can individuals retain control over their personal data? How can we guarantee that the data that we emit or that transit through us and the NICTs cannot allow formal identification or interpretation that escapes us? What is the degree of transparency? Open source code and documentation? Could the system be explainable in clear and popularized language in order to describe the way it produces its results, for example by communicating the nature of the services offered, the tools developed, the performance, and the risks of error?

With respect to digital data, the ethical framework for people and structures can be summarized according to four specific concepts (Davis and Patterson 2012):

– *identity*: what is the link between our offline and online identity?

– *confidentiality*: who should control access to digital data?

– *ownership*: who is the true owner of the data (subjective right, transfer of ownership, etc.), the rights to transfer them, and what are the obligations of the individuals and/or structures that generate and use these data? Does our existence consist of innovative acts on which we have copyright or other design rights?

– *e-reputation*: how can we identify which data is trustworthy and reliable?

The primary challenge is to give back to healthcare users the control of their information. At the heart of this reflection lies the positioning of the cursor around accountability and the ownership of data by stakeholders. Indeed, we are led to wonder about the responsibility of individuals in the case where the anonymization of data leads to a certain invisibility of individuals, who can clear individuals of certain rules of decorum. Finally, the fact that AI has a major impact on medicine is no longer in question. From now on, the debate is more towards the question of how much this impact will be positive or negative, for which person, in which way, in which places, and concerning what. In other words, it is no longer time to ask whether AI will answer is inevitably yes, but rather how, where, and when these positive and negative consequences will be felt (Floridi *et al.* 2018).

Finally, one of the central questions is to know that as healthcare users we will be able to choose which medicine we want to be treated by, and what services emanating from the digital ecosystem we want for the future of our healthcare system. How can we control and regulate algorithms and their uses in the future? Who will be the guarantor of ensuring that the digital rules defined will be respected? Is there a recognized repository of good ethical practices in the area of these processing algorithms? Are we moving towards a profound change in the doctor-patient relationship that would tend towards a tripartite doctor-AI-patient relationship where the machine will be a recognized and responsible medical actor? Will the functions of health professionals be modified as a result? If so, what future university training will be put in place to raise awareness and accompany the future doctors in this digital medicine?

On the other hand, if "the code is ethics" (because the current "weak" AIs only learn to learn thanks to humans), this means that the people who integrate ethics in NICTs are the publishers, designers, developers, or implementers of AI. Therefore, one may wonder whether it is ethically acceptable that only the manufacturer decides the parameters to set up to obtain a given response. Which organization, which roles, which rules, which policies on algorithms? Should this ethical character not be given back to politicians, to independent multidisciplinary committees, or to public or private regulatory bodies in charge of studying the relationships between human rights, technology, markets, and economic models in the 21st century?

Indeed, ensuring socially preferable outcomes from AI depends on resolving the conflict between incorporating the advantages and mitigating the potential disadvantages of AI, in short, simultaneously avoiding the misuse and underuse of these technologies. In this context, the value of an ethical approach to AI and technology more generally is more striking. Compliance with the law is simply necessary (it is the minimum required), but significantly insufficient (not the maximum that can be done). By analogy, it's the difference between playing by the rules and playing well, so you can win the game. Taking an ethical approach to AI gives what we define here as a "double benefit". On the one hand, ethics allow organizations to harness the social value promised by artificial intelligence. This is the advantage of being able to identify and exploit new opportunities that are socially acceptable or preferable. On the other hand, ethics allow organizations to anticipate and avoid or at least minimize costly mistakes. This is the benefit of preventing and mitigating actions that prove to be socially unacceptable and therefore rejected, even when they are legally unchallengeable. It also reduces the opportunity costs of choices not made or options not entered for fear of mistakes.

The double advantage of ethics can only work in an environment of public trust and clearly established responsibilities more broadly. Public acceptance and adoption of AI technologies will only be possible if the benefits are seen as significant and the risks seen as potential but avoidable, minimizable or at least something one can be protected against, through risk management (e.g. insurance) or repair. These attitudes will in turn depend on public participation in the development of AI technologies, transparency in how they work, and regulatory and remedial mechanisms. In this way, an ethical approach to AI can also be seen as an early warning system against risks that can endanger entire organizations. The clear value to any organization of the double advantage of an ethical approach to AI amply justifies the expense of commitment, openness, and contestability that such an approach requires.

The ethical questions relating to AI that most often come up concern autonomy, decision-making capacities, learning, the acceptable level of delegation to AI, the preservation of community interests, emotional and social interactions, imitation of the living, the repair and augmentation of the human, the dilution of responsibilities (who is responsible: the designer, builder, seller, operator, user, or autonomous agent?), the creation of a legal entity for an autonomous digital agent.

Today, society has not really established universal rules or guidelines to help integrate the moral standards or human values that humanity conveys into AI. With the exponential growth of digital technology, it is now urgent to find a consensus around a universal ethical foundation in order to be able to communicate and explain, in a transparent way, the actions of autonomous intelligent systems. The challenge is to acquire an optimal degree of confidence, given the scenarios in which human beings use them. Because of the conceptual complexities related to moral "values" and "principles", it is difficult to envisage and apprehend calculation structures that directly correspond to universal human values. However, if we associate ethical norms and rules with these universal principles, it is easier to envisage explicit ethical standards in such AIs. Indeed, these ethical rules can be identified as pragmatic instructions to act in a defined way in defined contexts.

Such a system of ethical standards is not simple to put in place and raises some mandatory questions (Floridi *et al.* 2018).

8.5. Framework based on general ethical principles associated with AI

The ethical issues discussed in section 8.4 apply to all forms of AI, whether physical robots (such as assistive robots or self-driving cars) or software-based AI (such as expert medical diagnostic support systems, intelligent personal assistants, or algorithmic chat robots such as chatbots). In order to create autonomous machines that improve human well-being and benefit society, it is essential that their design methodology integrates moral values associated with ethical principles. Such a vision of respect for people will inevitably lead to a change in the current approaches to AI development for organizations. Thus, the ethical reflections associated with these socio-technological systems must embody the most important moral ideals of human rights, give priority to the optimal benefit for humanity and the natural environment, and reduce and anticipate the risks and adverse impacts of AI on humanity.

Therefore, faced with this issue that surrounds the care and use of AI, the quality and harmony of the latter depend on the prioritization of purposes. This is why we have to face certain dilemmas like providing a quality of meaning and purpose in the accessibility of medical data while ensuring the protection of personal data. AI does not have to define itself as the source of ethics, because the latter goes beyond it. However, it can tend to it and sanction unethical actions. This questioning refers to the very foundations of ethics. Are there universal values that apply to everyone? Can the singularity of individual consciousness be transposed to a transversal instrument with a collective and multidisciplinary vocation such as an autonomous system? It is from the following questions that our reflection will be based in order to develop an intellectual approach – the questioning oriented towards an ethics of ends and means and the moral foundations of AI.

When we go through articles and works on ethics, we are soon to feel giddy in the face of the abundance of references and underlying social values used by the authors: “well-being”, “quality of life”, “pleasure”, “happiness”, “concern for others”, “compassion”, “empathy”, “care”, “altruism”, “responsibility towards others”, “community solidarity”, “sharing”, “mutuality”, "interdisciplinarity", "precaution", "respect for others", etc. This multiplicity of social values of all kinds has the inconvenience of creating confusion in people's minds. How to sort through all these values of society in order to identify the principles that bring them together and that allow for a clear discussion and analysis on the subject? What are the guiding principles and rules, the adjustment variables whose ethical values would be accepted by the whole community? Finally, "how can a medical imaging company bring added value, efficiency in the management of the patient?" (Bonhomme and Pinaudeau 2007). If we consult the international bioethical literature, we find that four constants come back from country to country. Thus, references to the principles of "autonomy", "beneficence", "non-maleficence" and "justice" appear tirelessly in all the books, whatever their place of origin, their culture, their beliefs, philosophy, or religion.

In the field of healthcare, a medical decision must be rational and must be methodically constructed by a few simple, coherent, clear, and predefined ethical principles. The notion of accompaniment has emerged in humanism. This social dimension of healthcare allows patients to regain some of their autonomy by taking them out of their passivity and mobilizing their resources. We are, therefore, in a relationship where people are at the center, where they are respected, and where socio-educational and socio-curative approaches must be developed in the same way as socio-therapeutic action. It is in this sense that the social environment will restore its hospitalizable value.

As we have just seen above, the term "principle" is intended to give broad guidelines for action and to set attitudes. It designates a fundamental orientation that inspires action. For a very long time, philosophers had the objective of "reducing all moral requirements to a single principle" (Ogien 2007) by taking inspiration from their glorious predecessors, Aristotle[4], Kant[5], Bentham[6] or Mill[7]. Nowadays, our modern society has several major principles that are both stable and few in number. Two books are references on the subject of ethical principles in health: *Public Health Communication Interventions* (Guttman 1996) and *Principles of Biomedical Ethics* (Beauchamp and Childress 2001). The latter book has, moreover, been the

4 The supreme good.

5 Good will.

6 The well-being of all.

7 The principle of non-injury.

first to establish and identify these four main ethical principles. According to Beauchamp and Childress, the locus of ethics is that of conscience, of questioning, of dissent, which must be framed by these four fundamental universal principles. This universality seeks to reveal itself to us through our concrete and practical realizations.

It was during the drafting of the Belmont Report that these four major principles of bio-medical ethics (respect for personal autonomy, beneficence, non-maleficence, justice) were formalized in North America for the first time. However, as soon as they were formalized and even before defining them, the authors of this report emphasize that these principles represent a framework for reflection whose application is not self-evident: "These principles cannot always be applied in an indisputable manner to resolve particular ethical problems. The objective is to provide an analytical framework to guide the resolution of ethical issues arising from research involving human subjects"[8] (Amann and Gaille 2007).

For Lazare Benoroyo, "these ethical principles of bioethics – drawing their sources in part from outside the field of Hippocratic ethics – have tended to devitalize the links that unite ethics and medicine" and to call into question the legality of the cardinal ethical aim that traditionally guided the production of healthcare[9]. According to Beauchamp and Childress (2001), consideration of the particular case makes it possible to give the principle a precise meaning without which it can be difficult to apply it correctly. According to the authors, "specification (by the case) is a way of reducing the over-generality of a norm, of giving it a greater capacity to guide action, while keeping it in line with the moral significance of the original principle."

Thus, whether one is situated in the recent history of North American medical ethics or in the more ancient history of ethical philosophy, the articulation of the case and the principle has always been affirmed as necessary and fruitful for a reflection of an ethical nature. These principles, therefore, impose a moral obligation, but they leave room for the creativity of the actors in the search for and elaboration of solutions without imposing a canonical scale of values. As they are not *a priori* hierarchized among themselves, it is the health professionals who will have to prioritize them in

8 Belmont Report.

9 Interview by Jean-François Mondot in *Les cahiers de Science & Vie; Naissance de la médecine*, 121(February–March 2011), 114.

the search for solutions to conflict situations. In this sense, this approach leaves room for the freedom and creativity of those involved (see Box 8.2).

Principle 1: Beneficence

Vocations: Beneficence contributes to individual and community well-being. It must meet two very specific rules: the action undertaken must be beneficial and useful, that is, have a positive benefit-cost ratio. It preserves human dignity and ensures the preconditions for life on our planet by preserving a good environment for the future of our future generations (see the notion of sustainable humanity). This principle is directly associated with respect for human dignity, which implies that individuals are treated with respect as persons, rather than simply as concerted actors.

Questions: How can we ensure that AI does not violate human rights? Once algorithms start to outperform the human being (especially in medicine, via medical diagnosis in dermatology and/or radiology), is it unethical not to use algorithms? How can it be ensured that AI serves and protects well the physical and moral integrity of humans, as well as our personal and cultural identity?

Principle 2: Autonomy

Vocations: Autonomy refers to the fact that people give themselves their own rule of conduct, since the Greek terms *autos* and *nomos* mean "self" and "law, rule", respectively. This principle aims to involve the patient in the decision-making process in order to make decisions autonomously without external influence (see the notions of *free and informed* consent and human free will). With AI the situation becomes a bit more complex; when we integrate AI in a human practice based on intelligence, we inevitably must promote the autonomy (moral, functional, political) of all human beings and the control of the autonomy of the algorithmic system. In order to guarantee human intervention, mechanisms should be put in place to ensure responsibility and accountability.

Questions: How can we ensure that AIs are accountable and maintain the individual freedom of individuals? How can we ensure that human beings who interact with AI systems can maintain complete and effective self-determination over themselves? Often judged infallible and "neutral", don't AIs pave the way for overconfidence and the temptation for everyone not to fully exercise their responsibilities? How can we deal with the new forms of dilution of responsibility that AI implies? How can we be sure that AI protects against surveillance, coercion, manipulation, or deception, whether direct or indirect?

Principle 3: Non-maleficence

Vocations: The purpose of non-maleficence is to avoid harming the person for whom one is responsible and to spare him/her from harm, suffering, damage, or even physical, psychological, financial, or social consequences that would be meaningless to him/her. AI-specific damage can result from the processing of data about individuals (i.e. how it is collected, stored, used, etc.). Its purpose, therefore, implies that one does good and refrains from doing harm. This principle appears in the Hippocratic maxim *primum non nocere*[10], whose consequence is to do good to patients and keep them away from evil and injustice. Privacy is characterized as being intimately linked to access and control over the use of personal data. Under these conditions, confidentiality, privacy, security, protection, and precaution are notions directly associated with this principle of non-maleficence. Inclusiveness and socio-cultural diversity are key ingredients of harm prevention to ensure the adequacy of these information systems to all genders, cultures, ages, life choices, etc.

Questions: how can we ensure that AI is transparent and explainable? How can we ensure that AI avoids any discrimination, manipulation, or negative profiling? How can we ensure that AI protects society from ideological polarization and algorithmic determinism?

Principle 4: Justice

Vocations: Justice has the vocation to share the available resources among all people[11]. This principle is closely linked to the notions of equality and equity, which intervene directly in the process of a judicial decision. Its mission is to promote prosperity and preserve solidarity. Ideally, all actions should aim at perfect equality, but depending on the circumstances and the nature of individuals, equity is often required in order to establish priorities and a certain hierarchy in the actions to be carried out. This principle has a scope that can be described as "macro-ethics" concerning all patients, whereas the three previous principles have a much more individual and relational dimension considered as "micro-ethics". This principle seeks to eliminate all types of unjust discrimination, to ensure that the use of AI creates contributions, assets, and benefits that are shared (or at least shareable) to avoid the development of further social damage and degradation. Equality also encourages adequate respect for the inclusion of minorities, who are traditionally excluded,

10 "First, do no harm."

11 Resources in time, money, or energy.

including workers and consumers. Finally, this principle of justice also requires those who develop or implement AI to comply with high standards of accountability.

Questions: How can we educate, train, and raise awareness about the benefits, challenges, and risks of AI for society? How can we understand and anticipate new issues around bias, socio-cultural diversity, discrimination, and exclusion? Although segmentation and profiling have certain advantages for the individual, how can AI significantly affect community logics essential to the life of our societies (democratic and cultural pluralism, risk pool)? (See the notion of algorithmic fragmentation: personalization and individualization versus community and societal logics.)

Box 8.2. *Vocations and questions related to ethical principles*

Moreover, according to Pierre Le Coz (2009), these four cardinal principles simply play an identifying role, allowing the discussion to avoid making a mistake. In any case, they are not intended to solve all ethical problems. One principle formalizes a value of an "intuitive, subjective, and imprecise" nature by giving it a verbal outline. The principle will allow the value to give a readable and easily shared meaning in a discussion or analysis. Ethics is not imperialist; it is rather the means to answer the question of how we can together. Establishing principles helps bring order and coherence to social values.

However, it is important to nuance the universal aspect of these four ethical principles in terms of their applicability. Indeed, as Pierre Le Coz (2009) pointed out, "each State is referred to its history, its culture, its morals, and it would be violently unrealistic to try to wrest it away from them in the name of an abstract universal. This is why it does not seem conceivable to impose universal norms by obliging this or that state to respect all demands. [...] States cannot limit themselves to modelling themselves on one another. They are always returned to the solitude of their choice, forced to take decisions of which none, in the end, fully satisfies us, since there is always a value that is subordinated, if not sacrificed to another, as we see with the problem of embryo donation. Each State must be determined according to the values to which it is most attached." It should then be noted that, in particular contexts, tensions, and conflicts may arise between these principles from an individual and societal point of view, and vice versa. There is, therefore, no way to deal with such trade-offs.

8.6. Algorithmic responsibility

According to us, responsibility is the fundamental structure of subjectivity; it is what makes a human a subject. Here too, responsibility is not reciprocal; one is responsible for others, for what is not one's own doing. This notion illustrates the principle that individuals held responsible for a nuisance on the political or legal level have an obligation of justification or compensation in one form or another. However, such individuals can only be held liable if they have some degree of control, in the sense that they have facilitated or caused the harm or are able to prevent or mitigate it (through insurance or otherwise). From a legal point of view, liability is realized on the one hand through the concept of the obligation to provide reparation (for example, through damages), and on the other hand through the ability to assume the consequences of one's actions.

In the digital context, the notion of responsibility becomes undeniably more complicated to identify and position. The most telling example is without question that of the responsibility of AI at the controls of the autonomous cars that are constantly multiplying on our roads. What choice will the machine make when faced with an insoluble traffic dilemma or an accident? Should it prefer to protect its passengers at the expense of pedestrians crossing the street, even if they are particularly vulnerable (elderly, children, or disabled people)? Or is it rather the opposite? Why choose one type of human life over another? Who would then be legally responsible? The owner or driver of the self-driving car? One of the manufacturers of components such as sensors or directional systems? The AI engineer of the vehicle? The brand, equipment manufacturer, or car manufacturer? The designer or developer of AI? We are witnessing a competition between self-driving car manufacturers according to their ethical decision on board. The regulations associated with responsibility vary from one country to another around the world. Some people propose the concept of "distributed responsibility", which would concern more players than conventional non-intelligent vehicles. All of this inevitably leads to complex situations in terms of global AI-related jurisdiction.

Thus, the accountability of responsibility for an algorithmic decision-making device is complicated by the fact that it is often not clear who has a degree of control necessary to be held legally or politically accountable. We can give the case of developers of algorithmic tools who sometimes know nothing about the use and future implementation of their tools. Conversely, the person(s) who integrate algorithmic systems into applications can only partially understand how they work. Should responsibility lie with the people who developed and coded the algorithm? What is certain is that it is increasingly difficult for the programmers themselves to predict or fully understand how the algorithm makes its decisions. So, it seems complicated to put all the blame on AI designers alone. But we consider that people who design and launch AI applications should at least be responsible for the operation of the systems they have developed. At the same time, those responsible should also look for public and private actors who buy the expert systems and/or intelligent machines and use them to offer their services without even understanding how they work. In this case, algorithmic liability must be reinforced by procedural guarantees and the rule of law. Internal checks and audit panels can be evaluation and regulation tools in this direction. Finally, it is also fundamental that anyone whose rights are violated by automated decision-making processes should be able to benefit from effective appeal systems.

8.7. Conclusion

Technological developments have driven many changes in the way we interact, inform ourselves, work, and think about the world. The digital revolution that society is going through, therefore, requires the acquisition of new skills, particularly in the field of medicine. AI-related tools have innumerable advantages and assets for both the patient and the doctor. However, these technical advances and the processing of digital data also represent ethical risks. The growing awareness of the power that automatic medical decision systems can have raises as many hopes as legitimate fears. These intelligent machines tend to change the role of the healthcare professional in the medical decision-making process, or even make it disappear. Some of the difficulties are also the consequence of the "black box" phenomenon, which AI professionals are now obliged to open in order to make the results obtained explainable. The ethical questions that these tools generate are at the center not only of trust in these artificial devices, but also of stakes in economic terms. AI represents a new reality for healthcare users, and the lack of transparency in this sector could undermine the fiduciary relationship between patients and healthcare providers. One of the challenges of improving an AI algorithm is based on machine learning technologies that allow it to learn from its errors. It is essential that algorithm designers be aware of the value judgments that impact their development. The way the algorithm is built is supported by values and imagined by people. For this, it is essential to have an approach based on the ethics of AI according to its purpose in order to better understand it, challenge it, and adjust it to improve it. Indeed, some AI may accentuate discriminations, biases, categorizations, risks of re-identification (hence loss of confidentiality and privacy) and individualization of society. Digital data will increasingly become associated with us, like a second skin, in order to better classify and discriminate us with the drifts associated with it. This is why we should not underestimate the risk of a "digital divide" illustrated by several dividing lines (social, industrial, economic, even spatial-temporal), and covering multiple realities.

We are convinced that medicine will always integrate an essential part of human relations and will never be able to rely totally on "decisions" made by algorithms, even highly efficient and reliable ones, but devoid of nuance, empathy, and compassion (Hervé and Stanton-Jean 2018). In this light, it is necessary to rethink our approach to digital life, the use of AI and its impacts in the healthcare sector. Protecting privacy requires that users of the tools of this digital revolution become more accountable for their actions. Individuals must be able to understand their digital environment in order to become masters of their applications. If a detailed ethical framework is not put in place, then the ethical glass ceiling will have exploded and we will not be able to change anything.

Between technophile unconsciousness and technophobic negation, only a thoughtful and restrained government-sponsored reflection with common sense and restraint will allow humanity to fully benefit from these technological advances. Under these conditions, it is necessary to provide an ethical framework and support that articulates the human and technical processes related to AI. Our digital ethics based on the four universal ethical principles thus constitutes an adequate mode of regulation of doctor-patient-AI behaviors based on the respect of moral values that are considered indispensable. Algorithms must be ethical and moral from their elaboration to their use, since the responsibility belongs to the designers as well as to the owners. Intelligent artificial agents must become partners, as a decisive contribution to decision support and therapeutic strategy. Thus, it is essential to give a legal entity to these AIs through an algorithmic ethical conscience. In our opinion, this notion of responsibility corresponds to the cornerstone of the hardening around algorithmic systems. It is the "ethics by design", that is, integrating ethical recommendations from the design stage and within the code lines of an AI. Consequently, we cannot rely exclusively on the responsibility of the proponents of these changes, nor on the dynamics of AI research, to avoid slippages, drifts, or even the trivialization of abusive uses of these techniques. It is at the level where the majority of digital choices in current life are generated, at the level of the individual, that the ethics of the digital world is inscribed. This is why education about this new digital responsibility is essential. To do this, we need to impose the requirement of responsibility on citizens socially by adopting an approach that is too normative for a more ethical approach. As a result, awareness and education campaigns will have to evolve in order to ensure that new generations are informed and trained to understand these technological innovations and the issues involved in the types of decisions associated with them, but also in the use and security of their personal data. In order to understand, prepare, and accompany it in the best possible way, our society will have to equip itself with an adapted moral and human framework by creating a new way of thinking, reflection, responsabilization and a new way of conceiving value and work.

8.8. References

Amann, J.P. and Gaille, M. (2007). Approche par les principes, approche par les cas : les limites philosophiques d'une opposition. *Éthique et santé*, 4, 195–199.

Balagué, C. (2018). De l'éthique des algorithmes et de l'intelligence artificielle. Livre blanc vade-mecum sur la gouvernance des traitements de données numériques, ADEL, 87.

Beauchamp, T.L. and Childress, J. (2001). *Principles of Biomedical Ethics*, 5th edition. Oxford University Press, New York and Oxford.

Bonhomme, D. and Pinaudeau, D. (2008). Imagerie médicale : des innovations au service de l'optimisation et de l'efficience. *IRBM News*, 29(2), 20–25.

Colloc, J. (2018). De l'intelligence artificielle mimétique aux systèmes autonomes : quels objectifs ? Quels enjeux éthiques ? Livre blanc vade-mecum sur la gouvernance des traitements de données numériques, ADEL, 62.

Davis, K. and Patterson, D. (2012). *Ethics of Big Data: Balancing Risk and Innovation*. O'Reilly, Sebastopol.

Floridi, L., Cowls, J., Beltrametti, M., Chatila, R., Chazerand, P., Dignum, V., Luetge, C., Madelin, R., Pagallo, U., Rossi, F., Schafer, B., Valcke, P., Vayena, E. (2018). AI4People – An ethical framework for a good AI society: Opportunities, risks, principles, and recommendations. *Minds and Machines*, 28, 689–707.

Gu, L., Kropotov, V., Yarochkin, F. (2017). The fake news machine: How propagandists abuse the Internet and manipulate the public. Research document, TrendLabs.

Guttman, N. (1996). *Public Health Communication Interventions: Values and Ethical Dilemmas*. Sage Publications, Thousand Oaks.

Hervé, C. and Stanton-Jean, M. (2018). *Innovations en santé publique, des données personnelles aux données massives (Big data) : aspects cliniques, juridiques et éthiques*. Dalloz, Paris.

Le Coz, P. (2009). Place de la réflexion philosophique dans la décision médicale. *Bulletin de l'Académie nationale de médecine*, 193(2), 499–510.

Marcinkowski, A. and Wilgaux, J. (2004). Automates et créatures artificielles d'Héphaïstos : entre science et fiction. *Techniques & Culture*, 43–44.

Nye, D.E. (2008). *Technologie & civilisation : 10 questions fondamentales liées aux technologies*. FYP Éditions, Limoges.

Ogien, R. (2007). *L'éthique aujourd'hui : maximalistes et minimalistes*. Gallimard, Paris.

Terry, N. (2014). Health privacy is difficult but not impossible in a post-HIPAA data-driven world. *Chest*, 146(3), 835–840.

Zolynski, C. (2015). Big Data : pour une éthique des données. *I2D – Information, données & documents*, 2, 25–26.

9

Legal Focus on the Notions of Telemedicine and E-Health

9.1. Introduction

No one will deny today that new information and communication technologies have been widely introduced in our hospitals, clinics, and doctors' offices. Doctors who are now connected are vigorously accompanied on a daily basis by their patients, who sometimes require 24-hour medical surveillance.

However, this digitization of the singular colloquium has developed differently and with varying frequency depending on the country. The leadership belongs to the anglophone countries, particularly the United States, which is now in the running for a healthcare Big Data treatment, while in Europe, and particularly in France, questions are being asked about the consequences of a possible implementation of a highly regulated Open Data healthcare system.

The approaches are undeniably different. This difference is not well understood by doctors, who would like to develop scientific research projects like their anglophone colleagues, but who feel constrained by an opaque standard, patients – who are adept at quantified self[1] and remote medical coaching – or even industrialists or start-ups, who are forced to

Chapter written by Lina WILLIATTE.

1 System allowing the patient to self-measure.

consider where to develop their project according to the degree of normative constraint imposed by countries.

The actors are legitimate in denouncing fundamentally different norms, in that they confer, according to their libertarian nature or not, competitive advantages that cannot be made up for. Nevertheless, the jurist is able to explain these diverse normative conceptions according to the legislative traditions of the countries and their policies for the protection of fundamental rights. Fundamentally divergent traditions, therefore, explain the normative framework applicable, on the one hand, to the development of medical practices and services via new technologies (section 9.2) and, on the other hand, to the processing and use of the resulting data (section 9.3).

9.2. Telehealth: a different adoption depending on the country

An in-depth analysis of current uses and practices in the sector of healthcare reveals that, depending on the country, the meaning given to the word used to qualify the act is different. Thus, while the qualification is identical, the action carried out by its author may, depending on the country, fall into another category of act and therefore into another category of norms. This divergence of terminology also gives rise to diverse normative conceptions. The example of telemedicine and e-health demonstrates this.

9.2.1. *A word with different meanings in different countries*

Today, it cannot be disputed that terms, expressions, words are used indifferently and without distinction of meaning to qualify acts, tendencies, and practices that are globally relevant to telehealth. A recent study (Gallois and Rauly 2015) shows that the terms telemedicine, telehealth, and e-health are used as synonyms (Crigger 2006), whereas in some cases they refer to a remote medical practice and define the act of care (Chandra *et al.* 2013) and in others, they designate the tool and therefore the intermediation for the production of the service (Kerleau and Pelletier-Fleury 2002) or health-related online commerce (Kirsch 2002). Different meanings are given to the words, which are not without impact on the applicable legal framework and on the legislator's perception of the said act. To illustrate this, let us take the typical case of telemedicine.

9.2.1.1. *Telemedicine: the French particularity*

Two conceptions of telemedicine are classically opposed: thus, in developed countries, telemedicine is essentially clinical, whereas in developing countries telemedicine is more informative (Simon 2013). Clinical telemedicine is understood as "a professional activity that puts in is the use of digital telecommunications to enable doctors and other medical professionals to perform medical procedures for patients at a distance" (Croels 2006). While informative telemedicine is defined as "an interactive audiovisual communication service that organizes the dissemination of medical knowledge and protocols for patient care and treatment with the aim of supporting and improving medical activity" (Simon 2013).

France is one of the first countries to have established a legal basis for the practice of telemedicine through Law No. 2009-879 of July 21, 2009, known as the HPST[2] Law and its decree of October 19, 2010[3], updated in 2018[4]. These two fundamental texts enshrine a clinical approach to telemedicine, defining it as a medical act performed by health professionals via information and communication technologies. In other words, telemedicine in France is a medial act performed by a healthcare professional whose effectiveness is recognized and which guarantees the best health safety in terms of proven medical knowledge. This definition draws a clear boundary with the conception of telemedicine in other countries, which understand it as any "healthcare service" provided via new technologies. The difference in terminology, although minimal, is fundamental in that one refers to a medical act and the other to a medical service. From this difference in terminology stems a specific applicable regulatory framework. However, in France, telemedicine is governed by legislation specific to it, whereas at the European level, telemedicine falls under the more general category of "e-health medical services"[5].

The French conception of telemedicine makes it a medical act performed by health professionals via information and communication technologies. This principle is confirmed by article R.6316-1 of the French Public Health Code of France, according to which telemedicine includes "medical acts

2 *Hôpital, patient, santé, territoires* (Hospital, patient, health, territories).

3 No. 2010-1229 *JORF* No. 0245 of October 21, 2010.

4 Decree of September 13, 2018, No. 2018-788 relating to the modalities of implementation of telemedicine acts.

5 This is the case, for example, in Germany: http://www.science-allemagne.fr.

performed remotely by means of a device using information and communication technologies".

The decree of 2010 gives a list of acts relating to telemedicine:

– teleconsultation, which allows the medical professional to give a remote consultation to a patient;

– tele-expertise, which allows the medical professional to seek the opinion of one or more medical professionals remotely on the basis of medical information related to the management of a patient;

– remote medical monitoring, which allows the medical professional to remotely interpret the data necessary for the medical follow-up of a patient and, if necessary, to make decisions regarding the management of this patient;

– medical tele-assistance, which allows the medical professional to assist another healthcare professional during a procedure;

– medical regulation, which is the doctor's response provided within the framework of medical regulation (SAMU[6]).

Moreover, to be acceptable, the telemedicine project must take into account the deficiencies in the provision of care due to the insularity and geographical isolation of the territory (Art. L6316-1 of the French Public Health Code[7]).

Thus, in France, telemedicine has been conceived by legislators as a "tool" that must meet the objectives of organization, continuity, permanence, and safety of care, and also fundamentally as a medical act; in this respect, the conditions for practicing medicine must be provided for and respected.

As such, the 2010 decree requires project leaders to respect the fundamental rights of the patient and the obligation of healthcare professionals to meet the legal requirements for the practice of medicine as set out in the public healthcare code and the code of medical deontology. All of this is assessed and verified by the authorities, which may result in responsibilities[8].

---

6 *Service d'aide médicale d'urgence*, Emergency Medical Assistance Service.

7 *Code de la santé publique*, French Public Health Code.

8 Primarily: civil liability to compensate a patient for harm suffered as a result of the failure to comply with the standard or ordinal liability for the offending healthcare professional.

Until 2018, telemedicine procedures were not covered by health insurance, which has had a major impact on the launch of telemedicine in France. Since the decrees of 2018, only two acts are covered. The conditions for reimbursement by the health insurance, however, are in addition to those provided by the 2010 decree. These conditions mark even more the difference between the practice of telemedicine and e-health practices. To be convinced of this, we should take the example of medical teleconsultation.

9.2.1.2. *Example of teleconsultation covered by the health insurance system*

Nearly 10 years after the coming into force of the first law in France that provided the first legal basis for the practice of telemedicine[9], certain acts provided for in the decree implementing said law dated October 19, 2010[10], are now part of ordinary social security law. However, among the five acts provided for by the text, only two of them are concerned: teleconsultation and tele-expertise[11]. Remote monitoring, still in experimentation, will certainly be the next act covered by the Social Security Code after the results of the ETAPES expeditions are analyzed. Tele-assistance, on the other hand, is not yet on the agenda of the social security financing laws.

Nevertheless, while teleconsultation is now part of the acts reimbursed by the social security, this coverage is subject to conditions defined by the decrees of August 1 and 16, 2018[12].

Special attention will be paid to the fact that the conditions set out below are necessary for the health insurance to cover the teleconsultation procedure; however, the fact that they are not met does not make the teleconsultation procedure an illegal act, provided however that said act complies with the conditions prescribed by the decree of October 19, 2010, updated by the decree of the September 13, 2018.

9.2.1.2.1. Conditions to be met for teleconsultation that complies with legal requirements

Article L6316-1 of the French Public Health Code defines telemedicine as a form of remote medical practice using information and communication

9 Law of July 29, 2009-879 known as the HPST law.

10 Decree No. 2010-1229.

11 Only teleconsultation will be dealt with in this chapter.

12 Order of August 1, 2018 NOR:SSAS1821639A and August 16, NOR:SSAS1822647A.

technologies. Telemedicine links one or more healthcare professionals to each other or to a patient, which necessarily includes a medical professional and, where appropriate, other professionals providing care to the patient. Therefore, telemedicine necessarily implies the presence of a medical professional, such as a doctor, a dental surgeon, or a midwife. In this respect, telemedicine differs from the telecare provided for in Article 13 of the *Ma Santé 2022* bill. The ambition of telecare is to create, on the territory, a true collective care that associates healthcare professionals from all healthcare professions and not only medical professionals. More specifically, telecare allows remote patient care by pharmacists and paramedics. This practice does not apply to exchanges between remote medical assistants and/or pharmacists via ICTs[13], without contact with the patient.

Telemedicine acts must be performed with the free and informed consent of the patient. This consent requires prior information on the implications of telemedicine treatment for the patient compared to conventional treatment. In this respect, the patient must be informed about the telemedicine process in place (organization of medical care), the identity and quality of the professionals involved in the patient's care, the necessary confidentiality of the exchanges generated by the practice of telemedicine and the means implemented to guarantee this right, the security of the exchanges and circulation of the data that will be generated by the practice of the procedure, the process put in place for the respect of the rights that derive from data protection (in accordance with applicable laws in France[14]), the identity of the technological third party (supplier of the medical device used to perform the telemedicine procedure), and the operator or even the host of health data.

Moreover, articles R6316-3 and R6316-4 of the French Public Health Code require that the act of telemedicine be carried out under conditions that guarantee the authentication of the professionals involved in the act, who must have been trained beforehand not only in the use of ICTs required for the act of telemedicine, but also in the actual practice of telemedicine[15]. The process must also guarantee the identification of patients and, if necessary, their preparation, and even their training for the act.

13 Information and Communication Technology.

14 Law no. 78-17 of January 6, 1978 amended in 2004; Law for a Digital Republic 2016; GDPR 2016 enforceable in 2018; Law of June 20, 2018; Decree of August 1, 2018, and rewriting order no. 2018-1125 of December 12, 2018; Decree no. 2019-536 of May 29, 2019.

15 Article R6316-9 of the French Public Health Code.

Once the telemedicine procedure is completed, a report must be recorded in the patient's medical record[16].

Finally, Article R6316-10 of the French Public Health Code reminds organizers and healthcare professionals who use ICTs that to practice telemedicine they must guarantee to the patient that the use of ICTs complies with interoperability and security standards[17].

It should also be noted that since the decree of September 13, 2018[18] came into force, the establishment of a telemedicine activity is no longer subject to a contract with the Regional Health Agency (*Agence régionale de santé*, ARS). Indeed, the 2010 decree had made this contract a means for the ARS to verify that the regulatory conditions were met for the launch of the telemedicine activity and above all that it met a healthcare need of the territory. As this requirement has been removed, it does not, however, mean that any telemedicine project must identify and justify the healthcare need it intends to meet.

9.2.1.2.2. Conditions of coverage by health insurance for medical teleconsultation

If we had to summarize these conditions in a few words, we could then indicate that in order to be reimbursed by the health insurance, the act must be proposed in compliance with the coordinated healthcare path. This condition is explained by the fact that telemedicine is not intended to "replace" the traditional doctor, or to "offer" only dematerialized medical care. Telemedicine has been designed to compensate for medical deserts and help healthcare professionals improve patient care and access to care. In this respect, it cannot be a solution aimed at disorganizing the healthcare system. To ensure this, the decrees of August 2018 make the attending physician the master of the game. Thus, only he or she can decide to use a teleconsultation for a patient whom he or she has been seeing (for at least 12 months) and who has already had the opportunity to meet or refer the patient to a

16 Specifically, Article R6316-4 of the French Public Health Code provides that the patient's file kept by each medical professional involved in the telemedicine act must include: the report on the performance of the act, the medical acts and prescriptions carried out within the framework of the telemedicine act, the identity of the healthcare professionals participating in the act, the date and time of the act, and any technical incidents that occurred during the act.

17 As required by article L1110-4-1 of the Public Health Code.

18 No. 2018-788 relating to the modalities of implementation of telemedicine acts.

teleconsulting doctor when the teleconsultation is not carried out with him or her. Let us specify, for all practical purposes, that the decrees open up teleconsultation more generally to any doctor exercising a liberal activity under a contract, whatever his or her sector of practice and medical specialty. On reading this condition, the question was raised as to whether teleconsultants could be hospital practitioners. This is a relevant question, insofar as the texts are specifically aimed at private practitioners.

Nevertheless, this is explained by the fact that the August 2018 decrees were adopted after the signature of Amendment no. 6 to the 2016 Medical Convention in June 2018, which only concerns private practitioners. The General Directorate for the Organization of Healthcare therefore specifies that teleconsultations carried out by doctors employed by healthcare institutions, but only in the context of outpatient consultations, and doctors employed by healthcare centers are also covered by the health insurance system as long as they are offered in accordance with the healthcare pathway[19].

With this clarification, and in order to guarantee the framework imposed by the decrees, it is stipulated that the use of teleconsultation must be carried out in alternation with so-called face-to-face consultations. This desire to promote the maintenance of physical or visual contact, although dematerialized, is also found in the condition of video transmission. In fact, only teleconsultations carried out by videoconference are recognized by the health insurance as entitling the patient to reimbursement by the latter; this excludes teleconsultations by telephone and, with them, platforms for phonic medical teleconsultation. Particular attention must be paid to the choice of the tool that will make it possible for the telemedicine act to be carried out[20]. Telemedicine doctors will have to ensure that this tool allows them to fulfill their professional obligations, among which is professional secrecy. Therefore, they will have to be careful that this tool allows for a secure and reliable connection, that it offers a secure messaging system to communicate in writing with the patient or colleagues, and that it makes it possible to trace invoices for the acts performed. The data generated by teleconsultation will

19 https://solidarites-sante.gouv.fr/soins-et-maladies/prises-en-charge-specialisees/telemedecine/article/la-teleconsultation.

20 It should be noted that the decrees provide for a flat rate for the structure dedicated to video transmission equipment of 350 euros and an additional flat rate of 150 euros (for the acquisition of certain connected devices such as the tensiometer, the list of which must be published by UNCAN).

have to be processed in accordance with the Data Protection Act recently amended by the Act of June 20, 2018, and stored securely. Finally, the whole system must be offered under conditions that respect the security and interoperability standards for data transmission and exchanges. These obligations are imposed on teleconsultants who commit themselves to their patient.

On this point, it is also up to the telemedicine doctor to ensure that the patient has the necessary equipment to carry out the videoconference and that it is located on a geographical area that allows a good quality internet connection[21].

Finally, once performed, the teleconsultation act must be the subject of a report drawn up by the teleconsulting physician, which he or she must archive in his or her patient file.

9.2.1.2.3. Temperaments in the coordinated healthcare pathway

The decrees have provided for the hypotheses of access to teleconsultation outside the healthcare pathway. These hypotheses concern patients under the age of 16 as well as directly accessible medical specialties (gynecology, ophthalmology, stomatology, oral surgery or maxillofacial surgery, psychiatry, neuropsychiatry, and pediatrics). In addition, the requirement to follow a coordinated healthcare pathway does not apply to patients who do not have a designated treating physician or whose treating physician is not available within the time frame compatible with their state of health. It is up to the patient to justify the unavailability of his or her treating physician by any means. In this hypothesis, recourse to teleconsultation is ensured within the framework of the territorial organization. These may be CPTS[22], ESP[23], MSP[24], CDS[25] or any other territorial organization that offers a coordinated telemedicine response open to all healthcare professionals in the territory. On this point, let us also mention Rider no. 15 of the National Pharmaceutical Convention signed on

21 These conditions, which are difficult to verify for telemedicine, will have to be the subject of an information note for patients indicating the conditions of access to teleconsultation.

22 *Communautés professionnelles territoriales de santé* (territorial health professional communities).

23 *Équipes de soins primaires* (primary care teams).

24 Multi-professional care homes.

25 *Centre de santé* (health center).

December 6, 2018, which allows pharmacies to be access points, in exchange for a refund, for the medical teleconsultations offered in the territory[26].

In any case, the telemedicine doctor thus requested must draw up a report of the teleconsultation, a copy of which he or she will keep and must send a copy to the attending physician and/or the physician who requested the procedure.

The teleconsultation is billed by the teleconsulting doctor at the same rate as a face-to-face consultation and surcharges may be added under the same conditions.

These regulatory constraints are, therefore, forging a full-fledged identity for telemedicine, which differs from e-health services.

9.2.2. *E-health: a service provision*

E-health is defined as a health service provision that brings together a provider and a consumer. More generally, it is mainly a question of personal services linked to the information society, in particular e-commerce. The scope of application is vast: remote observation of patients treated at home by healthcare providers, medical tele-advice, health information available on the Internet, health or well-being coaching (mobile health), etc. These services, which are designed as a service and not as a medical act, are excluded in France, from the scope of application of the 2010 decree and are instead covered by the European directive on the protection of health and safety at work of June 8, 2000, known as the E-commerce Directive, transposed in France by the law of June 21, 2004, on digital trust[27].

Consequently, the normative constraints respond less to the imperatives of organization, permanence, and safety of care, like the texts applicable to telemedicine practitioners, than to the free circulation, ease of implementation, and remuneration of services. Taken as a whole, e-health projects are easier to implement because they are less constrained from a regulatory point of view. Does this mean that the country's conception of its

26 FSPF press release from December 6, 2018.

27 The objective of this law was to create a legal framework to ensure the free movement of information society services.

telemedicine practice may affect its economic development and attractiveness? The answer is unconditionally positive, except to add that the quality of the practice and the service provided to the patient derives from the constraints on the project. The example of medical teleconsulting is illustrative on this point.

While in France, the medical tele-advice is not part of the acts provided for by the decree of 2010, and therefore cannot be qualified as an act of telemedicine, it is because its conception does not allow to protect on the one hand the person in demand, and on the other hand the professional solicited. Thought of as a commercial service, teleconsulting is, therefore, a part of e-health and is, therefore, less protective of the patient's rights than of the consumer's rights. The reverse is also true for the health professional, who is, therefore, considered as a service provider subject to the constraints of e-commerce.

Thus, the protection of the actors and beneficiaries of medical activities and services carried out via ICTs depends on the applicable standard. The normative constraint then becomes a strategic development tool. The example of data processing resulting from these new practices is another example.

9.3. Standard applicable to data

Telehealth and its various forms of implementation, insofar as they involve the use of information and communication technologies, intrinsically generate data, that is, raw information revealing a certain activity or state at a specific time.

No one will deny that in recent years there has been an acceleration in the production of both national and supranational legislation relating to the use of data; this observation is revealing of the challenges that the processing of digital data represents today. Whether these challenges are economic, financial, societal, or legal, data is without a doubt at the heart of the daily concerns of entrepreneurs. And rightly so, because far from being just raw information, its processing can be the source of a serious violation of people's fundamental rights. This is why a normative framework is indispensable.

In France, it is the French law "Informatique et Liberté" of January 6, 1978[28] that laid down the fundamental principles applicable to the computer processing of personal data. This law was first amended by the law of August 6, 2004[29], the main purpose of which was to transpose the European Directive of October 24, 1995[30] into French law. This same directive followed a recommendation of the Council of Europe, which had clearly stated the need to harmonize the provisions of the member states with respect to data processing in order to limit the obstacles to the free movement of data within the European Union.

In spite of these texts, different practices have been noted within European countries, some member states having proved more permissive than others; development facilities are denounced by actors constrained by a stricter national standard in this area.

It was not until the Charter of Fundamental Rights of the European Union that the right to protection of personal data was enshrined in European legislation[31]. Adopted by the Nice Intergovernmental Conference, the Lisbon Treaty gives it a binding scope[32], the whole having been enshrined in the European Regulation of April 27, 2016, on the protection of individuals with regard to the processing of personal data and on the free movement of such data[33].

The legal value of a European regulation is more binding than that of a European directive. Indeed, if a directive establishes a flexible framework that allows member states that have committed to apply it to draw inspiration from it when legislating on their territory, the European Regulation is more enforceable. Consequently, the State's margin of interpretation and discretion is much more limited, so that the national law to be adopted in

28 Law No. 78-17.

29 Law no. 2004-801.

30 Directive 95/46/EC on the protection of personal data.

31 Charter of Fundamental Rights of the European Union, published in the *Journal officiel des Communautés européennes* No. C364/1 of 18/12/2000.

32 Treaty on the European Union and Treaty on the Functioning of the European Union which adopted the Treaty of Lisbon signed on December 13, 2007, published in *Journal officiel* No. C326 of 26/10/2012, pp. 0001–0390.

33 No. 2016/679, *JOUE* No. L119 of May 4, 2016, p. 1. This Regulation directly applicable in the national legislation of the Member States repeals Directive 95/46/EC, which is considered obsolete.

application of the said Regulation is likely either to supplement it or to specify it, but in no case to contradict it. This is the very essence of the text of the laws of 2016 "for a Digital Republic" (October 7, 2016, No. 2016-1321) and of 2018 (June 21, 2018, No. 2018-493).

Therefore, while it can be said that the French and European legal framework is now converging on the founding foundation of personal data protection, it must be emphasized that there are still particularities specific to France.

9.3.1. *General framework*

Beforehand, it should be recalled that unlike our neighbors across the Atlantic subject to common law, in Europe and therefore in France, no property right has been recognized on the data. Indeed, the data is not legally qualified as a "thing or object", it cannot, therefore, benefit from the prerogatives usually granted to owners. Therefore, any possibility of claiming a right of ownership of the data is excluded, and therefore any right of purchase or sale is excluded.

According to the European vision, data is issued from the legal personality of a natural person. It belongs to the category of subjective rights. Like a person's identity, it benefits from the same legal protection as information relating to a person's private life.

The right to privacy of individuals is one of the most protected rights in our normative system. Consecrated by Article 12 of the Universal Declaration of Human Rights and taken up in Article 8 of the European Convention on Human Rights, in France, it is contained in Article 9 of the Civil Code, which was recognized in 1995 as having constitutional value[34].

Consequently, any collection, processing, use, transfer, circulation, etc. of personal data is subject to the prior information and consent of the person from whom it originates.

9.3.1.1. *Qualification of data*

The application of this principle implies that the data is personal data, with the capacity of identifying a person.

34 *Norme supérieur*. January 18, 1995, No. 95-352 DC. *JO* January 21, 1995.

Anonymous data, therefore, does not require the consent of the person from whom it originates for its processing. However, it is still necessary to be able to qualify the data as "anonymous data". This is an assertion that today does not seem to be easy to make, since the performance of IT solutions and tools makes any assumption of absolute anonymization difficult. For this reason, lawyers recommend that the information and consent of the person be made a principle applicable to all processing, even if it only concerns so-called anonymized data.

In any case, the burden of proof of consent lies with the person responsible for processing.

The request for consent must be presented in a form that distinguishes it from other questions that the data controller may ask and must be formulated in a form that is understandable, accessible, and in clear and simple terms. Moreover, the consent thus obtained must have been given freely, that is, to say without coercion, manipulation, or false information, as is the case with a service provider who makes the provision of a service or the performance of a contract conditional upon the consent of the person to the processing of his or her data, even though such processing is not necessary for the performance of the service sold or the execution of the contract.

9.3.1.2. *Special cases*

– *For the person concerned*: it is mainly a question of reporting the situation of a minor child. The European Regulation has not prohibited the processing of data concerning them. Nevertheless, it has set some limits intended to secure it.

Thus, the processing of personal data of a minor is lawful when he or she is at least 16 years old. Below that age, the consent of the holders of parental authority is required.

It is the responsibility of the data controller to provide proof of compliance with these conditions.

– With *regard to the qualification of the data*: if the processing of personal data is authorized, as long as the informed person consents to it, the principle is reversed when the processing concerns so-called sensitive personal data.

Any data revealing racial or ethnic origin, political opinions, religious or philosophical beliefs, or trade union membership, as well as the processing of genetic or biometric data for the purpose of uniquely identifying a natural person, data concerning health or data concerning the sexual life or sexual orientation of a natural person, shall be qualified as sensitive.

Processing of so-called sensitive data is prohibited. This principle is subject to the exceptions provided for in Article 9 Paragraph 2 of the GDPR[35]; among them, the explicit consent of data subjects to the processing of their data for purposes authorized by the European Union. However, the CNIL, the supervisory authority, must authorize its processing prior to the start. In other words, the person's consent is not a sufficient condition in itself; for the processing of sensitive data, it is imperative to file a request for authorization with the CNIL, which will only grant it subject to a guarantee of protection of the person's privacy and the legitimacy of the processing as well as its purpose.

9.3.2. *Rights of the data subject: founding principles of personal data processing*

The data is part of a person's private life. Therefore, the rights attached to it are equally protected. This protection implies compliance with a number of requirements that the data controller must guarantee.

Thus, the person whose data are processed must be informed of:

– the identity and contact details of the data controller, its representative or, if applicable, the Data Protection Officer (DPO);

– the right of access to the processed data, the right of rectification, the right of deletion, the right of opposition, the right to limit the processing, the right of data portability;

– the purposes of the processing, the duration of data retention, the existence of automated decision making, including profiling;

– the recipients of the data, if a data transfer to a foreign country (Europe or outside Europe) is going to be carried out;

– the right to lodge a complaint with a supervisory authority.

35 European Data Protection Regulation.

9.3.2.1. *A right to information for…*

People who consent to the processing of their data must, in order to give informed consent, be informed of the purposes of such processing. Although seemingly easy to achieve, this requirement is not easily met in the field. Indeed, data controllers and/or project leaders do not think sufficiently far in advance about the potential of their project. As a result, at the time of its launch, they use the data for a different purpose, so that they never think very differently from the one consented to by the data subject. Although justifiable, legally this behavior can be analyzed as a failure of such a nature as to make the data controller responsible.

Moreover, this right to information also concerns the right of any person to know the final destination of one's data and especially if they will be brought to cross the borders of France, Europe, or beyond:

– the transfer of data is envisaged outside French borders, but within the European Union. The obligation for European States to be in compliance with the RGDP by May 2018 at the latest is likely to secure the protection of personal data when such data is processed in a country that has committed to the same level of protection as France. To this end, a European Data Protection Committee has been set up primarily to ensure the consistent application of the Regulation within the Union;

– or the transfer of the data is envisaged outside the borders of Europe. This transfer is only possible if the European Commission has determined by decision that the third country in question provides an adequate level of protection. In the absence of a conformity decision by the Commission, the controller or processor may only transfer the data to a third country if it has provided appropriate guarantees for the protection of the rights of individuals. These guarantees may be a legally binding and enforceable instrument between authorities, binding corporate rules, standard data protection clauses adopted by the Commission or by a national supervisory authority approved by the European Commission, a code of conduct or a certification mechanism.

9.3.2.2. *A right of access to the data for…*

At any time, the person has the right to obtain from the data controller any information that allows him/her to assert his/her rights. In this case, the purpose is to verify the transparency and fairness of the processing. The person is, therefore, entitled to obtain from the data controller, as soon as possible, the correction of data concerning him/her, if it proves to be inaccurate. The person may also obtain the limitation of the processing when he/she contests the accuracy of the data concerning him/her or when he/she identifies unlawful processing. It may also require the deletion of the data, either because they are no longer necessary in view of the purpose of processing, either because the individual has withdrawn consent and/or objects to the processing of the data, either because the processing proves to be unlawful. Nevertheless, the person may be refused the execution of this right when the processing of the data meets imperatives of public interest or the exercise of the right to freedom of expression and information[36].

9.3.2.3. *A right to portability of data for…*

This is one of the novelties of the GDPR. The right to portability implies that any person whose data is processed in a computerized manner is entitled to retrieve the data he or she has provided to the data controller in a structured, commonly used, machine-readable format. However, this right is only applicable to computerized processing, which requires the consent of the person concerned (thus excluding computerized processing for purposes of general interest or in the exercise of the public authority vested in the data controller).

9.3.3. *The accountability principle*

Although previously the system was based on compliance with legal obligations, which it was up to the national authorities to control (in this case, the CNIL for France), verify and sanction, if necessary, the GDPR modifies the postulate and puts the data controller in charge, upstream of the project.

36 Article 17(3) of the GDPR specifically provides that the right to erasure does not apply if the processing is necessary "(1) for exercising the right of freedom of expression and information; (2) for compliance with a legal obligation which requires processing by Union or Member State law to which the controller is subject or for the performance of a task carried out in the public interest or in the exercise of official authority vested in the controller; (3) for reasons of public interest in the area of public health […]; (4) for archiving purposes in the public interest […]; (5) for the establishment, exercise or defense of legal claims."

It is now the responsibility of the latter to implement data processing in compliance with the normative requirements and to detect any possible flaws, to report and apply corrective measures. Consequently, the data processor must carry out a self-diagnosis, based on an impact analysis, of its data processing system both on its security and its legitimacy. In the event that the processing presents a high risk, the data controller must present measures to the CNIL aimed at reducing it. Failing this, the CNIL may accompany the data controller to ensure compliance; if necessary, sanctions may be imposed. On this point, the GDPR has also innovated. Thus, if a data controller or a subcontractor deliberately or negligently violates its obligations, the total amount of the administrative fine may amount to 10 million euros or, in the case of a company, up to 2% of the total annual worldwide turnover of the previous year. This penalty may amount to up to 20 million euros or, in the case of companies, up to 4% of the worldwide annual turnover of the previous financial year if the violation relates to the basic principle of processing and in particular to the conditions applicable to consent and the rights of individuals.

The severity of the sanction demonstrates the resolution of the European legislator to enforce the legal framework of computerized data processing. A framework that ultimately enshrines two new principles:

– the principle of accountability for the data controller, who is now responsible for the lawfulness, legitimacy, and security of his or her data processing, not only vis-à-vis the supervisory authority (the CNIL[37]), but also vis-à-vis the person whose data he or she is processing;

– the principle of empowerment[38] of the people whose data is processed. By enshrining a protective foundation of rights, the legislator has thus enabled the person concerned to exercise control over the processing of his or her data. The purpose of this control is to make them responsible for the management of their data.

---

37 *Commission nationale de l'informatique et des libertés* [National Commission for Data Protection and Liberties].

38 The granting of power to the person so that he/she can act himself/herself in regards to his/her data.

9.4. Conclusion

It is clear that we are in the process of constructing a law on the processing of computerized data. A right that contractors are advised to master before the launch of their project, because experience has shown that any incident resulting from non-compliance with the normative framework applicable to data processing is the cause of an image damage that causes the company's relationship of trust with its customers to shift to a relationship of mistrust, a shift from which it is difficult to recover *a posteriori.*

9.5. References

Chandra, A., Pettry Jr., C.E., Paul, D.P. (2013). Telemedecine from a macromarketing viewpoint: A critical evaluation with proposed licensing strategies. In *Government Policy and Program Impacts on Technology Development, Transfer and Commercilization, International Perspectives*, Marshall, K.P., Piper, W.S., Wymer Jr., W.W. (eds). Routledge, New York.

Crigger, B.J. (2006). e-Medicine: Policy to shape the future of health care. *The Hastings Center Report*, 36(1), 12–13.

Croels, J.M. (2006). *Le droit des obligations à l'épreuve de la télémédecine*. Presses universitaires d'Aix-Marseille, Aix-en-Provence.

Gallois, F. and Rauly, A. (2015). Télémédecine et comparaison des systèmes de santé : questionnements méthodologiques. In *Colloque international recherche & régulation 2015*. LADYSS, 10–12 June, Paris.

Kerleau, M. and Pelletier-Fleury, N. (2002). Restructuring of the healthcare system and the diffusion of telemedicine. *The European Journal of Health Economics*, 3(3), 7.

Kirsch, G. (2002). The business of eHealth. *Journal of Medical Marketing: Device, Diagnostic and Pharmaceutical Marketing*, 2, 106–110.

Simon, P. (2013). *La télémédecine ce n'est pas du e-commerce*. Communication, ANTEL, Ordre national des médecins.

List of Authors

Jérôme BÉRANGER
Inserm 1027 – Bioethics
Paul Sabatier University
Toulouse
France

Valentin BERTHOU
Laboratoires Roberval et Costech
University of Technology
Compiègne
France

Alpha Ahmadou DIALLO
Ministry of Health
Conakry
Guinea

Loïc ÉTIENNE
Medical Intelligence Service
Paris
France

Corinne GRENIER
KEDGE Business School
Marseille
France

Rym IBRAHIM
InCIAM
Aix-Marseille University
Marseille
France

Stéphane OUSTRIC
Conseil de l'Ordre des Médecins
de la Haute-Garonne
Paul Sabatier University
Toulouse
France

Susana PAIXÃO-BARRADAS
KEDGE Business School
Marseille
France

Dominique PON
Clinique Pasteur
Toulouse
France

Roland RIZOULIÈRES
Inserm 1106
Marseille
France

Marie-Ève ROUGÉ-BUGAT
DUMG
Rangueil Faculty of Medicine
Paul Sabatier University
Toulouse
France

Anthéa SÉRAFIN
Occitanie Data
Toulouse
France

Lina WILLIATTE
Catholic University of Lille
France

Index

Other titles from

iSTE

in

Innovation, Entrepreneurship and Management

2021

ARCADE Jacques
Strategic Engineering (Innovation and Technology Set – Volume 11)

BOBILLIER CHAUMON Marc-Eric
Digital Transformations in the Challenge of Activity and Work: Understanding and Supporting Technological Changes (Technological Changes and Human Resources Set – Volume 3)

BUCLET Nicolas
Territorial Ecology and Socio-ecological Transition (Smart Innovation Set – Volume 34)

DIMOTIKALIS Yannis, KARAGRIGORIOU Alex, PARPOULA Christina, SKIADIS Christos H
Applied Modeling Techniques and Data Analysis 1: Computational Data Analysis Methods and Tools (Big Data, Artificial Intelligence and Data Analysis Set - Volume 7)
Applied Modeling Techniques and Data Analysis 2: Financial, Demographic, Stochastic and Statistical Models and Methods (Big Data, Artificial Intelligence and Data Analysis Set – Volume 8)

DISPAS Christophe, KAYANAKIS Georges, SERVEL Nicolas, STRIUKOVA Ludmila
Innovation and Financial Markets
(Innovation between Risk and Reward Set – Volume 7)

HELLER David
Performance of Valuation Methods in Financial Transactions (Modern Finance, Management Innovation and Economic Growth Set – Volume 4)

UZUNIDIS Dimitri, KASMI Fedoua, ADATTO Laurent
Innovation Economics, Engineering and Management Handbook 1: Main Themes
Innovation Economics, Engineering and Management Handbook 2: Special Themes

2020

ACH Yves-Alain, RMADI-SAÏD Sandra
Financial Information and Brand Value: Reflections, Challenges and Limitations

ANDREOSSO-O'CALLAGHAN Bernadette, DZEVER Sam, JAUSSAUD Jacques, TAYLOR Robert
Sustainable Development and Energy Transition in Europe and Asia
(Innovation and Technology Set – Volume 9)

BEN SLIMANE Sonia, M'HENNI Hatem
Entrepreneurship and Development: Realities and Future Prospects
(Smart Innovation Set – Volume 30)

CHOUTEAU Marianne, FOREST Joëlle, NGUYEN Céline
Innovation for Society: The P.S.I. Approach
(Smart Innovation Set – Volume 28)

CORON Clotilde
Quantifying Human Resources: Uses and Analysis
(Technological Changes and Human Resources Set – Volume 2)

CORON Clotilde, GILBERT Patrick
Technological Change
(Technological Changes and Human Resources Set – Volume 1)

CERDIN Jean-Luc, PERETTI Jean-Marie
The Success of Apprenticeships: Views of Stakeholders on Training and Learning (Human Resources Management Set – Volume 3)

DELCHET-COCHET Karen
Circular Economy: From Waste Reduction to Value Creation
(Economic Growth Set – Volume 2)

DIDAY Edwin, GUAN Rong, SAPORTA Gilbert, WANG Huiwen
Advances in Data Science
(Big Data, Artificial Intelligence and Data Analysis Set – Volume 4)

DOS SANTOS PAULINO Victor
Innovation Trends in the Space Industry
(Smart Innovation Set – Volume 25)

GASMI Nacer
Corporate Innovation Strategies: Corporate Social Responsibility and Shared Value Creation
(Smart Innovation Set – Volume 33)

GOGLIN Christian
Emotions and Values in Equity Crowdfunding Investment Choices 1: Transdisciplinary Theoretical Approach

GUILHON Bernard
Venture Capital and the Financing of Innovation
(Innovation Between Risk and Reward Set – Volume 6)

LATOUCHE Pascal
Open Innovation: Human Set-up
(Innovation and Technology Set – Volume 10)

LIMA Marcos
Entrepreneurship and Innovation Education: Frameworks and Tools
(Smart Innovation Set – Volume 32)

MACHADO Carolina, DAVIM J. Paulo
Sustainable Management for Managers and Engineers

MAKRIDES Andreas, KARAGRIGORIOU Alex, SKIADAS Christos H.
Data Analysis and Applications 3: Computational, Classification, Financial, Statistical and Stochastic Methods
(Big Data, Artificial Intelligence and Data Analysis Set – Volume 5)
Data Analysis and Applications 4: Financial Data Analysis and Methods
(Big Data, Artificial Intelligence and Data Analysis Set – Volume 6)

MASSOTTE Pierre, CORSI Patrick
Complex Decision-Making in Economy and Finance

MEUNIER François-Xavier
Dual Innovation Systems: Concepts, Tools and Methods
(Smart Innovation Set – Volume 31)

MICHAUD Thomas
Science Fiction and Innovation Design (Innovation in Engineering and Technology Set – Volume 6)

MONINO Jean-Louis
Data Control: Major Challenge for the Digital Society
(Smart Innovation Set – Volume 29)

MORLAT Clément
Sustainable Productive System: Eco-development versus Sustainable Development (Smart Innovation Set – Volume 26)

SAULAIS Pierre, ERMINE Jean-Louis
Knowledge Management in Innovative Companies 2: Understanding and Deploying a KM Plan within a Learning Organization
(Smart Innovation Set – Volume 27)

2019

AMENDOLA Mario, GAFFARD Jean-Luc
Disorder and Public Concern Around Globalization

BARBAROUX Pierre
Disruptive Technology and Defence Innovation Ecosystems
(Innovation in Engineering and Technology Set – Volume 5)

DOU Henri, JUILLET Alain, CLERC Philippe
Strategic Intelligence for the Future 1: A New Strategic and Operational Approach
Strategic Intelligence for the Future 2: A New Information Function Approach

FRIKHA Azza
Measurement in Marketing: Operationalization of Latent Constructs

FRIMOUSSE Soufyane
Innovation and Agility in the Digital Age
(Human Resources Management Set – Volume 2)

GAY Claudine, SZOSTAK Bérangère L.
Innovation and Creativity in SMEs: Challenges, Evolutions and Prospects
(Smart Innovation Set – Volume 21)

GORIA Stéphane, HUMBERT Pierre, ROUSSEL Benoît
Information, Knowledge and Agile Creativity
(Smart Innovation Set – Volume 22)

HELLER David
Investment Decision-making Using Optional Models
(Economic Growth Set – Volume 2)

HELLER David, DE CHADIRAC Sylvain, HALAOUI Lana, JOUVET Camille
The Emergence of Start-ups
(Economic Growth Set – Volume 1)

HÉRAUD Jean-Alain, KERR Fiona, BURGER-HELMCHEN Thierry
Creative Management of Complex Systems
(Smart Innovation Set – Volume 19)

LATOUCHE Pascal
Open Innovation: Corporate Incubator
(Innovation and Technology Set – Volume 7)

LEHMANN Paul-Jacques
The Future of the Euro Currency

LEIGNEL Jean-Louis, MÉNAGER Emmanuel, YABLONSKY Serge
Sustainable Enterprise Performance: A Comprehensive Evaluation Method

LIÈVRE Pascal, AUBRY Monique, GAREL Gilles
Management of Extreme Situations: From Polar Expeditions to Exploration-Oriented Organizations

MILLOT Michel
Embarrassment of Product Choices 2: Towards a Society of Well-being

N'GOALA Gilles, PEZ-PÉRARD Virginie, PRIM-ALLAZ Isabelle
Augmented Customer Strategy: CRM in the Digital Age

NIKOLOVA Blagovesta
The RRI Challenge: Responsibilization in a State of Tension with Market Regulation
(Innovation and Responsibility Set – Volume 3)

PELLEGRIN-BOUCHER Estelle, ROY Pierre
Innovation in the Cultural and Creative Industries
(Innovation and Technology Set – Volume 8)

PRIOLON Joël
Financial Markets for Commodities

QUINIOU Matthieu
Blockchain: The Advent of Disintermediation

RAVIX Joël-Thomas, DESCHAMPS Marc
Innovation and Industrial Policies
(Innovation between Risk and Reward Set – Volume 5)

ROGER Alain, VINOT Didier
Skills Management: New Applications, New Questions
(Human Resources Management Set – Volume 1)

SAULAIS Pierre, ERMINE Jean-Louis
Knowledge Management in Innovative Companies 1: Understanding and Deploying a KM Plan within a Learning Organization
(Smart Innovation Set – Volume 23)

SERVAJEAN-HILST Romaric
Co-innovation Dynamics: The Management of Client-Supplier Interactions for Open Innovation
(Smart Innovation Set – Volume 20)

SKIADAS Christos H., BOZEMAN James R.
Data Analysis and Applications 1: Clustering and Regression, Modeling-estimating, Forecasting and Data Mining
(Big Data, Artificial Intelligence and Data Analysis Set – Volume 2)
Data Analysis and Applications 2: Utilization of Results in Europe and Other Topics
(Big Data, Artificial Intelligence and Data Analysis Set – Volume 3)

UZUNIDIS Dimitri
Systemic Innovation: Entrepreneurial Strategies and Market Dynamics

VIGEZZI Michel
World Industrialization: Shared Inventions, Competitive Innovations and Social Dynamics
(Smart Innovation Set – Volume 24)

2018

BURKHARDT Kirsten
Private Equity Firms: Their Role in the Formation of Strategic Alliances

CALLENS Stéphane
Creative Globalization
(Smart Innovation Set – Volume 16)

CASADELLA Vanessa
Innovation Systems in Emerging Economies: MINT – Mexico, Indonesia, Nigeria, Turkey
(Smart Innovation Set – Volume 18)

CHOUTEAU Marianne, FOREST Joëlle, NGUYEN Céline
Science, Technology and Innovation Culture
(Innovation in Engineering and Technology Set – Volume 3)

CORLOSQUET-HABART Marine, JANSSEN Jacques
Big Data for Insurance Companies
(Big Data, Artificial Intelligence and Data Analysis Set – Volume 1)

CROS Françoise
Innovation and Society
(Smart Innovation Set – Volume 15)

DEBREF Romain
Environmental Innovation and Ecodesign: Certainties and Controversies
(Smart Innovation Set – Volume 17)

DOMINGUEZ Noémie
SME Internationalization Strategies: Innovation to Conquer New Markets

ERMINE Jean-Louis
Knowledge Management: The Creative Loop
(Innovation and Technology Set – Volume 5)

GILBERT Patrick, BOBADILLA Natalia, GASTALDI Lise,
LE BOULAIRE Martine, LELEBINA Olga
Innovation, Research and Development Management

IBRAHIMI Mohammed
Mergers & Acquisitions: Theory, Strategy, Finance

LEMAÎTRE Denis
Training Engineers for Innovation

LÉVY Aldo, BEN BOUHENI Faten, AMMI Chantal
Financial Management: USGAAP and IFRS Standards
(Innovation and Technology Set – Volume 6)

MILLOT Michel
Embarrassment of Product Choices 1: How to Consume Differently

PANSERA Mario, OWEN Richard
Innovation and Development: The Politics at the Bottom of the Pyramid
(Innovation and Responsibility Set – Volume 2)

RICHEZ Yves
Corporate Talent Detection and Development

SACHETTI Philippe, ZUPPINGER Thibaud
New Technologies and Branding
(Innovation and Technology Set – Volume 4)

SAMIER Henri
Intuition, Creativity, Innovation

TEMPLE Ludovic, COMPAORÉ SAWADOGO Eveline M.F.W.
Innovation Processes in Agro-Ecological Transitions in Developing Countries
(Innovation in Engineering and Technology Set – Volume 2)

UZUNIDIS Dimitri
Collective Innovation Processes: Principles and Practices
(Innovation in Engineering and Technology Set – Volume 4)

VAN HOOREBEKE Delphine
The Management of Living Beings or Emo-management

2017

AÏT-EL-HADJ Smaïl
The Ongoing Technological System
(Smart Innovation Set – Volume 11)

BAUDRY Marc, DUMONT Béatrice
Patents: Prompting or Restricting Innovation?
(Smart Innovation Set – Volume 12)

BÉRARD Céline, TEYSSIER Christine
Risk Management: Lever for SME Development and Stakeholder Value Creation

CHALENÇON Ludivine
Location Strategies and Value Creation of International Mergers and Acquisitions

CHAUVEL Danièle, BORZILLO Stefano
The Innovative Company: An Ill-defined Object
(Innovation between Risk and Reward Set – Volume 1)

CORSI Patrick
Going Past Limits To Growth

D'ANDRIA Aude, GABARRET Inés
Building 21st Century Entrepreneurship
(Innovation and Technology Set – Volume 2)

DAIDJ Nabyla
Cooperation, Coopetition and Innovation
(Innovation and Technology Set – Volume 3)

FERNEZ-WALCH Sandrine
The Multiple Facets of Innovation Project Management
(Innovation between Risk and Reward Set – Volume 4)

FOREST Joëlle
Creative Rationality and Innovation
(Smart Innovation Set – Volume 14)

GUILHON Bernard
Innovation and Production Ecosystems
(Innovation between Risk and Reward Set – Volume 2)

HAMMOUDI Abdelhakim, DAIDJ Nabyla
Game Theory Approach to Managerial Strategies and Value Creation
(Diverse and Global Perspectives on Value Creation Set – Volume 3)

LALLEMENT Rémi
Intellectual Property and Innovation Protection: New Practices and New Policy Issues
(Innovation between Risk and Reward Set – Volume 3)

LAPERCHE Blandine
Enterprise Knowledge Capital
(Smart Innovation Set – Volume 13)

LEBERT Didier, EL YOUNSI Hafida
International Specialization Dynamics
(Smart Innovation Set – Volume 9)

MAESSCHALCK Marc
Reflexive Governance for Research and Innovative Knowledge
(Responsible Research and Innovation Set – Volume 6)

MASSOTTE Pierre
Ethics in Social Networking and Business 1: Theory, Practice and Current Recommendations
Ethics in Social Networking and Business 2: The Future and Changing Paradigms

MASSOTTE Pierre, CORSI Patrick
Smart Decisions in Complex Systems

MEDINA Mercedes, HERRERO Mónica, URGELLÉS Alicia
Current and Emerging Issues in the Audiovisual Industry
(Diverse and Global Perspectives on Value Creation Set – Volume 1)

MICHAUD Thomas
Innovation, Between Science and Science Fiction
(Smart Innovation Set – Volume 10)

PELLÉ Sophie
Business, Innovation and Responsibility
(Responsible Research and Innovation Set – Volume 7)

SAVIGNAC Emmanuelle
The Gamification of Work: The Use of Games in the Workplace

SUGAHARA Satoshi, DAIDJ Nabyla, USHIO Sumitaka
Value Creation in Management Accounting and Strategic Management: An Integrated Approach
(Diverse and Global Perspectives on Value Creation Set –Volume 2)

UZUNIDIS Dimitri, SAULAIS Pierre
Innovation Engines: Entrepreneurs and Enterprises in a Turbulent World (Innovation in Engineering and Technology Set – Volume 1)

2016

BARBAROUX Pierre, ATTOUR Amel, SCHENK Eric
Knowledge Management and Innovation (Smart Innovation Set – Volume 6)

BEN BOUHENI Faten, AMMI Chantal, LEVY Aldo
Banking Governance, Performance And Risk-Taking: Conventional Banks Vs Islamic Banks

BOUTILLIER Sophie, CARRÉ Denis, LEVRATTO Nadine
Entrepreneurial Ecosystems (Smart Innovation Set – Volume 2)

BOUTILLIER Sophie, UZUNIDIS Dimitri
The Entrepreneur (Smart Innovation Set – Volume 8)

BOUVARD Patricia, SUZANNE Hervé
Collective Intelligence Development in Business

GALLAUD Delphine, LAPERCHE Blandine
Circular Economy, Industrial Ecology and Short Supply Chains (Smart Innovation Set – Volume 4)

GUERRIER Claudine
Security and Privacy in the Digital Era (Innovation and Technology Set – Volume 1)

MEGHOUAR Hicham
Corporate Takeover Targets

MONINO Jean-Louis, SEDKAOUI Soraya
Big Data, Open Data and Data Development (Smart Innovation Set – Volume 3)

MOREL Laure, LE ROUX Serge
Fab Labs: Innovative User (Smart Innovation Set – Volume 5)

PICARD Fabienne, TANGUY Corinne
Innovations and Techno-ecological Transition
(Smart Innovation Set – Volume 7)

2015

CASADELLA Vanessa, LIU Zeting, DIMITRI Uzunidis
Innovation Capabilities and Economic Development in Open Economies
(Smart Innovation Set – Volume 1)

CORSI Patrick, MORIN Dominique
Sequencing Apple's DNA

CORSI Patrick, NEAU Erwan
Innovation Capability Maturity Model

FAIVRE-TAVIGNOT Bénédicte
Social Business and Base of the Pyramid

GODÉ Cécile
Team Coordination in Extreme Environments

MAILLARD Pierre
Competitive Quality and Innovation

MASSOTTE Pierre, CORSI Patrick
Operationalizing Sustainability

MASSOTTE Pierre, CORSI Patrick
Sustainability Calling

2014

DUBÉ Jean, LEGROS Diègo
Spatial Econometrics Using Microdata

LESCA Humbert, LESCA Nicolas
Strategic Decisions and Weak Signals

2013

HABART-CORLOSQUET Marine, JANSSEN Jacques, MANCA Raimondo
VaR Methodology for Non-Gaussian Finance

2012

DAL PONT Jean-Pierre
Process Engineering and Industrial Management

MAILLARD Pierre
Competitive Quality Strategies

POMEROL Jean-Charles
Decision-Making and Action

SZYLAR Christian
UCITS Handbook

2011

LESCA Nicolas
Environmental Scanning and Sustainable Development

LESCA Nicolas, LESCA Humbert
Weak Signals for Strategic Intelligence: Anticipation Tool for Managers

MERCIER-LAURENT Eunika
Innovation Ecosystems

2010

SZYLAR Christian
Risk Management under UCITS III/IV

2009

COHEN Corine
Business Intelligence

ZANINETTI Jean-Marc
Sustainable Development in the USA

2008

CORSI Patrick, DULIEU Mike
The Marketing of Technology Intensive Products and Services

DZEVER Sam, JAUSSAUD Jacques, ANDREOSSO Bernadette
Evolving Corporate Structures and Cultures in Asia: Impact of Globalization

2007

AMMI Chantal
Global Consumer Behavior

2006

BOUGHZALA Imed, ERMINE Jean-Louis
Trends in Enterprise Knowledge Management

CORSI Patrick *et al.*
Innovation Engineering: the Power of Intangible Networks

Printed and bound by CPI Group (UK) Ltd, Croydon, CR0 4YY
15/09/2026
14962361-0002